Bonnie Prince Charlie

A Life

This book is dedicated to the memory of the author's father, who died in Warsaw on 9 August 2009

Bonnie Prince Charlie

A Life

PETER PININSKI

AMBERLEY

First published 2010

Amberley Publishing Plc
Cirencester Road, Chalford,
Stroud, Gloucestershire, GL6 8PE
www.amberleybooks.com

ISBN 978 1 84868 194 1

British Library Cataloguing in Publication Data.
A catalogue record for this book is available from the British Library.

Typeset in 10.5 pt on 13.5 pt Garamond Premier Pro.
Typesetting by Fonthill.

Printed and bound in the UK.

Contents

Guide to Polish Pronunciation

Polish pronunciation looks as difficult to the newcomer as Gaelic. However, it is simple, regular, and stress is always on the penultimate syllable.

Vowels:

a	as in 'and'	e	as in 'end'	i	as in 'mean'
o	as in 'hot'	u	as in 'shoot'	y	as in 'hit'

Consonants, like English except for:

c = 'ts' like 'hits'
j = 'y' like 'yes'
w = 'v' like 'love' – or 'f' like 'woof' if at the end of a word

Pairs of letters that produce a single sound:

cz = 'ch' like 'cheat'
ch = 'ch' like 'loch'
rz = like 'zh' or the 'je' of the French 'je suis'
sz = 'sh' like 'shilling'

Accents:

ą	as in 'faun'
ę	as in 'lent' ... both ą and ę are nasal
ć or ci	like the 'ch' of 'cheat' but more delicate
ł	like the 'w' in 'weather' or 'pew'
ń	like the 'ñ' in 'mañana' but nasal
ó	like the 'oo' in 'pool'
ś or si	like the 'sh' of 'shilling' but more delicate

ż	like the 'je' of 'je suis' but harder
ź or zi	like the 'je' of 'je suis' but more delicate

... delicate means the sound is formed just behind the teeth.

Examples:

Lwów	:	Lvooff	Leszczyński	:	Lesh chin ski
Grzymałów	:	Gzhy ma woof	Nikorowicz	:	Nee ko ro veetch
Warszawa	:	Var sha va	Radziwiłł	:	Rad zhee viw

Foreword

Professor Bruce Lenman, who wrote the foreword for the present author's book, published in Britain in 2002, entitled *The Stuarts' Last Secret – The Missing Heirs of Bonnie Prince Charlie,* coined the apt expression 'the industry of Stuart charlatanism', referring to successive nineteenth- and twentieth-century charlatans who made exotic claims to be royal Stuart descendants. Because the existence of Bonnie Prince Charlie's grandchildren and descendants was kept so strictly and successfully secret, these charlatans could operate in an information vacuum and, until more recently, were not denounced by serious historians otherwise occupied with mainstream politics, of which the exiled Stuarts ceased to be a part after the disaster at Culloden.

These fraudulent claims created a high credibility hurdle, which had to be jumped in order to satisfy academics that *The Stuarts' Last Secret* was not another case in point. That is why the book, containing unknown documentary evidence this author was fortunate enough to discover, had to be lengthy and detailed, heavily footnoted, with archival references given in full, a preface by a second professor of history, Waldemar Łazuga of Poznań University, and with appendices as well as a postscript. Furthermore, the previously unpublished information had to be presented almost as if before a court of law, rather than related as history, and both the direct and circumstantial evidence was complex and extensive. Hugh Massingberd wrote in his review of 25 May 2002 in *The Spectator* that *The Stuarts' Last Secret* constituted proof 'to surely the most sceptical pedant's satisfaction'; however, the reader needed to be an expert not to find the book difficult and challenging.

The present work aims to tell the story of Prince Charles Edward Stuart, his daughter Charlotte, Duchess of Albany, and their heirs, including the information given in the earlier book but presented in short, simple and smooth form. Those wishing to pursue specific lines of enquiry, check some area in greater detail, or see from what source or archive various facts and quotations originate may easily do so by referring to the 2002 publication.

Since 2005, this author has had the privilege of writing for the Stewart Society's annual publication, *The Stewarts*. The 2009 volume contains another piece entitled 'The Last Stuarts – More Secrets', which begins:

> Anyone who has conducted archival research and then published will know that you have to pick the moment when further work will not substantially change your conclusions. So you publish. Yet you know that details remain out there, awaiting discovery, taunting from their archival hideouts. You carry on digging and, maddeningly, out they crawl, too late to be included. Some are minor details, others significant. The master copy of your book becomes peppered with frustratingly unpublished hand-written notes in red ink.

The present work, therefore, takes the opportunity to include additional information discovered after the publication of *The Stuarts' Last Secret*, which the author hopes will make this book of interest not only to new readers but also to those familiar with the earlier one.

Back in the late eighteenth century, the secret of Prince Charles' grandchildren was so well-kept by his daughter, Charlotte, and the father of her children, Prince Ferdinand de Rohan, that not even the Hanoverian spy, Sir Horace Mann, found out. Indeed, only a few of those closest to the Stuarts and Rohans knew. It wasn't until Alasdair and Henrietta Taylor's research in the mid-twentieth century, Professor George Sherburn's biography of Charlotte's son in 1960, and the publication of *The Stuarts' Last Secret* in 2002, that the truth emerged. Previously, the information vacuum not only gave rise to Lenman's 'industry of Stuart charlatanism', but often led to comical mistakes being made by journalists and writers of popular history, causing confusion insofar as they have been repeated by later writers, thus becoming 'established facts'. To give just three examples:

Aglaë – one of Prince Charles' granddaughters is often referred to as Aglaë, because that is the name Charlotte Stuart used for her in letters sent to her mother in Paris written after 1784 when living with her father in Italy. However, all Charlotte's letters were written in code as a precaution against Hanoverian spies, about which she explicitly warned Ferdinand. He was 'my friend', her children were her 'little flowers', her family was the 'garden', her son was 'he who is in the country', the other daughter was 'V.', occasionally 'Marie-V.', etc. Consequently, if Charlotte used the name Aglaë openly in her encoded letters, then obviously Aglaë was also a code and therefore the one name her daughter was definitely NOT called! In fact, this author managed to discover details of the daughter's wedding, evidence in memoirs from her husband's family, her death certificate, and a letter, all published in *The Stuarts' Last Secret*, all proving that her real name was the eminently more Stuart name of Charlotte.

Zemire – some writers have claimed that Prince Charles' other granddaughter was called Zemire, because Charlotte once wrote asking her mother '... and how is Zemire?' But they should have read all her letters. Then they would have known that there were three names Charlotte didn't need to encode: Jacquot, Moustache and Zemire. Because those were the names of her family's pet dogs!

The Château de Beaumanoir legend – in 1977, another author wrote of Charlotte's two daughters: 'Nothing more was heard about the two Stuart girls beyond the fact that they both died unmarried at the Château de Beaumanoir near Tours. Aglaë died in 1823 and Marie in 1825, and they were buried at Saint Cyr-sur-Loire.'

Although that book gave no archival source whatsoever, the claim has often been repeated by later writers who never checked the archives for Beaumanoir in the Commune de Fondettes at the *Archives Départementales d'Indre et Loire* at Chambray-les-Tours for which the records of death for 1820-32 are complete but contain nothing at all to support this claim.

And yet, curiously enough, the author was quite right that a certain Marie Stuart of Albany did actually die at the Château de Beaumanoir in the Commune de Fondettes near Tours. And she actually was unmarried. At that time, she was staying with Beaumanoir's owner, Alexander MacAlister, who generously paid for her tomb. And that tomb really is at the New Cemetery of Saint Cyr-sur-Loire. But the author was absolutely wrong that this Marie was Prince Charles' granddaughter. She couldn't possibly have been. Because this Marie didn't die in 1823, nor in 1825. In fact, she wasn't even born till 1824 – forty-five years after the death of her supposed mother, Charlotte Stuart! But if you go to the *Registre des Décès* for the Mairie de Fondettes (no. 28, 23.VIII.1873), you will see that Marie Stuart of Albany died a full half-century later, in 1873, on 22 August. As anyone who has tried to decipher dates from old tombs knows, a century of rain and frost hardly makes for easy reading where badly weathered stone is concerned, and 1873 is easily mistaken for 1823 ... especially if you don't check the records.

So who was this mysterious Marie Stuart of Albany?

During the nineteenth century, there lived two brothers, John Carter Allen and Charles Manning Allen, sons of naval officer Thomas Hay Allen by Catherine, daughter of Owen Manning, Vicar of Godalming. They were born in Wales, but later, calling themselves 'Sobieski-Stuart', claimed to have been born at Versailles as grandsons of Bonnie Prince Charlie. Today, they are denounced by historians as exotic charlatans and described by the *Dictionary of National Biography* as 'demonstrably false'. After John's death in 1872, his brother proclaimed himself Charles Edward Stuart, Count of Albany, and lived until 1880. This younger of the two imposters had a son and three daughters, two of whom died childless, one of whom was called Marie. And it was this Marie, NOT Charlotte Stuart's, who died at the Château de Beaumanoir near Tours, who was buried at Saint Cyr-sur-Loire, and who gave rise to this often-repeated but much-confused legend.

Prologue

It was spring of the year 1683 and a vast Turkish army had moved out of Belgrade and was fast approaching Vienna. There in the frightened heart of Europe, Leopold, the Holy Roman Emperor, appealed throughout the continent for help. But no one's aid did he seek more than that of King John III Sobieski, King of Poland and Hammer of the Turks. To him he wrote: 'It is not so much Your Majesty's troops that we need, as Your Majesty's presence. For we are sure that your person at the head of our armies and your name alone, which is held in awe by our common foe, will mean defeat for them.'

The fearless warhorse relished no prospect more. On 1 April, he signed an agreement of military assistance with the Imperial Ambassador, Count Waldstein, in which he would receive 1,200,000 ducats and supreme command of the allied forces of Europe if he came in person to lead the relief. The Polish king organised his forces and moved south towards Vienna, which by mid-July was being besieged by a Turkish force of no less than 65,000 Turkish soldiers, 15,000 Tartars, and thousands of other people. Inside the locked gates of the encircled city, the defence under Count Rüdiger von Starhemberg was helpless.

The Polish army of 21,000 arrived at Vienna on 12 September in two columns led by Field-Marshals Nicholas Jerome Sieniawski and Stanislas Jabłonowski. En route, they had stopped at the great Monastery of Częstochowa, where Sobieski was given the sabre his grandfather, Field-Marshal Stanislas Żółkiewski, had left there years before as a votive offering. Then, upon arrival at the siege, the king assumed supreme command of the 65,000-strong Christian army. In one of his rare historical essays, J. B. Morton lets us glimpse the opposing protagonists:

> Upon a bay horse came the Polish king, sitting in his saddle heavily, corpulent, but of majestic bearing, his moustaches still dark, his eyes full of intelligence and humour; his figure even more conspicuous by reason of the tunic of sky-blue silk which he wore. Beside him was the boy, Prince James, his son, in breastplate and helmet. There followed the melancholy Lorraine, and the heads of all the princely Houses of the Germanies ... The still confident Kara Mustapha reclined in his tent and took coffee. At the opening of the tent his bejewelled horses awaited him.

Battle was joined. Then came the decisive moment. Sobieski's seasoned eye surveyed the field, and he summoned the commander of his elite Polish heavy cavalry. The king pointed to the very centre of the enormous wealth-laden Turkish encampment. There stood a vast white tent comprising no less than forty-five silk-hung rooms. It was that of the Grand Vizier himself. As his cavalry captain peered into the distance, Sobieski told him to prepare the heavy cavalry to charge. Morton describes the sight of the 3,500 Polish winged hussars as they thundered down the small valley on the right flank led by the king himself on an Arab charger:

> As the pace quickened, and the horses broke from a trot into a gallop, the Turkish leaders saw in the forefront of the squadrons a figure that seemed to absorb into itself all the long story of Christendom in arms and the awful majesty of the Faith embattled. They saw the royal standard and the shield borne before him, and at the knowledge of his presence they lost their hope. Word spread through the ranks that the Polish king was leading the charge ... As they drew near, there was added to the thunder of the hoofs the terrifying sound of the huge vulture and eagle wings fastened to their shoulders. In their ranks rode the high nobility of Poland, and behind them pressed the Pancernes, in shirts of mail, soldiers less splendid to the eye, but no less fierce in battle, no less tried ... There was no resistance to the shock of the charge. Everything in its way went down, whilst Lorraine and Waldeck turned the right wing of the Turks, and Jabłonowski the left. It is recorded that Kara Mustapha, in despair, said to the Khan of the Crimean Tartars: 'And cannot you help me?'; to which the Khan replied: 'I know the King of Poland. I told you that if he came, there would be nothing for us to do but retreat.'

The next day, 13 September, Sobieski wrote to his French-born wife, Marie Casimire:

> God be blessed for ever! He has given our nation victory. He has given it such a triumph as no past century has ever seen! All the artillery, the whole Moslem camp, all its uncountable riches have fallen into our hands. The approaches to the town, the neighbouring fields, are all covered with the infidel dead and the remainder is in flight and stricken with panic ... Their tents, all their carriages are taken, et mille d'autres galanteries fort jolies et fort riches, mais fort riches, I have not yet seen all the booty, Il n'y a point de comparaison avec ceux de Chocim. Four or five quivers alone, mounted with rubies and sapphires, are worth many thousands of ducats. You will not then, my love, say to me, as the wives of the Tartars say to their lords when they return without booty: 'You are no warrior, for you have brought me nothing. It is only he who is in the forefront of the fight that can get hold of anything.'

To the Pope, Sobieski sent the green banner of the Prophet. Kara Mustapha, however, was promptly executed by the Sultan. The Polish historian, Ladislas Konopczyński, was not exaggerating when he said that 'on 12 September 1683 King John III decided not only the fate of Austria, but of all Christendom'. Lord d'Abernon described it as one of the eighteen battles that changed the course of world history.

Some months later, in February 1685, in the opposite corner of Europe, King Charles II died and his younger brother succeeded to his three thrones, crowned as James VII of Scotland and II of England and Ireland.[1] Thus was James the fourth Stuart King of England and Ireland and the twelfth King of Scots since his ancestor Walter, hereditary High Steward of Scotland, married Princess Marjorie in 1315, daughter of Scotland's legendary hero, King Robert the Bruce, victor of Bannockburn. James was the heir of an unbroken bloodline stretching back through the great dynasties of Stuart, Bruce and Canmore, some say even to Fergus Mor MacErc, King of Dalriada a millennium and a half ago.

But James was crowned at a time of narrow-minded religious antagonism. In France, Louis XIV's regime was both anti-Protestant and expansionist. His bitter opponent was the Calvinist Stadtholder of Holland, William of Orange. The latter was both James' nephew and son-in-law. Yet James had converted to Catholicism and was set upon implementing an unpopular domestic policy of equality for Catholics and most other religious minorities, despite the majority of his English subjects being Protestant.[2]

As for William of Orange, he feared two things: that James would become drawn into a military alliance with France, thus changing the balance of power in Europe against the Protestant block; and that, as James was still without a male heir, the Stuart succession in favour of William and his wife was threatened by his policy of ecumenism.

William had been manipulating domestic British politics for some time prior to mid-1688 when James' second wife, the Catholic Mary of Modena, gave birth to a legitimate male heir. The birth of James Francis Edward Stuart was the signal for William to implement a plan he had prepared earlier to keep Britain in the Protestant camp by force. Some weeks later, the Dutch Stadtholder invaded England. King James fled into exile in France, where his cousin Louis XIV unwaveringly supported him and the Stuarts' rights, usually against the advice of his ministers. Louis gave his support not only because he genuinely liked his Stuart cousins, but because he recognised the principle of inheritance by the divine right of kings and was staunchly Catholic. This last point created a dilemma for the Stuarts. The only European power really able to help militarily was France. However, both King James and his son rightly believed that Louis would immediately stop all support if they were to convert to Protestantism – yet that was precisely what the majority of Jacobite supporters in Britain wanted.

But, in 1685, had one known that, in 1719, the great Polish King John III's granddaughter, Marie-Clementina Sobieska, would marry King James VII & II's son and heir, James Francis Edward Stuart, one would have been forgiven for presuming that nothing but a glorious future could possibly await this young and handsome royal couple.

Who would have dreamt that, within one short century, the illustrious royal House of Stuart would not only have lost their united thrones of Scotland, England and Ireland to mere German Electors (of Hanover), but that their native country would have lost its sovereignty to England; that the Stuart family would have become extinct; and that the only member of its last generation – a Duchess called Charlotte (of Albany) – would be dead?

Who would likewise have thought that, within that same short century, the Sobieski family would not only have failed, after such a victory as Vienna, to place even one of their three sons on the united thrones of Poland and Lithuania, but have lost them instead to mere German Electors (of Saxony); that their native country would have lost its sovereignty to Russia, Prussia, and Austria; that the Sobieski family would have become extinct; and that the final member of its last generation – a Duchess called Charlotte (de Bouillon) – would be dead?

For the descendants of the Stuarts and the Sobieskis, the only thing this magnificent first half of the 1680s heralded was the beginning of their decline and fall. History had prepared a multiplicity of fates with which to mock the yet-unborn descendants – poisoned inheritances of preceding generations – destructive events outside their own control.

And so it was that, after William of Orange's invasion of Britain in November 1688, the exiled Stuarts held their courts in France, the Lorraine, and Italy. Though sometimes subject to financial constraints, they were not the poverty-stricken, bickering, infiltrated places of Hanoverian propaganda. The Court of James VII & II at Louis XIV's enormous Château de St Germain was 'a large and magnificent establishment, culturally rich, politically important, and enjoying regular social contact with the Court of France'; whilst the Court of James VIII & III in Rome was 'maintained with considerable splendour'.[3] And from all of these places, each generation of the Stuart family launched repeated attempts to regain their thrones, every one plagued by that family's legendary bad luck.

I

Papa Wagner: The Prince's Parents 1717-1719

The Church is in ruins, the State is in jars
Delusions, oppressions and murderous wars
We dare na weel say't but we ken wha's to blame
There'll never be peace till Jamie comes hame.

Robert Burns

In late 1717, the young Irish veteran of the Jacobite uprising of 1715, Charles Wogan, had been instructed to find the most eligible bride possible for the exiled King James VIII of Scotland and III of England and Ireland – the only legitimate son of James VII & II. Finding a bride was not an easy task, for despite the donations and other income that James received from France, Spain, the Vatican and elsewhere, he needed vast amounts to pay for his court with all its attendant exiles, whose pensions he granted and maintained with extraordinary generosity.

James' life had hitherto been exemplary, totally unstained by sordid affairs. But none of his matrimonial plans had succeeded. He had fallen passionately in love with his d'Este cousin, the eldest daughter of his uncle, Rainaldo III, Duke of Modena, but been refused. Similarly, a political match with the daughter of the Russian Tsar, Peter the Great, had been turned down. Notwithstanding the antiquity of the House of Stuart and their kinship with nearly all the major ruling families of Europe, few were prepared to cross Hanoverian England.

Finally, vetted by the Duke of Ormonde, Wogan had come up with what seemed a coup. None of the three daughters of Prince James Sobieski, god-child of King Louis XIV of France and son of the hero-King John III of Poland, were married. With the Battle of Vienna still within living memory, that name bore the lustre of greatness, whilst the girls' mother, Hedwig Elisabeth, was a Princess of Bavaria-Neuburg, closely related to the imperial Habsburgs, a string of reigning German princes, and by marriage to the Kings of Portugal and Spain as well as the Grand Duke of Tuscany and the Duke of Parma. Such close connections with the greatest figures of Catholic Europe were of enormous significance, given that they followed the lead of the Vatican, which continued steadfastly to regard the Stuarts as the true Kings of Scotland, England and Ireland and the Hanoverians as usurpers.

Of the Sobieski princesses, Marie-Casimire was the unloved eldest, aged twenty-four but 'astonishingly solemn', according to Wogan. She would die a spinster in 1723. The second was Marie-Charlotte, but 'beyond all measure gay'. It was she who would become the last of the Sobieskis and, in 1723, marry Prince Charles de La Tour d'Auvergne, Duke de Bouillon. But the youngest was the sixteen-year-old Marie-Clementina, god-daughter of Pope Clement XI and considered by the Irish matchmaker to be 'sweet, amiable, of an even temper and gay only when in season'.

Not without significance for King James was the fact that Clementina's dowry was 600,000 livres d'or of rental income which Prince James Sobieski had invested in the Hôtel de Ville in Paris, as well as 250,000 livres owed to him by King Augustus II of Poland, and the entire income from the leasehold of the huge Szawle estate[4] comprising 6,000 farms and 70,000 hectares. In addition, there was the fabulously valuable Sobieski jewellery, which included two famous rubies, each reputedly as large as a pigeon's egg, and the prospect of still greater wealth after the death of the girl's father, for Prince Sobieski had no male heir. In time, most would go in support of the Jacobite Cause, but for the present, it seemed the perfect answer to James' problems.

The matrimonial agreement was concluded at Oława[5] on 22 July 1718, but once it became known that the Stuart king was to marry and therefore might continue the rightful senior royal line, King George I went apoplectic[6]. He put a bounty on James' head, pressurised his ally, the Holy Roman Emperor Charles VI (notwithstanding the fact that Clementina was Charles' first cousin) to intervene and prevent the marriage, whilst simultaneously offering to add £10,000 to Clementina's dowry if she could be forced to marry any German prince at all. The Habsburg ruler co-operated by firstly threatening the fifty-one-year-old Prince Sobieski with exile from his Castle of Oława in Silesia and secondly by arresting Princess Clementina and her mother, together with their escort and retinue, all of whom he imprisoned at the Castle of Ambras near Innsbrück.

Not only were James and Wogan outraged, but all Europe was scandalised. The Pope, various princes, and the relatives of the Stuarts and Sobieskis protested to the Emperor about such treatment of his own aunt and her daughter, but Charles VI's hands had been firmly tied by George I. However, the Hanoverian and Habsburg rulers underestimated the Poles, Irish and Scots, whose genius in such circumstances grows in proportion to the scale of the obstacle.

James was overworked with the preparations for Cardinal Alberoni's Spanish invasion plans aimed at a Jacobite restoration. Nevertheless, at the end of January 1719, immediately before leaving to go and join the Spanish fleet on 8 February, he entrusted the task of rescuing his future bride to Wogan, with the single condition that Prince Sobieski agree whatever plan was devised. Wogan's mission was so secret that not even the Pope knew about it. As an eighteen-year-old, the Irishman had escaped from Newgate Prison after the 'Fifteen in a group of thirteen prisoners led by Brigadier William Mackintosh of Borlum. Armed with this experience, he masterminded the ingenious escape of the royal prisoners. Travelling incognito and passing himself off as a doctor, he found his way into the cells where the prisoners were being held and quickly agreed a plan with the teenage Polish princess. Within nineteen days, he was at Sobieski's residence at Oława, posing as Mr Wagner, an English tourist.

At first, Sobieski agreed to Wogan's plan, but then changed his mind and, through his treasurer, offered him the present of a Turkish snuff box taken by his father from the tent of the Grand Vizier at the Battle of Vienna. Frustrated by his failure, the Irishman refused to accept it. The next day, Sobieski invited him for a private lunch, during which he said such a refusal was a measure of nobility and that he would, after all, place his daughter's care in Wogan's hands.

Proceeding to the headquarters of the Irish Legion with Sobieski's valet, Wogan co-opted his uncle, Major Richard Gaydon, the gigantic Lucas O'Toole, and Captain and Mrs John Misset with their French maid, Jeanneton. The latter dressed up as Princess Clementina and the group broke into the prison whilst the guards were drinking below. There they left the maid behind and escaped with Clementina through the pouring rain and into the night. Soon, they discovered that they had left behind not only the maid, who later rejoined her employers, but also a large package containing Clementina's Sobieski jewellery and yet more from the Stuarts which had been sent by King James to Oława. The panic-stricken O'Toole rushed back to where the package had been left and mercifully found everything as they had left it.

The Jacobite, John Walkinshaw, also appears to have helped in the preliminary marriage negotiations with Prince Sobieski and was later sent to Vienna by King James to protest to the Emperor about the latter's detention of his bride.

The Irish team heaped praise upon the little Polish teenager for her bravery and charm, and, with the man Clementina now called 'Papa Wagner', continued over the Brenner Pass and arrived at the safety of Bologna where the aged Cardinal Curzio Origo literally danced with joy when Wogan announced that he had brought the king's fiancée. There, on 9 May 1719, the marriage between James and Clementina took place by proxy. In less dramatic style, the journey continued on to Rome, where the Irishmen were honoured by the Roman Senate and no less so by James himself after returning in August from the abortive Spanish attempt, with no choice now but to reconcile himself to exile in the shade of the Vatican – an association he knew only too well would damage the Stuart Cause.

The Pope then leased from the Marchese Muti and refurbished one of the largest palaces then available in Rome, which had rooms suitable for a royal court as well as a garden, and placed it at the young couple's disposal. Thereafter, it was called the Palazzo del Re and stands at the northern end of the Piazza dei Santissimi Apostoli[7]. By coincidence, it was next door to the Palazzo Odescalchi, vacated just five years before by Clementina's grandmother, Queen Marie-Casimire of Poland, the destructive but much-adored wife of King John III. James himself arrived back from Spain on 28 August and awaited his bride at the Cathedral of Montefiascone near the southern shore of the Lago di Bolsena to the north of Rome. Finally, at midnight on 3 September 1719, Bishop Sebastiano Bonaventura celebrated the marriage of the thirty-one-year-old James Francis Edward Stuart, rightful King of Scotland, England and Ireland, the only son and heir of King James VII & II by Princess Mary d'Este, daughter of Alphonso IV, Duke of Modena, and the seventeen-year-old Princess Marie-Clementina Sobieska, daughter of Crown Prince James Louis Sobieski of Poland and Princess Hedwig Elisabeth of Bavaria-Neuburg.

In London, the outwitted George I and his Hanoverian government fumed in impotent rage.

2

The Road Home: Upbringing in Rome 1719-1745

Oh there were mony beating hearts
And mony a hope and fear
And mony were the pray'rs put up
For the young Chevalier.

anonymous

After their marriage, James and Clementina held their exiled court at the Palazzo del Re. The Pope also granted the young couple the use of the Palazzo Savelli at Albano, set in the hills to the south of the city, near a lake with wooded slopes. It was an idyllic summer residence. Outside the doors of the Palazzo del Re lay the most fashionable and gossipy capital of Europe. The Italians placed little emphasis on formal education, more on heraldry and music, and most on chivalry and appearances. They welcomed into their midst the huge numbers of visitors to Rome and were breezily free from the rigid snobbery that suffocated Paris. Here beat the heart of Catholicism at whose Papal Court reigned a relaxed and carefree attitude. Attending it were dozens of cardinals, many of whom were younger sons of Europe's foremost aristocratic families, having often started their careers in this exalted rank if they hadn't inherited much at home.

With their exiled court, the wealthy, young, good-looking James and Clementina made a strange comparison. In front of their palace stood a Papal guard, one of only three in all Rome apart from the Vatican and the Quirinale. Yet, within, James, though himself a Catholic, nevertheless maintained the Stuart tradition of religious toleration and surrounded himself with large numbers of Protestants, kept two Protestant chaplains and a Protestant chapel. Clementina was also different, as she was unusually intense and devout in her worship. James' religious even-handedness was echoed in his words that he didn't want to 'become an apostle, but a good king of all my subjects'. He worked hard and was meticulous in answering his vast correspondence, which took him three to four hours daily. His seriousness, reserve and patience seemed an oasis of calm amid the throng of British exiles that formed this community-in-exile.

Fascinated by all this was not only most of Roman Society, but also the Hanoverian spies who hovered about them, led first by Baron Philip von Stosch under his pen-name, John Walton, and later by Sir Horace Mann. Their work cost the British taxpayer a large amount of money and consisted in the ruthless pursuit of every tiny detail of the lives of the Stuarts and their court, no matter how intimate.

Then, just sixteen happy months after the Stuarts married, in the late afternoon of Tuesday 31 December 1720, there occurred an event for whose discovery no spy was required. After six long days of labour, during which the Pope had offered up special prayers and provided consecrated baby linen, Clementina became mother to a baby boy. Ahead of his time and breaking with tradition, James was categoric that only women could be present in the bed-chamber itself. Thus, either there or immediately outside, the birth was witnessed by four cardinals as well as sundry princesses and ambassadors. One hour later the little Stuart Prince of Wales was baptised Charles Edward Louis John Casimir Silvester Severino Maria by the Bishop of Montefiascone. His names recalled his beheaded great-grandfather, England's sainted king, the great kings of France, Spain and Poland, as well as the saint upon whose day he was born. A royal salute was fired from Castel Sant'Angelo and the Pope immediately sent greetings and presents as did the Courts of France and Spain. Rome and all Jacobite centres throughout Britain and Europe burst into unbridled celebration and even the ten-year-old Louis XV of France is said to have clapped his hands for joy. Few could imagine a better welcome for the New Year. Thus was born the child whom Giulio Cesare Cordara said was 'reared from infancy never to forego the desire or the hope of recovering the Crown' – who would become, as Sir Walter Scott later wrote:

> one of those personages who distinguish themselves during some single and extraordinarily brilliant period of their lives, like the course of a shooting star, at which men wonder, as well on account of the briefness as the brilliancy of its splendour.

Meanwhile, the Hanoverians began their lifelong attack on the infant, which would not cease even with his death, circulating satirical medals by the notorious anti-Semite, Christian Wermuth, with inscriptions such as:

> Rome offers in place of a king, one whom without witness Sobieska has brought forth, a child surviving in misery, deformed!

To his government, Walton reported that the prince had been born a cripple and his mother would never be able to bear another child. And whilst letters of congratulation were flowing in to the baby's delighted parents from various courts and heads of state, Westminster was sending out diplomatic notes of protest, the pettiness of which made a laughing stock of the Hanoverian regime. It was foolish to try and take the moral high ground at such a time, for the South Sea Bubble was in the process of bursting – a financial fraud of huge proportions perpetrated by key members of the pro-Hanoverian Whig government and, without doubt, by the Hanoverian royal family itself. The latter were saved from its consequences only by the brilliant handling of Sir Robert Walpole. No less unsavoury were the dreadful relationships of George I and his family. He and his son were infamous for their public fights and squabbles, whilst the repeatedly unfaithful king had scandalised all Europe by imprisoning his long-suffering wife for decades when she finally did the same to him.

It was now that Walpole commenced his long premiership, constructing a ruthlessly efficient but corrupt political system to keep the Whigs in power and the Stuarts out. Yet their propaganda did not fool everyone. One Anglican minister invited to the Protestant chapel at the exiled court was astonished to discover that 'King James is a virtuous and upright man, so distant from any form of bigotry and opposed to any religious discrimination whatsoever that never is a word spoken on that subject in his house'. Likewise, the young Whig, Lord Blandford, the Duke of Marlborough's heir, noted that James 'talks with such an air of sincerity that I am apprehensive I should become half a Jacobite if I continued these discourses any longer'.

Shortly after, James became embroiled in another Jacobite conspiracy, this time centred on London itself – testimony to the deep dissatisfaction felt even in the capital of the Hanoverian Whig administration. It was organised under the leadership of the London lawyer Christopher Layer and, in England, included the Duke of Norfolk, the Earls of Orrery and Stafford, Lords Bathurst and Lansdowne, as well as Sir Henry Goring and Sir William Wyndham. Others were the Earl of Mar and General Dillon in Scotland and the Earl of Arran in Ireland. But the long-famous Stuart bad luck struck again. Just at this time, the supportive Pope Clement XI died and was replaced by the hostile Innocent XIII. In desperate need of a financing source, James turned to the French regent, the Duke of Orléans. But he had long held a petty-minded grudge against the Stuarts and promptly informed the British government, albeit on condition that no one involved would be executed as a consequence. The Hanoverians promised, then broke their word.

Later, on 6 March 1725, the four-year-old Prince Charles gained a younger brother, who was christened Henry Benedict Maria Clement Thomas Francis Xavier and became the Duke of York. Yet just as the birth of two male heirs and the exemplary morality of the Stuarts had been the greatest boost to the Jacobite Cause, so now occurred a disaster. James and Clementina's early marital happiness was shattered by postnatal problems and their respective characters were ill-suited to the consequences. He was wrapped up in his work, meticulous and pedantic; she was captivating, impulsive, over-sensitive and impatient. He regarded his role as one in which he should educate his young wife; she found this patronising and felt she understood life at least as well as he did. What they did share was stubbornness.

Having taken offence at James not long after Charles' birth, Clementina left her husband and rushed off, ostensibly to take the waters at Lucca. After a while, she quietened down and returned, having written: 'I am trying to overcome my naughty temper, so as to appear to you the best girl in the world.' Next time round, things were worse.

Towards the end of her second pregnancy, James decided to start Charles' formal education. He dismissed the boy's nurse, the arch-Catholic Miss Dorothy Sheldon, General Dillon's niece, and replaced her with the Protestant James Murray, Earl of Dunbar, and the Catholic Sir Thomas Sheridan. From then on, and especially after

Henry's birth, inflamed by the destructive Mrs Sheldon, the devout Clementina worked herself up into a fury directed against the Protestants with whom James had surrounded himself. In particular, she accused her husband of letting his Secretary of State, John Hay, Earl of Inverness, and his wife, Marjorie, 'come between them' – implying that James was having an affair with Lady Inverness. She furthermore protested hysterically that her son was being brought up a Protestant, despite the fact that the Pope himself had approved James' choice for their son's tutors. In addition, though not without reason, given the customs of the time, she was embittered that James would not allow her to choose her own household for her suite of rooms located directly above his, but was forced to share her husband's. Matters reached a head when Clementina demanded the dismissal of all those she found offensive, stating that she would 'rather suffer death than live with people who have no religion, honour or conscience'. As this was not forthcoming, she left her husband on 15 November 1725 for the Ursuline Convent of St Cecilia just across the Tiber.

All the courts of Europe reverberated with the scandal and George I and Walpole made gleeful capital of it, to James' mortification. Eventually, the exiled king partially compromised, but only after much misunderstanding and infuriating interferences by third parties, including Pope Benedict XIII, whose emissary-bishop James threatened to throw out of the window, and whose Cardinal Alberoni he left speechless by acidly telling him that he was forgetting himself.

Despite repeatedly asking the advice of his most trusted older Italian lady friends, James remained exasperated and bewildered by his wife. Perhaps his mistaken decision to deny Clementina the right to her own household betrayed his fear that there was something about her he knew he could never control. Whatever the case, he kept up a relentless but patronising attempt to pacify his wife, though no angel himself. For whilst Clementina had been hurling accusations against him, he had unwisely published their private correspondence and provocatively appeared at the opera with the flirtatious Marjorie Hay. However, in January 1728, after James had taken the two boys off to distract them with a string of balls and other festivities in Bologna and at last agreed to Clementina's justifiable demand to choose her own household, the family became reunited and began to live together once more in the Palazzo del Re.

Yet the detail of their separation is not as relevant as the effect it had on those involved. For James, it was a disorienting humiliation which deepened his stoicism and served only to increase the distance between him and his first-born. For Clementina, whether physiological or psychological in origin, it had a devastating effect. She developed a religious fixation and isolated herself more and more from all around her. She ate progressively less, prayed ever longer, stopped bothering to dress properly, and became duplicitous and manipulative, which James interpreted as 'the finest dissimulation and hypocrisy'. Soon she turned skeletal in appearance, her periods became irregular, and she began to suffer from malnutrition. It would be centuries before doctors would recognise anorexia nervosa, whilst at the time, some believed her behaviour to be a form of saintly abstinence. When Clement XII became Pope in 1730, Clementina developed a spiritual passion for him and surrounded herself by priests who encouraged her asceticism. It was hardly the cure for a problem which had made her unrecognisable as the fearless teenage princess who had escaped with such *élan* from imprisonment at Innsbrück with Papa Wagner's team of extraordinary Irishmen. Finally, having spent the last four years of her life visiting hospitals, looking after the sick and distributing alms to the poor, the emaciated young woman died in the middle of January 1735 from scurvy caused by malnutrition. She was only thirty-three.

Those who have lived through the stress of anorexia will realise what sort of a scar this must have left on Charles and Henry. When Clementina left them in November 1725, it was already for the second time in Charles' four years of life. Henry was abandoned as a baby of only eight months. Their mother didn't return for three years, and when she did, she became a waif-like religious recluse, distant and fragile, still capable of dazzling charm, but not of maternal warmth. About her hung the fear of some approaching tragedy, terrible and unfathomable. The main point of contact between mother and sons was music. Nor did the children witness anything of the love that binds a man and woman, for their parents led separate existences. And though Charles and Henry seemed happy and boisterous, throughout their childhood, there had been no let up from the traumatising atmosphere of their mother's self-destruction culminating in her death when they were fifteen and nine respectively. In a letter written by Charles, he promised his father to 'be very dutiful to Mamma, and not jump in her presence'. He was seven.

The Pope ordered that King John Sobieski's granddaughter be buried with full state honours and James Murray wrote that 'the princes are almost sick with weeping', having spent hour after hour praying at their mother's bedside during her final days. Clementina's embalmed body lay in state for three days as crowds queued to pay their last respects to the person they considered holy. Finally, adorned with the emblems of royalty, her body was 'temporarily' interred in the crypt of St Peter's to await the day which would never come, when her remains could be laid to rest in the native soil of the land of her husband's ancestors. Her heart was placed by the Franciscans in an urn in the Basilica dei Santissimi Apostoli near the Palazzo del Re, and for years, the faithful attributed miracles to her intercession.

During James' time in Bologna, one or two key things had changed. George I had died in June 1727, and James had gone to the Lorraine to see how the land lay, but France told him firmly to leave, peace having broken out in Europe. In addition, Cardinal Fleury had taken over the reins of power in that all-important country, but was ill-disposed to the Stuarts. Unfortunately for James, Fleury would live until 1743, throughout which time, he maintained the Duke of Orléans' anti-Stuart policy. As a consequence, George II succeeded without obstruction.

The results of the two boys' education under the cool, humourless Murray and warm, fatherly Sheridan proved very different. Henry was a diligent academic and deeply interested in learning. Charles was not. Yet this in no way annoyed the latter, indeed it encouraged him, and the brothers became close. When only two, Charles was described by John Hay as 'healthy and strong' and one who 'runs about from morning till night'. A year later, Hay added that 'he is a great musician and plays on his violin continually'. At four, Charles stubbornly refused to kneel when presented to the Pope. Two and a half years later, his cousin James FitzJames[8] wrote of Charles:

> Besides his great beauty he was remarkable for dexterity, grace and almost supernatural address. Not only could he read fluently, he could ride, fire a gun; and, more surprisingly still, I have seen him take a cross-bow and kill birds on the roof and split a rolling ball with a bolt ten times in succession. He speaks English, French and Italian perfectly and altogether is the most perfect prince I have ever met in my life.

Apart from his marksmanship, horsemanship, musical talent and love of dancing, it seems Charles' favourite sport was golf, at which he excelled. But when forced to study, his vitality and exuberance became transformed into anger, usually directed against his tutor. His spelling was notoriously bad and a subject for constant reproach from a father who, despite his pedantry, was not above taking his sons for midnight spins in his carriage, boating on Lake Albano, or visiting festivals in Rome, where he would lavish them with ice cream.

Yet there was one subject about which Charles was passionate, which he not only learnt to perfection but which filled him with an all-embracing inspiration he radiated to others – that he was the heir to the lawful King of Scotland, England and Ireland and that it was his destiny to restore his father and family to their rightful position. Everything Charles did became transformed into some step towards the fulfilment of this mission. From the age of ten, he had been privy to his father's secret political activities. And then, at the age of fourteen, he gained his first experience of war. Under the tutelage of his cousin James FitzJames, who had just become the 2nd Duke of Berwick and Liria, he was appointed general of artillery at the siege of Gaeta, which was being conducted by the Spanish to the south of Rome. He took his duties very seriously and even served in the trenches. The soldiers adored him for his vivid interest in their problems, about which he talked with the various nationalities in English, German, French, Italian and Spanish. Afterwards, Berwick wrote to Charles' father: 'I wish to God that some of the greatest sticklers in England against the family of Stuart had been eye witness to that siege, and I am firmly persuaded that they would soon change their way of thinking.' Even the Hanoverian spy, Walton, irritated with the prince's success, wrote to his masters that 'everyone is saying this boy will one day become a far greater adversary of the House of Hanover than his father ever was'.

Then began the frustration which would become the bane of his life. All the early marriage plans of this period came to nothing. No army would accept him for fear of Hanoverian reprisals. His mother's cousin, the Holy Roman Emperor Charles VI, refused him permission to serve in the Turkish wars. He was even denied a visit to Poland where his Sobieski grandfather lived and who, until his death in December 1737, kept up a regular correspondence with him and had specific plans for his two grandsons.

Just three months prior to his daughter's death, the elderly Prince James Sobieski left Oława and returned to the ancient family seat of Żółkiew, north-east of Lwów in southern Poland. From there, he corresponded with the Russian Tsarina Anne in order to gain her support for his two Stuart grandchildren in his attempt to have their princely status formally incorporated within Poland. This parliamentary process, known as the *indygenat*, related to the recognition and acceptance of foreign nobles into the ranks of the Polish-Lithuanian nobility, giving them all the rights of that class. For Sobieski saw his grandsons' future in Poland as heirs to his massive landed estates based on Oława near Wrocław, Tiegenhof near Gdańsk, and Żółkiew near Lwów. But the *indygenat* was essential if Charles and Henry were to inherit, because only those who belonged to the Polish-Lithuanian nobility could own land in that country. From the Castle of Żółkiew on 1 March 1735, Prince James wrote to the Tsarina Anne of:

> the tragic death and loss to me of Clementina, the Queen of His British Royal Highness, my most beloved daughter for whom I will grieve throughout eternity, who on the 18th of January, by the will of our Lord, left this Earth. She has however left me, her desperate father, the particular consolation of her two sons, my most beloved grandsons, whom into your Imperial Majesty's protection I humbly ask you receive, that through the intervention of your all-powerful Imperial Majesty they might receive the *indygenat* at the next session of the Polish Parliament.

Terminated by the old prince's death, nothing ever came of his plans. All more purposeful avenues being closed, King James organised for his sons a tour of the courts of the northern Italian states where Charles' tact and kindness astounded his long-abused tutors. Using the title 'the Count of Albany', he met his uncle, Charles Albert, Elector of Bavaria and impressed him by his lack of pretension about his role at the siege of Gaeta. Received by the highest and mightiest, Charles' triumphant tour so infuriated the Hanoverians that they expelled the Venetian Ambassador from London and issued formal protests to the courts of Tuscany and Genoa. But that only increased the aura of fascination surrounding the handsome, young Stuart prince.

Bursting with energy, Charles had to survive more than five years of inactivity in Rome before the international situation began to swing in favour of the Jacobite Cause. Though the pro-Stuart English Catholics and Tories had been more or less silenced by the Hanoverians, disaffection in Scotland was rife. For during the late 1730s and early 1740s, popular feeling had become inflamed against Westminster by the abuse of the early Black Watch units known as the Highland Companies, which were now being sent to fight Hanover's wars on the Continent, despite having been promised that they would only serve at home. Britain found herself at war with Spain from 1739 over the issue of access to Spanish-dominated American territories, and also with France from 1740 over the Austrian succession. In addition, the anti-Stuart Cardinal Fleury died in 1743, and France began to feel that a Stuart restoration might be a better alternative to the House of Hanover, which kept involving Britain in the Continent's affairs.

Against this background, an association of Jacobite leaders was formed in Scotland in 1738. The 'Concert of Gentlemen' comprised James, 3rd Duke of Perth, and his uncle, Lord John Drummond (the future 5th Duke), the Earl of Traquair's heir Lord Linton, and his brother John Stewart, Lord Lovat, Donald Cameron of Lochiel and his father-in-law Sir James Campbell of Auchenbreck, and William Drummond of Balhaldy[9]. In March 1741, they signed a letter to Cardinal Fleury asking for French help and announced the readiness of Scotland to rise.

One of these men was the initiator of an important transformation that occurred about this time. In the 1730s, there were precious few Scots at King James' court in Rome, and those there were, the young Prince Charles thoroughly disliked, especially his tutor James Murray, together with John and Marjorie Hay, whom he blamed for his parents' separation. Charles' father saw himself as English, and relations between the two of them were not good because Charles resented the fact that his father was obviously closer to his younger brother Henry. Seeing all this, the two Drummond brothers, James and John (3rd and 4th Dukes of Perth respectively), decided it was time to remind the Stuart princes of their family's origin, that Charles was heir not only to the thrones of England and Ireland but, in particular, to his family's ancient Kingdom of Scotland. So, in 1739, John gave Charles a Highland targe, helmet, breastplate, dagger and pistols, whilst in 1740, James sent him a suit of Highland clothes in bright red and black tartan, and Henry was given a book of Highland dances – the Drummonds well knowing that both Stuart boys enormously enjoyed dancing and were famous for doing so extremely well. This made a powerful impression on Charles, who demonstrated his extrovert nature in 1741 by sensationally appearing in Highland dress at two balls in Rome, one given by Cardinal Armand de Rohan. None of the guests had ever seen anything like it before! Delighted to contrast himself with his 'English' father and younger brother, Charles wrote in thanks to the Drummonds, adding that 'now I can dress like my friends'. He also began to display the Scottish Order of the Thistle with the Cross of St Andrew, whereas previously he had usually been seen wearing only the English Order of the Garter.[10]

Not long after, in 1743, Louis XV's emissary, John Butler, returned from England with the news that the time seemed propitious for a French invasion based on a Stuart restoration strategy. So the French king sent Balhaldy to Rome to suggest to the fifty-five-year-old James that his eldest son come to Paris to act as nominal commander of a force under Europe's greatest strategist, the first marshal of France, Count Maurice de Saxe, a natural son of King Augustus II of Poland. Charles was full of enthusiasm, and after much hesitating, his father agreed. The plan was to land ten thousand troops near London and announce an initiative to depose the corrupt Whig regime as well as the deeply unpopular Hanoverian dynasty without making any territorial demands at all. It was assumed that one significant battle would be fought and won under de Saxe, who would then be replaced by the Tory Duke of Ormonde, whereupon the disaffected would flock to the Stuart banner. Significantly, no diversionary attack was planned for Scotland.

Charles' journey on 8 January 1744 from Rome to Paris was so secret that not even Henry was informed. He bade farewell to his father, little knowing that it would be for the last time, and set off on a 'hunting' expedition. His tutor Sheridan caused a distraction by falling from his mount, whereupon the prince got out of his coach, took off his wig, put on a mask and dark cloak and rode off on a black horse into the night with an attendant and two servants. Word was relayed back that he had suffered an accident and was staying at Frascati to recover. In fact, posing as a Spanish officer, he made his way via Savona and Antibes to Paris with astonishing speed and organisational efficiency. He wrote to his father upon arrival: 'Mr Graham has been very careful of me ... both he and the two servants have suffered by my impatience to arrive.'

By mid-February, Walpole's spies already knew that Charles was in Paris, had been warmly greeted by the king, and was being visited there by the leading Jacobites from nearby St Germain who, after the departure of Charles' father in 1712 and the death of his grandmother in 1718, had remained at the former exiled Stuart court. At Westminster, the English prime minister spoke of 'the Young Pretender being in France and of the designed invasion from thence, in concert with the disaffected here'. He demanded that troops be sent for 'in the greatest haste'. Though lazy and apt to change his mind, Louis XV proceeded with the plan and sent the Marshal de Saxe to Gravelines, where Charles, under the name of the 'Chevalier Douglas', was to rendezvous during the first week of March. From there, he went to Dunkirk, where fifteen ships, five frigates, and seven thousand troops awaited him. However, a Frenchman spying for the English revealed the plans, and Admiral Sir John Norris was waiting when the French ships put to sea. In addition, a violent storm suddenly broke out, wreaking havoc. Twelve French vessels were lost, seven of them with all hands, and more were damaged. This was all the encouragement the French needed to give up and invade Flanders instead.

The whole thing may have been nothing more than a cynical diversion, but Charles stayed on the coast until April, awaiting developments which did not come, whereupon he left for Paris. His father urged him to be patient and return to Rome. But, determined to press on, Charles' mood was one of growing frustration as he spent his time in the capital as well as the country houses of Northern France.

It was at this period that his friendship began with his de La Tour cousins. This family comprised his highly influential courtier uncle, the Duke de Bouillon, who had been one of Louis XV's closest friends, and Charles' youthful first cousins, Godefroy-Charles, Prince de Turenne, and his sister Louise, who had just married Prince Jules-Hercule de Rohan, eldest son of the Duke de Montbazon. De Bouillon's wife, Princess Charlotte Sobieska, had died in Warsaw just four years before. She had been Charles' aunt. And whereas Charles had inherited the rights to his Sobieski grandfather's Silesian estates and fabulously valuable jewellery, she had inherited the vast Żółkiew property near Lwów, which she sold in 1739 to their nearest Polish-domiciled cousin, Prince Michael Radziwiłł, grandson of King John Sobieski's sister.

The fateful year of 1745, known in the Highlands as *Bliadhna Thearlaich*[11], brought with it a change of significance. The prince's angry humiliation at the Stuart Cause being treated as the plaything of foreigners transformed his patient obedience of his father into a determination to take fate into his own hands. Another change was his new orientation towards his mother's relations. It was now that Charles began to demonstrate that wherever his dynamic character came from, it was certainly not from his cautious father.

However, whilst his charisma, stamina, will-power and self-belief may have been pure Sobieski, the prince was just twenty-five, inexperienced and possessed of none of the military acumen, and therefore authority, of his heroic ancestor. Maintaining complete secrecy, even from his father, he fell in with a circle of wealthy men, mainly descended from exiled Irish families. Foremost among them was Antoine Walsh, a French naval officer, slave-trader and ship-builder whose father had commanded the vessel that brought King James VII & II to France after the Battle of the Boyne. Just as Charles was tired with the French Court, which refused to receive him openly, so was he impressed by these decisive businessmen. They, in turn, fell for his persuasive charm and agreed to make large loans and organise ships and arms in support of a plan whereby a small invasion would trigger a rising intended to force France to commit herself once she saw what an opportunity had presented itself.

It was a bold strategy. Initially, the French turned a blind eye, knowing that even a complete flop would have a beneficial diversionary effect. The timing seemed good. In May, the Marshal de Saxe had inflicted a serious defeat on the English at Fontenoy. Even Walpole was incensed by the flippancy of the Hanoverian king and Prince of Wales at his country's losses in a war he considered theirs:

> Our army in Flanders is running away and dropping to pieces by detachments taken prisoner every day; whilst the king is at Hanover, the regency at their country seats, not five thousand men in the island, and not above fourteen or fifteen ships at home! Allelujah!

Charles acquired two ships, the sixty-four-gun man-o'-war *Elisabeth* with 760 troops, and the sixteen-gun frigate *du Teillay*. Together, they carried a cargo of 3,500 muskets, 2,400 broadswords, twenty pieces of artillery, ammunition, and a cash reserve of 4,000 louis d'or – all paid for by loans Charles had procured and the pawning of the Sobieski jewels. Having spent his last few days on the de Bouillons' estate at Navarre, Charles left three letters to be sent immediately upon his departure. To his father he finally revealed the secret, to the King of France he wrote in emotional terms that he hoped would encourage support, whilst the Spanish Court quickly responded to his appeal, sending four ships with arms, men and money as well as Irish troops serving in their army.

On 21 June, the prince boarded the *du Teillay* at St Nazaire. With him were the legendary 'Seven Men of Moidart' – two Scots, one Englishman and four Irishmen. They were Duke William of Atholl, Aeneas MacDonald, the Paris-based banker, Francis Strickland, from an old and loyal Westmoreland family, Sir Thomas Sheridan, George Kelly, the parson and intriguer, Sir John MacDonald, an ageing cavalry veteran of the French Army, and John William O'Sullivan, who had very useful military experience. But though Prince Charles in his account of the Rising states,

'I landed with seven men', in fact, there were more, including Abbé Butler, a relation of the Duke of Ormonde, and also a servant of Cameron of Lochiel called Duncan Cameron from Barra, who knew the Hebridean seaways.

Again, fate went against the Stuarts. By chance, Antoine Walsh's squadron came upon the newly refitted HMS *Lyon* off the Lizard. Already, Charles' reliance upon the help of others prevented him from exercising authority. Walsh refused to assist the *Elisabeth*, which took and gave a day-long pounding, with the disastrous result that she had to limp back to port with over 200 wounded or dead. Charles' ship was now on its own.

The barren land of the Hebrides was sighted on 23 July, and Walsh dropped anchor off the Isle of Barra, whence MacDonald returned alarmed, having learned that his brother-in-law Roderick MacNeil of Barra was away and the arch-Jacobite Sir Hector MacLean of Duart had just been arrested. The Duke of Atholl and Sheridan wanted to return, but Charles was adamant and Walsh backed him up.

Further blows lay in store. On the Isle of Eriskay, Alexander MacDonald of Boisdale told the prince to go home, to which he replied that he had already done precisely that by coming to Scotland. And the two key chiefs of Skye, Sir Alexander MacDonald of Sleat and Norman MacLeod, 19th Chief of Macleod, refused to rise. All three were shocked that they were expected to risk the appalling English treason laws for an expedition with no backing at all.

Undaunted, Charles sailed for the mainland, landing at Loch nan Uamh[12] in the Catholic Jacobite district between Arisaig and Moidart. There, Angus MacDonald of Borradale was no less horrified than the island chiefs by the lack of support. Nevertheless, a stream of the influential came to hear the composed and confident Stuart prince over the course of the next two weeks.

On 6 August, Charles wrote to Louis XV announcing his arrival and appealing for help, having told his father a couple of days earlier that 'the French Court must now necessarily take off the mask, or have eternal shame on them; for at present there is no medium'. Some support was forthcoming from the MacDonalds, but the principal person to be won over was the strongest man in all Lochaber, Donald Cameron, Younger of Lochiel, the acting chief whose elderly father, Lord Lochiel in the Jacobite Peerage, had for years been an exile in France. It was Lochiel who in early 1745 had stressed that the French must provide a minimum of 6,000 troops, as anything less would be suicidal and few would rise. On the way to Borradale from his great wooden house at Achnacarry, Lochiel called on his brother, John Cameron of Fassiefern, whose home was on the north shore of Loch Eil. The latter was disturbed when he heard how few men and arms the prince had brought with him. Doubting his sibling's head would rule his heart, he said, 'Brother, I know you better than you know yourself. If this prince once sets his eyes upon you, he will make you do whatever he wishes.'

He was right. For Lochiel was persuaded less by the argument that Scotland was scarcely defended and that, in the event of failure, he was guaranteed a French regiment that would bring him more income than his estate, but more by Charles' challenging words:

> In a few days, with the few friends that I have, I will erect the Royal Standard and proclaim to the people of Britain that Charles Stuart is come over to claim the Crown of his ancestors, to win it, or perish in the attempt; Lochiel, who, my father has often told me, was our firmest friend, may stay at home, and learn from the newspapers the fate of his prince.

Before he had any evidence that the Cameron clansmen would actually arrive, Charles displayed his utter determination by sending Walsh's ship back to France. It had been his only means of escape.

Without doubt, Charles had already used the argument that French help would be forthcoming, for which he had no firm evidence, but of which he was convinced. Yet, even so, it was extraordinary that he won over MacDonald of Kinlochmoidart, MacDonald of Clanranald, MacDonald of Glencoe, MacDonald of Keppoch, and Stewart of Ardsheil. Also striking was that 'we remained several days at anchor in this bay, and Highlanders were perpetually arriving to see the prince to whom they proved so faithful that, though all the inhabitants of the neighbourhood knew that he was there, no one thought of going to announce it to the English Governor of Fort William'.

Then came the first real test. On Monday 19 August 1745, in Glenfinnan, at the head of Loch Shiel, the Royal Standard was to be unfurled. Charles arrived there mid-morning to find it deserted save for two shepherds. He went and waited in silence in a small hut. After some time, 150 clansmen of MacDonald of Morar came in with Rob Roy MacGregor's son, James Mor. They were an inconsequential band. For hours, the prince waited, but no more arrived. Then, at about four in the afternoon, the distant sound of the pipes began to be heard, growing in volume as they came nearer. The MacDonalds stood in silence, and Prince Charles came out from his hut to listen. It was Clan Cameron marching to their ancient war-pibroch, 800 of them, from the braes of Lochaber, Ardnamurchan and Sunart with Young Lochiel at their head. The strongest man of Lochaber had kept his word. Behind him strode two of his younger brothers, Alexander, who served as Catholic chaplain, and Dr Archibald. Further back marched the various officers and gentlemen of the clan as well as the standard-bearer and so on, right down to the humblest. Finally, they were joined by some 350 more from MacDonald of Keppoch's clan and seventy Royal Scots.

Charles walked amongst the Highlanders and began to hear the Gaelic in which he would be reasonably fluent a year later, having been taught by the poet and Jacobite captain, Alasdair MacMhaighstir Alasdair. Amid his 1,200-strong army, one thing was now clear, Charles Stuart was indeed come home at last and the 'Forty-Five was on.

Late that afternoon, to wild hurrahs, the aged Duke William of Atholl unfurled the Jacobite Standard of white, red and blue silk, which had been blessed by Bishop Hugh MacDonald, and proclaimed King James VIII, then Charles as regent. The latter looked on, radiant, flanked by Lochiel, Keppoch, John Gordon of Glenbuchat, Father Colin Campbell, and the prince's new secretary and old friend, John Murray of Broughton.

Almost at once, the Highland Army, raised against all the odds, marched off, stopping on 22 August at Kinlochiel, where Charles was upset by George II's baseness in announcing a bounty of £30,000 for him, dead or alive. Encouraged by his supporters, he replied in like terms. From there, his army moved on along the northern shore of Loch Eil, staying overnight at Fassiefern House on the 23rd, exactly one month since the *du Teillay* had dropped anchor off Barra. John Cameron of Fassiefern was no Whig, as his later involvement in the Elibank Plot proved, but since 1735, he had been a burgess of Glasgow and was a shrewd businessman. Having advised his elder brother not to join the prince, he had departed for the Glenorchy home of his father-in-law, John Campbell of Achalader. It may well have been agreed between the Cameron brothers that Fassiefern should keep himself 'clean', so that in the event of failure, one of them would be able to salvage something of the family's property – a common practice. Fassiefern went on to help his family and clansmen, both politically and financially. Notwithstanding the secrecy in which this was done, he was robbed and imprisoned by the Hanoverians in 1746, 1751 and 1753, when the Governor of Fort William wrote to the Lord Justice Clerk that 'the uprooting of Fassiefern is what we ought to have chiefly in view'. Finally, Fassiefern was sentenced on trumped-up charges to ten years' banishment, whence he returned in 1763 and died in Lochaber in 1785.

So on 23 August 1745, the prince was entertained, not by John Cameron of Fassiefern, but by his wife Jean. Outside, overlooking the long expanse of loch and hills to the south, the bushes at the end of the lawn provided the Highland Army with the Stuart emblem of the white rose with which they adorned their bonnets and which became the campaign badge. The next day, the Highlanders marched on with pipes playing, following their prince through hill and glen, into legend, poem, and song.

3

The Rising: Glenfinnan to Culloden 1745-1746

Firm to his word and faithful to his trust
He bade not others go, himself to stay
As is the pretty, prudent, modern way
But like a warrior bravely drew his sword
And raised his target for his native lord.

Whig poem to Donald Cameron of Lochiel,
published on his death in exile in 1748.

Each man who joined the Stuart Rising knew the penalty foreseen by the English treason laws:

> They must be severally hanged by the neck, but not till they be dead, for they must be cut down alive; then their bowels must be taken out and burned before their faces; then their heads must be severed from their bodies, and their bodies severally divided into four quarters.

They also knew that the Hanoverians could muster an army of over 30,000 trained veterans, call upon the Dutch, with whom they had signed a mutual-defence treaty, buy in German mercenaries, and equip them all. For they had the full resources of the Treasury as well as the Navy to keep the French and Spanish at bay. That so many were prepared to take this risk speaks clearly of hatred of the Union as well as the 'wee, wee German lairdie'. And though the power of the Highland chiefs over their people was very considerable, nevertheless, this cut both ways, because not all chiefs wanted their clans to rise, who otherwise would have, and vice versa. Furthermore, the overall picture of Jacobite support was distorted by complex clan rivalries. However, national honour and loyalty towards their lawful king and dynasty, the willpower and charisma of Prince Charles, and, above all, the sheer bravery of the Stuart supporters are factors which it would be wrong to dismiss. In emphasis of this is the fact that a full fifty-seven years had elapsed since James VII & II had gone into exile and thirty-eight since the 'forced' union with England. How much more pragmatic it was to back the Whig regime and Hanoverian incumbents or just stay at home. And many were the Jacobite sympathisers who took this surely reasonable latter course.

Ten days after Duke William of Atholl had proclaimed his father at Glenfinnan, Charles' army had grown to 2,000 men, swelled by the time they reached the Great Glen by the Stewarts of Appin and the Glengarry MacDonnells. Ranged against it was the Hanoverian commander in Scotland, General Sir John Cope, who had twice that number and held the powerful fortresses of Edinburgh, Stirling, and Dumbarton. The general's aim was to concentrate his forces and, carrying extra arms for the volunteers he expected to join him, march north and take the strategic Corrieyairack Pass. Little of this happened. The Jacobites beat Cope to the high pass, and he was stunned to discover that, even on the territories of clans whose chiefs were Whig supporters, such as John Campbell, Earl of Breadalbane, no Scots volunteered to join the Hanoverians. Worse, many of Cope's own troops deserted to the Jacobites, informing them of his plans. Wrong-footed, the general shied away from giving battle in the Great Glen and made first for Inverness and then Aberdeen, whence his force returned to Dunbar by sea. To the south were two more Hanoverian dragoon regiments under the command of the aged General Joshua Guest. But they were not in a position to oppose the Highland Army, enlarged by Ewen Macpherson of Cluny with 400 of his clansmen, which marched rapidly to Perth, taken by Lochiel and 400 Camerons just prior to the arrival of the main body on 4 September. Instead, Guest's dragoons retreated to the coast and awaited Cope's arrival.

It was now that Charles' two most important generals joined the royal standard, the fifty-one-year-old Lord George Murray, the talented but temperamental younger brother of the Duke of Atholl and a veteran of both the 'Fifteen and the 'Nineteen, and the much younger, certainly more modest, James Drummond, Duke of Perth. They were also joined by a Drummond cousin, William, Viscount Strathallan, as well as David, Lord Ogilvy, and Laurence Oliphant of Gask.

Edinburgh was the next target, outside which 1,000 MacDonalds and Camerons were grouped ready to force entry to the city on 17 September. At daybreak, by chance, the Netherbow Port opened and a coach came out. Seizing the opportunity, the Highlanders charged through with Lochiel at their head, and the city of 40,000 offered no resistance. Later that day, James Hepburn of Keith, a veteran of the 'Fifteen, with sword drawn, led Prince Charles in Highland dress to his rooms at Holyrood. At Mercat Cross:

> The Heralds of Arms in their robes, the king's declarations read, all the windows of that fine street were full at every storey of men and women. When the heralds had finished there was a continual cry of 'God Bless the King!' from both sexes and the ladies to throw themselves out of the windows with white handkerchiefs in their hands, waving about like so many colours.

In less than two months, Charles was holding court and hosting balls at the ancient palace of his ancestors. The speed and scale of events seemed miraculous and a dramatic contrast to the Earl of Mar's passivity during the Jacobites' incomparably better opportunity in 1715. Four days later, the Battle of Prestonpans was fought. O'Sullivan described the scene:

> You can't imagine what courage the prince's activity, in setting every regiment in order, the joy that he had painted in his face, and talking some words of Gaelic to the men, inspired them all ... He drew his sword, 'Now Gents,' says he, 'the sword is drawn, it won't be my fault if I set it in the scabbard before you be a free and happy people' ... When the chiefs repeated to their men what the prince said all the bonnets were in the air and such a cry that it would be wherewithal to frighten any enemy.

Though Cope's army was the same size as the enemy's and positioned well, the battle lasted only a quarter of an hour. The Highlanders outflanked his forces thanks to the Jacobite officer, Lieutenant Robert Anderson, a local farmer's son, who showed Lord George Murray a secret path, known as the Riggonhead Defile, which led through some marshland. Armed with that crucial intelligence, Murray launched a ferocious infantry attack just before dawn and the Hanoverians fled with 1,200 killed or wounded and as many taken prisoner. Jacobite losses were minimal. Before the battle, the chiefs had implored Charles not to expose himself to danger, as it was 'only his presence that kept them all united and encouraged their men'. But he replied, 'Tis for that reason that they must see me. You all expose yourselves for the king and country's Cause and I am as much obliged to it as any of you.' During the fighting, O'Sullivan observed that 'as soon as the fire began he was in the midst of them'. Afterwards, Charles arranged medical treatment for the wounded of both sides, maintaining his chivalrous attitude towards the defeated with the words: 'I can't rest until I see my own poor men taken care of, and the other wounded too, for they are the king's subjects as well, and its none of their fault if they are led on blindly.' He was now in possession of all Scotland, though the castles of Edinburgh and Stirling remained garrisoned by Hanoverian guards.

Some Mackenzies came in at this point under George, Earl of Cromartie, as well as an Atholl Brigade formed by Duke William and Lord George Murray. So too did Lord Lewis Gordon with his clansmen, Gordon of Glenbuchat with more from his, whilst David Tulloch and John Hamilton raised another 480. Likewise came in Gordon of Aberlour, Stewart of Tinntinnar, and from the west, additional Camerons, MacDonalds of Keppoch, and MacGregors of Balquhidder. Besides them were Lords Balmerino, Elcho, Pitsligo, and Kilmarnock, as well as John MacKinnon of MacKinnon from Skye. Importantly, there also appeared the first fruit of Charles' strategy towards France when three French ships brought in a number of regular French troops, 4,000 guineas, and some field pieces that were added to their own, which included the guns captured from Cope at Prestonpans. One of the new arrivals was Lt Colonel James Grant, who now took command of the artillery. Another was the semi-official envoy of the French Court, the Marquis d'Eguilles. But, worryingly, he brought no clear indication of France's policy.

After an October spent recruiting, both to enlarge his army and compensate for the tendency of the Gael to wander off home after victory, the Jacobite Army was approaching 6,000. Charles' inexperience now prevented him from subduing his exuberant vitality. Indeed, the delay at Edinburgh for recruiting had actually narrowed the timing difference between the slow-moving French preparations and the Jacobite decision to invade England, carried by only one vote. But Charles pushed for further dynamic action to force the French to commit themselves and, as a consequence, the hesitant English Jacobites. Had he waited a few days, he would have been far better placed to co-ordinate his advance south with the French preparations. For, in November, the Duke of Perth's brother, Lord John Drummond, arrived from France with 800 men of the Royal Scots and some of the Irish Brigade, two squadrons of the Duke of FitzJames' cavalry, and an artillery company. More importantly, Drummond brought with him two letters from Louis XV at last promising more and early French military support for what Voltaire described as 'the world's greatest expedition'. Drummond also knew of the tremendous public enthusiasm in Paris that had greeted the news of the Jacobite victory at Prestonpans. However, he also knew of the ominous Hanoverian troop withdrawals from Flanders.

For the time being, however, Charles' strategy seemed to be working. But the French administration was proceeding at a snail's pace. Consequently, the lightning speed of the Jacobite advance worked against them. Usually marching on foot at the head of his men, the phenomenally fit and strong Prince Charles crossed the Esk into England on 8 November. Carlisle surrendered on 15 November almost before the siege had begun, with the total loss to the Highland Army of one life. Marshal Wade's force of 14,000 at Newcastle failed to give fight for the combined reasons of being tactically outwitted and bad weather, whilst General Sir John Ligonier's 10,000 in Staffordshire found themselves overtaken by the rapidity of events. With this, the latter fell ill and was replaced by the eighteen-stone Duke of Cumberland, a younger son of George II whose dismal command had caused the disastrous British defeat at Fontenoy.

Lord George Murray confused Cumberland, a day's march away at Lichfield, by a brilliant feint, which had his opponent heading off in quite the wrong direction, thereby opening up the road to Derby, which the Highland Army reached by 4 December. They were now within 130 miles of London and strengthened by the addition of 300 new recruits under Colonel Francis Townley, which formed the Manchester Regiment. O'Sullivan recalled that:

> We arrived the next day at Derby, where his Royal Highness was perfectly well received. Bonfires on the roads, the bells ringing. We arrived a little late. It was really a fine sight to see the illuminations of the town. The prince's reason for striking to the left towards Derby was that he expected by that to gain two days march on Cumberland and of consequence to arrive at London before him, that was always the prince's design, since Cumberland avoided to come to an action.

Wade and Cumberland's combined numbers were 24,000. However, they were behind the Jacobites, and Wade in particular was painfully slow moving. Now only a mixed bag of untried men at Finchley, no more numerous than the Highland Army, stood between Charles and the Palace of St James, where his father's birth in 1688 as a Catholic heir had triggered William of Orange's invasion of England. With Charles at Derby, the mood in the English capital was one of utter panic and would have been still worse had the government not had some luck. Just twenty-four hours before the news of the Jacobite victory at Prestonpans, 6,000 Dutch troops had landed from Flanders. This momentarily steadied a badly shaken London. Had they landed a day or two later, 'the confusion in the city of London would not have been to be described and the king's crown, I will venture to say, in the utmost danger', according to King George's prime minister, Thomas Pelham-Holles, 1st Duke of Newcastle. Soon after, Horace Walpole commented that, had the Marshal de Saxe landed with 10,000 men, he would have just walked into power, and that 'I look upon Scotland as gone'. Conversely, morale and confidence amongst the Scots could not have been higher. One officer wrote to his wife from Derby, 'Our whole army is in top spirits and we trust in God to make a good account of them.'

With Prince Charles poised to descend upon the capital, London believed itself caught in a co-ordinated pincer movement between the Jacobite Army in the north and a French landing due any day from the south. Fielding wrote that the Highland threat 'struck a terror into it scarce to be credited', Wade that 'England was for the first comer', and Walpole that 'there never was so melancholy a town ... I still fear the rebels beyond my reason'. Meanwhile, the Bank of England suffered a panic run on funds, which it tried to stem by making cash payments in burning-hot sixpences. On the other hand, the London Jacobites effortlessly put together a support fund of £10,000. Pro-Stuart wall posters started appearing on walls everywhere, whilst the Duke of Newcastle agonised as to whether he should declare for King James instead of his Hanoverian master, who, though striving to appear calm, ordered his ships to be laden with as many valuables as possible and kept at full alert in the Thames, ready for an eventual flight back to the Continent.

It was against such a background that Lord George Murray called Prince Charles to a meeting of the Council of War at Derby. The latter could scarcely believe his ears. All that day, the chiefs and commanders argued that, in the absence of support from the English Jacobites, who had failed to materialise, Charles' army should conduct a pragmatic retreat to Scotland and join up with Lords Strathallan and Drummond's force of nearly 4,000 at Perth. The council was more or less unaware of the panic in London and the precise state of the French preparations, which, had the fight been taken to the English capital, would have been catapulted into action and, whatever the effect, could only have swung things further Charles' way. As it was, the majority of the council felt isolated, exposed, and deep inside hostile territory. The prince was totally opposed, realising that a retreat could never be disguised as anything but a shameful defeat, which would destroy morale and reverse the magnetism of the 'winning side', towards whom the London mob would probably swing. Charles' first words to Murray were, 'To retire, Lord George? Why the clans kept me quite another language and assured me they were all resolved to pierce or to die!' As Murray commented later, 'His Royal Highness had no regard for his own danger, but pressed with all the force of argument to go forward.' But Charles lacked military credibility. Nor did he possess the dictatorial powers of his adversary, being at the head of a loose alliance of sometimes-jealous and independent-minded chiefs rather than a regular, disciplined standing army. Charles failed to carry the council with him, and according to Lord Elcho, 'fell into a passion and gave of the gentlemen that spoke very abusive language and said they had a mind to betray him'.

According to the usually well-informed Hanoverian spy Dudley Bradstreet, O'Sullivan was in favour of marching on London and so was the Duke of Perth. Family tradition in the Gordon and Moir families maintains that Sir William Gordon of Park and James Moir of Stoneywood were also in favour of the bolder course. But Charles it was who proved to be the one in tune with the ordinary clansmen and soldiers. For when the decision became clear to the rank and file, 'if we had been beat, the grief could not have been greater'. Of their prince, O'Sullivan commented, 'I never saw anyone so concerned as he was for this disappointment, nor ever saw him take anything after so much to heart as he did it.' And even if the men realised that the council's decision was understandable, it was clearer still that it ran contrary to the flow of logic governing all that had gone before. The Whig supporter, John Home, in his *History of the Rebellion*, commented, 'There were moments when nothing seemed impossible; and, to say truth, it was not easy to forecast, or to imagine, anything more unlikely than what had already happened.' No one better summed up the psychological transformation than the previously petrified Walpole: 'No one is afraid of a rebellion that runs away.' His smugness was the measure of his relief.

For the French too, everything was now changed. On 24 October, the Marquis d'Argenson had signed the secret Treaty of Fontainebleau between the Stuarts and France, committing the latter to military support. Before Charles had arrived at Derby, he had received a letter dated 26 November from his younger brother Henry. In it he wrote that the French foreign minister had assured him of Louis XV's firm resolve to invade England and that 'you might count on it being ready towards December 20th'. This was reinforced by the Minister for the Navy, who on 10 December wrote, 'We are at last on the eve of a mighty event. We have completed at Dunkirk and neighbouring ports all the necessary preparations for the embarkation of 12,000 men commanded by the Duke de Richelieu ... the disembarkation could take place before this month is out'.

Henry Stuart was not the only one anxiously waiting to sail. So were his cousins and *aides de camp*, Prince Godefroy-Charles de Turenne and Prince Jules-Hercule de Rohan. So too was George Keith, the 10th Earl Marischal. But when the French heard the news of the retreat on 29December, Richelieu seemed surprisingly keen to halt the preparations despite his king's continued insistence on helping his Stuart cousin. Louis was reduced to ordering Richelieu to sail at any cost. But by then foul weather and an English naval blockade was preventing the French fleet from leaving harbour. By 7 February, it was clear that the French invasion, which earlier had seemed destined for easy success, was doomed to failure. The French cancelled their plans and abandoned Charles and his army to their fate.

In his authoritative analysis entitled *The '45*, the Sandhurst senior military lecturer and authority on the Rising, Dr Christopher Duffy, considers the decision not to advance on London from Derby to have been a clear strategic mistake, in that, whilst success was not guaranteed, retreat ensured failure. Nevertheless, the withdrawal was conducted brilliantly by Lord George Murray, and the Scots successfully attacked Cumberland's vanguard at Penrith. Waiting for them at Perth was the second Jacobite force of some 4,000 men under Strathallan and Drummond, including clansmen raised by Lord Lewis Gordon, which had put to flight a Whig army near Aberdeen towards the end of December. But Charles foolishly acceded to Francis Townley's suicidal request to leave him and his Manchester Regiment to garrison Carlisle, even though his men wanted to proceed to Scotland. After their inevitable surrender, Cumberland began to reveal his savage nature.

On 26 December, the prince arrived at Glasgow, where he met a young woman whose family background could scarcely have been more closely associated with the Stuarts. She was Clementina, the daughter of John Walkinshaw of Barrowfield and Camlachie by Catherine, daughter of Sir Hugh Paterson of Bannockburn and Lady Jean Erskine. Clementina's grandmother Jean was the sister of 'Bobbing John' Erskine, the 6th Earl of Mar, whom James created Duke of Mar in 1715 despite his inept leadership of that year's Rising, after which both escaped together from Scotland to France. James then appointed him gentleman of the bedchamber and secretary of state from 1716-19. But many doubted Mar's loyalty as he swapped sides with alarming regularity – hence his nickname – and in 1717 betrayed James to George I's ambassador in Paris. Clementina's father, however, was beyond reproach and had been a Jacobite agent in Rome and James' Ambassador to Vienna in 1717, losing his estates in 1723 because of his Stuart loyalties.

Leaving Glasgow on 3 January, the Jacobites wasted time on a futile, misdirected siege of Stirling Castle, during which the prince stayed at Paterson's Bannockburn House, where he argued with the self-righteous Murray, whom he bitterly resented for the decision to retreat from Derby. But when the sadistic General Henry Hawley came to relieve Stirling, Murray took only twenty minutes to lead Charles' 8,000-strong force to victory at Falkirk on 17 January. It was a significantly more impressive battle than the earlier victory at Prestonpans. Of it, O'Sullivan wrote, 'There were a great many officers killed, for gold watches were at a cheap rate. Our loss was not considerable, we had more wounded than killed.' Having fled to Linlithgow the same evening Hawley wrote to Cumberland that his 'heart is broke'. Not that he seems to have had one. Walpole said of him, 'Frequent and sudden executions are his rare passion.' His own brigadier-major wrote that 'the troops dread his severity, hate the man and hold his military knowledge in contempt'. He was believed to be an illegitimate son of George I and therefore the natural uncle of the Duke of Cumberland, who soon after assumed overall command.

Two days later, Charles was back at Bannockburn with the Patersons and Clementina Walkinshaw, who was tending to the severe fever he had caught. Meanwhile, his brother Henry, still on the French coast impatiently awaiting the French fleet's sailing, had been abandoned by his cousins, Turenne and Rohan. Both had been itching to join the Jacobite campaign but had been ordered to rejoin their regiments in Flanders.

At the end of January, Charles suffered another blow. After the victory at Falkirk, which had again sent the Whigs in London into despair, Charles had begun to strain at the prospect of challenging Cumberland on the legendary field of Bannockburn itself. There, on 23-24 June 1314, his ancestors, King Robert the Bruce and Walter Stewart, High Steward of Scotland, had crushed King Edward II's threefold-greater forces of 18,500 men in the decisive battle of the Wars of Independence. Could anything better inspire the Jacobite Army? And such a lift was badly needed. For after Falkirk, a letter from General Cope had been found stating that London was no longer expecting the French to invade – news damaging to the Highland Army's morale. Yet, on 29 January, ostensibly worried by the number of clansmen who had gone off home and fearing the time it would take to rally them once more, Murray and the other commanders recommended throwing their heavier artillery pieces into the Forth and retreating into the mountain glens of the Highlands 'where we can be usefully employed the remainder of the Winter, by taking and mastering the forts in the north ... and in the Spring we doubt not but an army of 10,000 effective Highlanders can be brought together'.

John Hay of Restalrig had the thankless task of delivering this message to Prince Charles who 'struck his head against the wall till he staggered and exclaimed most violently against Lord George Murray'. Charles replied:

> Is it possible that a victory and a defeat should produce the same effects and that the conquerors should fly from an engagement, whilst the conquered are seeking it? Should we make the retreat you propose, how much more will that raise the spirits of our enemy and sink those of our own people? ... What opinion will the French and Spaniards then have of us, or what encouragement will it be to the former to make the descent for which they have been so preparing? ... And what will become of our Lowland friends? ... I can foresee nothing but ruin and destruction ... Why should we be so much afraid now of an enemy that we attacked and beat a fortnight ago when they were much more numerous I cannot conceive ... Has the shame of their flight made them more formidable?

This time, Murray did not succeed in repeating his well-ordered retreat from Derby. He wrote that it was 'but a flight and the men were going off like so many sheep scattered upon the side of the hill, or like a broken and fleeing army after a defeat'. He began to blame others. On 2 February, Prince Charles reviewed his re-grouped forces at Crieff. He was furious. No more than 1,000 men had left him. Relations with and within his high command degenerated into mutual recrimination and accusations of treachery.

As Charles had correctly foreseen, Cumberland's morale was now in the ascendant. However, the duke failed to catch the Highlanders and waited at Perth, whilst on 8 February, his brother-in-law, Prince Frederick von Hesse, landed at Leith with 5,000 German regulars. Of Scotland, Cumberland wrote that 'the greatest part of this kingdom are either openly or privately aiding the rebels and how it may be changed I don't know, at least immediately'. A little later, he added, 'I am now in a country so much our enemy that there is hardly any intelligence to be got.'

Charles and his force arrived at Inverness on 19 February, and he installed himself at Culloden House. His aim was to reduce or neutralise Forts William and Augustus, destroy or disperse the local Whig forces, take Inverness and hold as much of the coastline as possible.

Inverness was taken immediately. On 1 March, Fort Augustus surrendered to a siege conducted by Brigadier Stapleton and Lochiel's Camerons, Keppoch's MacDonalds and some of Drummond's men. But they couldn't do the same at Fort William from which they withdrew on 2 April. In addition, a Whig army of some two 2,000 men under John Campbell, Earl of Loudon was completely scattered. The balance sheet did the Jacobites credit. But luck turned against them. At the end of March, a small force under Lord Reay successfully ambushed a number of Stuart supporters who had just landed from France with desperately needed cash of £12,500 and large quantities of stores and ammunition. It all fell into the government's hands. This problem became a disaster when Lord Cromartie went with 1,500 men to try and retrieve the situation. Instead, they were taken prisoner. Their loss was a major blow, only partly offset by some minor successes of Murray and Drummond and the appearance of 200 new volunteers from Argyll under Charles MacLean of Drimnin and James MacLean, Younger of Ardgour, together with some Scots who had deserted from the Whig forces.

The German troops and 300 English cavalry under von Hesse were already at Dunkeld and Cumberland, with his well-fed and rested army of 9,000, was ready to move north from a one-month-long stay in Aberdeen. He left on 8 April, supported by the Navy's warships and supply ships. March had proved unkind to the Jacobites for other reasons. Charles fell ill and so did Murray of Broughton, who had been tirelessly efficient in organising provisions for the army. He had been replaced by the near-incompetent Hay of Restalrig and everything was now in short supply.

By 14 April, the Hanoverian Army reached Nairn, just ten miles from Culloden. The evening before, Charles' force had been rejoined by Lochiel, who had marched from Lochaber, and some of Glengarry's men from Sutherland. Now, with morale low and his troops exhausted and ill-fed, the prince agreed to O'Sullivan's proposal to give battle – something which had been repeatedly refused when morale had been high and victory fresh. Charles' had been the genius which had often sensed the possible when reason appeared to dictate otherwise. But desperation made him unreceptive to Murray's reservations concerning the choice of Drummossie Moor as a battlefield. For its flatness perfectly suited the Hanoverian artillery and lacked any slope from which the Highlanders might launch one of their devastating charges. Instead, Charles focused on the need to fight to the east of Inverness to prevent that town from falling into his enemy's hands, because that was where their provisions were stored. And apart from the moor at Culloden, there was precious little choice.

On the night of the 15th, MacDonald of Keppoch marched in with 200 men. With him came one last glimmer of hope, which reunited Charles and Murray – to launch a surprise night attack on the Hanoverian camp at Nairn. As Murray laid out the plan, he added, 'We have another advantage that people does not think of. This is Cumberland's birthday, they'll be as drunk as beggars!' The idea was inspired. But thanks to Hay's 'unaccountable negligence', as many as 2,000 near-starving men were away searching for food. Moreover, the rear of the column could not keep up with Murray, and they managed only six miles in six hours with four miles left to go at two o'clock in the morning. Finally, Murray took the decision to return to Culloden despite the fact that the prince sent word that he was very keen to press on. Hay rode up to Murray, who loudly criticised him for his failure to organise supplies. Furious, Hay rode back to Charles, accusing Murray of deliberately disobeying orders. The retreat was a mess, and the only result of the whole endeavour was to exhaust the army, which had not slept all night. Just as with the earlier decision to retreat from Derby, so too does Dr Christopher Duffy criticise Murray's decision not to press on with the attack at Nairn.

By ten in the morning, the men were barely awake and weak from hunger. Their number was down to 5,000 and the only good news was that Charles Fraser of Inverallochy had come in with 300 men and more were on their way under Simon Fraser, Master of Lovat. But just as he had done the previous day, Murray insisted that, in the forthcoming battle, the right wing should be given to his Atholl Brigade. This was more than undiplomatic. It outraged the MacDonald chiefs whose clan had held this honour for 450 years. Lochiel and Keppoch spoke out against giving battle that day. But Stapleton ruined any chance of pragmatism when he provoked the chiefs into fighting there and then by insulting them in words which Lochiel described as an 'odious and undeserved aspersion'.

About midday on the 16th, the two armies stood facing each other. The weather was freezing and the rain and sleet lashed by a gale. On one side were Cumberland's 9,000 fresh and well-ordered men. On the other, Prince Charles' exhausted, hungry, and dejected 5,300. On the Jacobite right, as he had so stubbornly demanded, was Murray's Atholl Brigade supported by Robertsons and Menzies. Next was Clan Cameron under Lochiel, then the Stewarts of Appin, the Frasers, the Mackintoshes, the Farquharsons, the MacLachlans, the MacLeans, the MacLeods, the Chisholms, and on the left, the infuriated MacDonalds of Clanranald, Keppoch and Glengarry. Behind them stood the second line, which included the French regulars. It was commanded by Lords Ogilvy and Lewis Gordon, Gordon of Glenbuchat, the Duke of Perth, and Lord John Drummond, with the Irish Picquets on the left wing and the cavalry in the rear under Lords Strathallan, Pitsligo, and Balmerino.

Just then, a single Highlander began to walk slowly forward. The ranks watched as the lone figure reached the enemy's front line. He gave up his weapons and asked to surrender to the Duke of Cumberland himself. He was taken through the bustle of the Hanoverian ranks, where he suddenly saw Lord Bury whom he took to be King George's son. Snatching a pistol out of the hands of an English soldier, he tried to shoot the grandly dressed young man, but missed. They killed him on the spot. Yet this Scottish hero knew that only some desperate act could save his prince and people now.

4

Drummossie Moor: Disaster, Flight & Exile 1746

On hills that are by right his ain
He roams a lonely stranger
On ilka hand he's press'd by want
On ilka side is danger
Yestreen I met him in the glen
My heart near bursted fairly
For sadly chang'd indeed was he
Oh! Wae's me for Prince Charlie.

William Glen

The Hanoverian artillery immediately proved its great superiority, taking full advantage of a site tailor made for it, tearing gaping holes in the Jacobite infantry who stood, enraged at their losses, waiting for the traditional order to charge: 'Claymore! Claymore!' The Jacobites couldn't reply. Even as the prince's horse was shot from under him and his groom killed, he left his forward troops for far too many minutes in that murderous assault. Perhaps it was because Murray was now disinclined to any order but his own, or perhaps he was waiting for the redcoats to commit themselves and repeat the mistakes of Prestonpans and Falkirk. Finally, Charles ordered the charge after Lochiel told Murray that 'he couldn't hold his men much longer'. The instruction was to be passed to the line by Lochlan MacLachlan of Inchconnel, but his head was ripped from its torso by cannon fire, delaying things further. So Brigadier Stapleton completed the task, with Ker of Graden and Sir John MacDonald rushing the order to the right and left wings respectively.

Clan Chattan burst forward, led by MacGillivray of Dunmaglass and his standard-bearer with pipers playing. They raced through the smoke and grapeshot towards the Hanoverian line screaming 'Loch Moy!' and 'Dunmaglass!'. Then charged the Camerons, Murrays, Frasers and Stewarts. But the usually ferocious MacDonalds, antagonised by Murray, were so out of sorts that they never even engaged the enemy and their attitude infected the Gordons and Farquharsons on their right. As the charge went in, an invisible piece of boggy ground forced the Jacobite centre to swerve to the right, blocking the best soldiers and squashing the Athollmen against a wall and then a dyke from which their flank was mercilessly fired upon by Wolfe's regiment. Having veered right, the centre now found it had moved into the heaviest fire of all. It was all going horribly wrong.

The Highlanders inflicted terrible damage and both Barrell's and Munro's regiments were split wide open. But the weeks spent by Cumberland's troops in mastering co-ordinated bayonet techniques to deal with the Highland style of fighting paid off. Now the Hanoverian counter-attack did greater damage still. Only three of Clan Chattan's twenty-one officers survived, whilst the Camerons' chief, Lochiel, lay helpless, his ankles smashed by grapeshot. Half the Stewarts of Appin were either killed or wounded, and eight of the chief's own family lay dead. MacLachlan of MacLachlan also fell and by him lay his son and heir. Only thirty-eight MacLeans survived. MacLean of Drimnin, learning from one son of the death of his other, attacked the Hanoverian line on his own, overcome with grief, killing one and wounding another before being hacked down. Now Charles' army was becoming outflanked on the left, and the MacDonalds and Farquharsons began to fall back, notwithstanding the cries of the Drummond brothers: 'Claymore! Claymore!' Devastated that his clan should turn and run, Keppoch tried to rescue the honour of MacDonald by charging the enemy with a few lone men. He was killed in a torrent of enemy fire. Then the Hanoverian cavalry charged. But the Jacobite second line, having let the retreating MacDonalds past, closed ranks again and checked the enemy's advance with accurate volleys, whilst Lord Lewis Gordon's regiment and the Royal Scots advanced again, led by the blood-stained Murray.

The day was already lost beyond hope. The Camerons and the right retreated steadily, though terribly exposed, fighting all the way, whilst the outnumbered Scottish cavalry gave them all the protection they could from the Hanoverian dragoons, despite dreadful casualties. Ogilvy and Murray now showed their mettle by continually turning on the enemy so as to keep them from coming close whilst the French troops coolly employed professional defensive techniques, skilfully slowing the Hanoverian advance. Old Lord Balmerino, broken, rode slowly towards the enemy and surrendered, knowing that only the scaffold awaited him now. Lord Strathallan, however, charged the massed ranks of enemy dragoons in a mad rage. He was cut to shreds with forty of his men.

The retreat was now general. Twenty-five minutes after the Jacobite charge had gone in, their dead and dying lay four deep in places. Accounts disagree with regard to Prince Charles' reaction. They vary from him being forcibly prevented from charging the enemy, to being seized with panic, and everything in between. Indeed, it may well be that amid such carnage, he felt each of these emotions in turn. Someone finally seized the bridle of his horse and pulled the stunned young man away, tears streaming from his hazel eyes.

The butchery carried out by Cumberland's execution squads on the Highland wounded as they lay helpless on and around the field of battle was disgusting – it had nothing in common with the *coup de grâce*. So too was the unspeakable punishment meted out to Jacobite prisoners, the indiscriminate murder, burnings and even roastings alive, gang rapes, wholesale pillage and wanton destruction that was wreaked upon the length and breadth of the Highlands for long after. This was not standard practice. It was savage and it was bad politics. Cumberland reacted to the ultra-loyal Hanoverian Lord President Duncan Forbes' suggestion of tempering the law with princely mercy by shouting, 'Laws? I'll make a brigade give the laws!' before describing him as 'arrant Highland mad … that old woman who spoke to me of humanity'. The Whig provost John Hossack urged General Hawley 'to mingle mercy with …', but got no further before being kicked from the room, down the stairs and out into the street.

Just as Charles' chivalry towards his prisoners and the Hanoverian wounded will always remain a credit to him, so will the violence after Culloden ever stain the name of Hanover. And though Charles was the initiator of the 'Forty-Five, it seems wrong to hold him personally responsible for the unforeseeable sadism that followed. Cumberland's own words written to the Duke of Newcastle after Culloden speak volumes: 'I tremble for fear that this vile spot may still be the ruin of this island and our family.'

The speed of events at Drummossie Moor and Charles' inexperience made him commit the cardinal mistake of failing to appoint a rendezvous for his army. A few assembled at Fort Augustus, whilst large numbers rallied at Ruthven in Badenoch, surprisingly full of fight. There were no less than 2,000 of them under Lord George Murray, the Dukes of Atholl and Perth, Lords John Drummond, Ogilvy and Nairne, Charles Stewart of Ardshiel and Colonel Roy Stewart. With determined leadership, their vengeance might have been terrible, and at the time, few considered Culloden decisive. Meanwhile, their prince had escaped along a line parallel with the southern shore of Loch Ness. One who went with him wrote:

> Our troops retired, some by Badenoch, some by Inverness and some by Ranach. The French ambassador and a great many of our volunteers gave themselves up at Inverness. Barisdale, the MacGregors and others that were towards Dornoch retired by Lord Seaforth's country. His R.H. took the road in the mountains of Ranach, and brought with him Sir Thomas Sheridan, O'Sullivan, John Hay and Sandy MacLeod, one of his *aides de camp*, and FitzJames' horse.

In fact, there was also Lord Elcho, O'Neil, and a Gaelic speaker from North Uist called Edward Burke. That night, Charles instructed MacLeod to write to Macpherson of Cluny:

> We have suffered a good deal; but we hope that we shall soon pay Cumberland in his own coin. We are to review to-morrow at Fort Augustus the Frasers, Camerons, Stewarts, Clanranalds and Keppoch's people. His R.H. expects your people will be with us at furthest Friday morning. Dispatch is the more necessary that His Highness has something in view which will make ample amends for this day's ruffle … For God's sake make haste to join us; and bring with you all the people that can possibly be got together.

O'Sullivan, also present that evening, described the moment to King James' agent in Paris in an encoded letter dated 26 July 1746:

> My associate and I after our unlucky shipwreck of the 15th of April last, retreated into a spot where we hoped to be able to collect a little of the remains of our property and to try and re-establish our business as far as was possible and thus to give time to our correspondent in France to arrange our affairs with our creditors and to extricate us from the awkward situation in which we were. But all the efforts we were able to make proved useless. Our property was too much scattered and in so many different hands that we were never able to gather together so much as half a farthing and we were so harassed by our creditors that we were obliged for our own safety to retire.

From Ruthven, where the 2,000 had rallied, came a letter written by George Murray a few hours after Charles' to Cluny:

> As no person in these kingdoms ventured more frankly in the Cause than myself and as I had more at stake than almost all the others put together, so to be sure I cannot but be very deeply affected with our late loss and present situation ... I thank God I have the resolution to bear my own and family's ruin without grudge.

Murray went on to issue a barrage of accusations against the prince, especially for coming without French aid and for the defeat at Culloden. Then he turned on O'Sullivan and Hay, blaming them for incompetence, before resigning with these words:

> I would of late when I came last from Atholl have resigned my commission, but all my friends told me it might be of prejudice to the Cause at such a critical time. I hope your R.H. will now accept my demission.

In the light of these words from his senior commander, written from where the main body of men had assembled, there can have seemed little point in any course other than that of returning to France to try and obtain the aid referred to by Murray. But Charles penned an ill-worded letter to the chiefs that misjudged the patriarchal culture of Gaeldom that ultimately looked to him for leadership. In an aloof style, he told the men to fend for themselves whilst he would try and make it back to France to raise support from that country which the Scottish leaders were already coming to feel had betrayed them – but which had always been, and still remained, crucial to success and which Charles consistently did everything in his power to secure.

Lochiel, joined in Lochaber by Murray of Broughton, saw clearly just how destructive to Jacobite unity Charles' proposed course would be and dispatched his brother, Dr Archie, to Arisaig to dissuade him. Lochiel wrote to Charles that his plan was 'dishonourable to himself and so harmful to the whole Scottish nation'. But Dr Archie was too late. Charles had sailed from Loch nan Uamh for the Outer Isles with

O'Sullivan, O'Neil, Father Allan MacDonald, Alexander MacLeod, Edward Burke, and seven boatmen on the evening of the 26th, two days earlier. Continuing the fight would prove impossible without the prince at their head. Yet fate now played a cruel trick. Just four days after Charles had stood in that very same place, the means to carry on arrived. Two frigates from Nantes dropped anchor in Loch nan Uamh with no less than 36,000 louis d'or and sufficient arms to sustain a campaign right through the summer.

Some chose to escape to France with the returning ships, such as Sir Thomas Sheridan, Lord Elcho, Lord John Drummond, and the dying Duke of Perth. But as Murray of Broughton wrote, 'Mr Cameron of Lochiel retired into a little hut with Mr Murray where he expressed unwillingness to desert his Clan' so as to 'raise a body of men sufficient to protect the country and to keep on foot during that summer until they should see whether or not the succours promised from France were really intended'. The plan was to take the newly arrived ships and news of the money and arms across to Charles and persuade him to return. But this was prevented by the sudden appearance of three Hanoverian frigates. The French ran for the Continent.

On the shores of Loch Arkaig, the chiefs from Barisdale and Moidart began to rally again. By 8 May, a convention had been called by Lochiel and Murray of Broughton. It included Lord Lovat, Clanranald, Lochgarry, Barisdale, Keppoch's nephew, Colonel Roy Stewart, and Gordon of Glenbuchat. They decided that their clans should gather at Lochiel's Achnacarry in the Braes of Lochaber on 15 May, whilst 'the Frasers of Aird and other loyal men north of the Ness shall join the people of Glenmoriston and Glengarry; and that the Frasers of Stratherrick, the Mackintoshes and Macphersons shall assemble and meet at the most convenient place in Badenoch'. The MacGregors, Menzies, and Glenlyon people were to march to Rannoch and join the local people and the Atholl men, whilst Glenbuchat and Roy Stewart were to rally Lords Lewis Gordon, Ogilvy and Pitsligo, the Farquharsons and the other northern Jacobites.

But Charles was no longer present. Nor were all made of the same stuff as Lochiel. At Achnacarry, 400 Camerons, MacLeans and MacDonnells from Barisdale came in with more Camerons to follow from Sunart and Ardnamurchan under Major Alexander Cameron of Dungallon. But before they could move off to join up with the MacDonalds of Keppoch at Braelochaber, Lochiel's force was caught in a pincer movement with 600 Hanoverians approaching from the south and 2,000 from the north. They retreated to the foot of Loch Arkaig, where they saw 'the melancholy and dismal prospect of the whole country on fire'. In the face of impossible odds, Lochiel ordered his force to melt into the hills and glens whilst he himself went to an islet on Loch Shiel adjacent to Cameron of Dungallon's house at Glenhurich. With that order, the 'Forty-Five was over.

In 1999, Professor Norman Davies wrote, 'After each of the Jacobite Risings, the draconian English law of treason was improperly introduced into Scotland, and prisoners illegally removed to England for trial.' Their horrific fate almost defies description. These were just two of Davies' examples to illustrate how 'in several respects the Act of Union was flagrantly breached'.

In 1991, Professor Michael Lynch commented that what had been extraordinary during the whole period from 1688 until 1746 was 'the incredible and repeated good luck of the London regime' and how 'truly marginal was the narrow gap which separated success from failure, whether in 1708 or 1745'.

Two hundred years earlier, Sir Walter Scott observed that 'if Prince Charles had concluded his life soon after his miraculous escape, his character in history must have stood very high'. He was referring to the five months following Culloden during which Charles was constantly on the run from the huge military and naval search encompassing the entire north-western seaboard. The price on his head was £30,000. Yet, though poverty reigned everywhere and 'we hang or shoot everyone that is known to conceal the pretender', as one English officer wrote, only one attempt to betray him was ever made. On the other hand, a string of individuals helped the prince, most of whom were later imprisoned. There was also an extensive underground intelligence system in which parents organised their innocent-looking children to ferry information to Charles and the others who were with him so as to keep them constantly informed of Hanoverian troop movements.

Charles crossed in early June from South Uist to Skye in a dramatic escape organised by a Hanoverian officer, Hugh MacDonald of Armadale, who told the prince that 'though an enemy in appearance', he was 'yet a sure friend in his heart'. Charles had dressed up as a maid of Armadale's stepdaughter, Flora MacDonald. Under his disguise, he wanted to hide a loaded pistol but Flora protested, saying that were he to be searched it would give the game away. Charles answered, 'Indeed, Miss, if we shall happen with any that will go so narrowly to work in searching me as what you mean, they will certainly discover me at any rate'. Flora was later imprisoned in the Tower of London. Then, upon parting with the prince as he was to leave Skye for Raasay in late June, Donald Roy MacDonald said that 'though Sir Alexander [MacDonald of Sleat] and his following did not join Your Royal Highness, yet you see you have been very safe amongst them; for though they did not repair to your standard, they wish you very well'.

Raasay offered no refuge, just another insight into Cumberland's policy. In the words of his successor, 'Nothing but fire and sword can cure their cursed, vicious ways of thinking ... for God Almighty's sake don't spare those whom you have in your power.' In May, the whole island had been plundered, burnt and pillaged without mercy. The laird's house had been reduced to ashes and every habitation on the island left in ruins except for two tiny villages that the Royal Navy officers had overlooked. The orders were given by Captain Ferguson, a man of evil reputation whose men marched through the island in three bodies, killing everything alive in their paths and leaving the animals' carcasses to rot so they couldn't be used for food. On the small rocky island of Rona, just north of Raasay, they raped a blind girl and horse-whipped two Highlanders so brutally that one died and the other never recovered. Then they returned to steal the clothes of the remaining poor of Raasay, kill what cattle had been missed the first time, and rape two more women, one of them crippled. This was now the rule throughout the Highlands and Isles, as John Prebble's *Culloden* chillingly records. Charles enquired of these horrors in detail, aghast at what he heard, whilst the cousin of the heirs of Raasay, Captain Malcolm MacLeod, told him of the cruelty meted out by Cumberland after Culloden. The stories were so appalling that Charles had difficulty believing them.

MacLeod had the further task of removing about eighty lice from the prince's body, noting that Charles never once complained at his discomfort and that, despite his awful condition, there was 'something about him that was not ordinary, something of the stately and the grand'. A couple of MacKinnon clansmen who had last seen Charles before Culloden recognised him and 'lifted their hands and wept bitterly'. O'Sullivan said that 'the prince was in a terrible condition, his legs and thighs cut all over from the briers; the midges or flies which are terrible in that country, devoured him and made him scratch those scars which made him appear as if he were covered with ulcers'.

By mid-July, having at times almost relished the extraordinary physical and mental hardships in which a bed at night was a rare comfort and food a scarcity, Charles was back on the mainland, moving from Moidart to Knoydart. There his small band had to break through a military cordon, the tightness of which was remarkable. From the head of Loch Eil to the top of Loch Hourn, there were camps at intervals of half a mile, sentries within shouting distance of one another, and patrols to maintain strict vigilance everywhere.

In the third week of July, Charles was joined at Corriegoe, north of Loch Cluanie, by a group of destitute men who had all served in his army and who took it upon themselves to become his bodyguard. They are known to history as the Seven Men of Glenmoriston, though in fact there were eight. They swore that their 'backs should be to God and their faces to the Devil; that all the curses the Scriptures did pronounce might come upon them and all their posterity if they did not stand firm to help the prince in his greatest danger'. They proved not only loyal but also strict disciplinarians. When Charles wanted to move on before they considered it safe, they threatened to tie him up rather than comply. He commented that 'kings and princes must be ruled by their privy council, but I believe there is not in all the world a more absolute privy council than what I have at present'.

On 23 August, a year to the day since Charles stayed the night at John Cameron's Fassiefern House, the latter's elder brother, Lochiel, hiding in Mullach Coire an Iubhar, discovered that Charles, the men of Glenmoriston, and a couple of others were hiding nearby, to the north of the ruins of Achnacarry, which had been burnt on Cumberland's orders. Exactly a week later, they were reunited at Ben Alder, east of Fort William. The still-crippled Lochiel tried to kneel before his prince. But Charles didn't allow him to. Two days later, Macpherson of Cluny returned, having been out looking for Charles. He too tried to kneel, but Charles stopped him and 'kissed him, as if he had been an equal'. They then all moved higher up the hill to a hide-out known as Cluny's Cage where they passed a week of relative comfort. Invisible from below, it was a wooden construction on two floors, roofed by turf and screened by a holly grove. Yet its view out was excellent. Seeing the mass violence, wholesale destruction, and widespread starvation caused by the Hanoverians, Lochiel said that Charles was 'cut to the heart by the evils the country had endured'. Women and children had been found on the hillsides dead from want. Lochiel's sister-in-law, Jean Cameron, recalled that many Highland women were forced to beg the Hanoverian soldiers for the guts and green hides of slaughtered cattle, which Cumberland's men had stolen from them in the first place. Then, whilst the women boiled this offal, the soldiers would sometimes amuse themselves by shooting at them, 'for diversion and for wagers etc'. Charles and his companions agreed he should leave for France so as to try and obtain help. Moreover, by appearing elsewhere, George II would see that his enemy was no longer in Scotland and hopefully send his troops back to the Continent.

Cluny's Cage was to be their winter quarters if a rescue ship from France did not come, and a chain of communications had already been set up, from Clanranald's South Uist and Moidart through the Camerons' Lochaber to the hide-out in Ben Alder. However, two ships from St Malo made it, the *Heureux* and the *Prince de Conti*. Charles, Lochiel, and Dr Archie Cameron, joined by Roy Stewart and Macpherson of Breakachie, travelled under cover of darkness to Loch nan Uamh during the six days from 13 September, passing ruined Achnacarry on the way. There they boarded two French ships and sailed into exile with about 100 others. Cluny Macpherson remained behind. In Charles' words, he was 'the only person in whom he could repose the greatest confidence'. The job with which he was entrusted was to prepare for the next Jacobite rising, which would never come. Cluny returned to the Cage, where he remained hidden by his clansmen for ten years. Finally, Prince Charles thanked the Highlanders who had escorted him by moonlight to the loch's shore and bade them a tearful farewell with the words: 'It'll not be long before I shall be with you'. Not only were the hills disappearing into the night, but so too was the ancient culture of Gaeldom. And he had been the instrument of its terrible destruction.

5

Expulsion from France: Love & Banishment 1746-1749

But I cannot forget, so I wait and wonder
How long will the thinly dividing window hold?
How long will the dancing drown the terrible anger
Of those, the unwanted, who peddle their grief in the cold
Wrapped in their own despair's thick and unkindly fold?

Maurice Lindsay

The very day Charles landed at Morlaix in Brittany, he wrote to his younger brother Henry asking him to arrange an immediate meeting with Louis XV. However, King James was already being advised by Colonel Daniel O'Brien, the Stuart representative at the French Court, that they were 'more of a mind to seek peace than think about a new expedition to Scotland'. Henry had been staying at the Navarre estate of his uncle, the Duke de Bouillon, but the two brothers were reunited at Fontainebleau. The shorter, ebullient younger prince rushed up and threw his arms around his taller, more serious sibling. Fearing this to be an assault, Lochiel drew his sword, but Charles turned quickly in protection, exclaiming, 'He's my brother!' They all appeared at court on 20 October. The prince was greeted with exceptional warmth by Louis and his queen, Princess Marie Leszczyńska, a cousin of Charles' mother. He was also fêted by the rest of the French royal family, Madame de Pompadour, Louis' ministers and a string of others. But Louis proved evasive about providing material help. The Stuart princes had even been required to attend incognito, as the Count of Albany and Baron Renfrew.

Charles was intensely frustrated, despite a reluctant public appearance on the 28th at the opera with Henry and de Bouillon at which the public exploded in wild applause. He sent Louis a forceful memorandum from his base at Clichy asking for an army of 18-20,000, arguing that their cause was one and the same. He also urged the French king to strike now whilst the Highlands were seething, before the far-reaching penal laws rapidly being introduced by Westminster could take full effect. He received no reply and repeated the message. Finally, Louis proposed 6,000 troops to his ministers. But, whereas Charles believed the French would sooner focus on England, Lochiel was for a re-run starting in Western Scotland in early 1747. At that time, Hanoverian spies were reporting a readiness to rise again amongst the people of Mull, Morvern, Appin, Sunart, Moidart, Arisaig, Knoydart, Glenmoriston, Glen Spean, and Glen Roy, not to mention the Cameron country around Loch Eil. Indeed, only the Glencoe MacDonalds 'seemed to be weary of rebellion'. But Charles rejected Louis' proposal, realising that it lacked critical mass, was only enough to distract the Hanoverians from Flanders and therefore careless of the Scottish lives which would be sacrificed.

Meanwhile, James was writing from Rome to his son, criticising him for pushing the French Court too aggressively. But time was slipping by, and despite his hero's welcome in France, Charles had nothing to show for his desperate efforts. In mid-October 1746, he wrote, 'How can you imagine that I can enjoy any pleasure or amusement when I have continually before my eyes the cruelty with which my poor friends are treated?'

The Treaty of Fontainebleau was now forgotten by the French Government and the cynical reason for its secrecy exposed. As they retreated ever further from giving support of any kind, so did Charles' frustration begin to boil over into anger directed against an ever wider spectrum of people. His mood blackened into an isolated explosive depression, for his character was not like that of his father, who stoically endured defeat, a fact underlined by James' wise but tedious letters urging his 'dear child' to be patient and prudent with the French Court. On his mother's side, Charles came from legendarily dynamic stock. The person Clementina Sobieska once had been when escaping from Innsbrück might well have understood her son now. But she was long dead, killed by her self-destructive anorexia.

Since birth, Charles had been immersed in the myth that the Stuarts' royal birthright had been granted by God and that he had been born to win back their thrones, which had been wrongfully taken away. But reality had turned out to be almost diametrically opposed to this childhood fairy tale, which had been smashed by a shocking avalanche of brutal reality. And there was no one with whom Charles could share the responsibility for the terrible things being done to the land and people that had once had been the beautiful, legendary theme of his youth. His inability to control his intense frustration was reflected in the hostility of his letter of 29 December 1746 to Sir James Steuart, his plenipotentiary for negotiations with the Court of France:

> If the ministers pretend that the king has a mind to undertake something in our favour, you are to demand proof of his sincerity. Let that be either his daughter in marriage or a large sum of money, not under a million. If you find them cold and backward, you are to communicate to them my orders to leave the court until matters are riper ... You are to concur in no measures which seem only to work the affairs of France by occasioning a diversion on the part of Great Britain, but on the contrary to take all possible measures to prevent and disappoint any such scheme.

Charles' great-grandmother had been a royal French princess. But to expect the hand of one now and to equate her to a sum of cash whilst displaying open contempt for Europe's greatest ruler was a worrying indication of Charles' mental state. Perhaps it was misguided bargaining, but he then went on to gracelessly refuse a French allowance for himself and Henry, expressing outrage at its modesty, preferring to live in penury and debt. He similarly rejected their proposal for a residence, which he described as 'scandalous'.

Frustrated by Louis and his ministers, Charles looked about frantically for a way forward. He even came up with the idea of marrying Tsarina Elizabeth of Russia, whose dowry would be 20,000 soldiers for an immediate invasion of England. For his brother, he had plans for a marriage to one of their rich Polish cousins and, on 27 November 1746, wrote to his father that Henry 'should not lose a minute's time ... If Prince Radziwiłł has any daughters of age, I should not think one of them to be an unfit match'.

In Rome, James was revisited by the same fear with which he had beheld the apparently unfathomable behaviour associated with his wife's anorexia. His eldest son was simultaneously a celibate young man, humbly attending confession and protesting devotional obedience to God, yet a veteran of the most appalling scenes of war, who was beginning to display a drinking habit already generating warnings from his friends by the end of 1746. Moreover, Charles' plans were becoming ever more divorced from reality, whilst his pathologically suspicious mind was severely testing the bond of trust with his father and brother as he moved towards self-imposed isolation. Just as James had once interpreted his wife's illness as dissimulation and hypocrisy, so now was he unable to comprehend the emotions twisting inside his son. He concluded that the explanation had to lie elsewhere and must be the work of 'wicked advisors'. His view was understandable, because he was still receiving letters such as Balhaldy's, which spoke glowingly of Charles in April 1747, but added, 'When I considered the animals about him, my heart was torn to pieces.'

Few of the good men remained. In November 1748, Balhaldy said of Lochiel, to whom Charles had kept his promise of a French regiment:

> It becomes cruel in me now to be obliged to begin to inform you of the loss Your Majesty has of the most faithful and zealously devoted subject who ever served any prince, in the person of Donald Cameron of Lochiel. He died the 26th of last month of an inflamation of the head at Borgues[13] where he had been for some time with his regiment.

Charles might have been helped by the venerable George Keith, Earl Marischal, whom he almost begged to come to Paris and act as his general agent. For James was now refusing to correspond via his son's 'wicked' secretary, George Kelly. However, Marischal diplomatically refused on the grounds of 'broken health'.

Recognising that relations between his two sons were degenerating, James tried to arrange for Henry to visit the Spanish Court. But when Charles found out, he adamantly refused to agree and instead went himself, unannounced, wildly hoping to gain military assistance and the hand in marriage of one of the king's sisters. But he failed completely and came back with nothing except even greater contempt for that court than the French one.

Upon returning to his incognito life in Paris, Charles continued to press Louis and his war ministry for action. But news of another variety was on its way. In May 1747, Henry secretly left Paris for Rome, informing the enraged Charles only when safely on his way. In that letter, he lied several times, fearing his brother's dominating tendencies, thereby 'confirming' to Charles that his suspicions concerning his family's loyalty were well founded. Henry said that his sole motive was to visit his father, that he would only be staying a fortnight, and referred to his return journey. In fact, there never was to be a return journey. James and Henry had decided to implement a plan for the latter's accession to the College of Cardinals. This was the real reason for Henry's sudden departure. And when Charles discovered it in June, he knew exactly what the effect on the Stuart supporters would be. It was not only a major propaganda gift which Hanover would gloatingly exploit by whipping up anti-Catholic religious phobia, but it ruled out Henry's prospects of providing heirs to the succession and represented his moral abdication. James also took the opportunity to give up. Almost with relief, he effectively retired from all political activity aimed at a restoration. About this time, he wrote to his heir, 'My age and infirmities increase ... I am really unfit to do anything but to pray for you.' Charles' response was brief: 'Had I got a dagger through my heart it would not have been more sensible ... my love for my brother and the Cause being the occasion of it.'

Yet no matter how justified he may have been in believing the timing of this decision to be catastrophic, nevertheless, he knew perfectly well that, since the late 1730s, Henry had been intended for the Church – if there was no realistic chance of a restoration – for the practical reason of securing the Stuarts' financial position. Notwithstanding, Charles proceeded to ignore his brother for twenty years and stopped sharing any private thoughts with his father, whom he placed in the same category as Louis XV. All had become his enemies, together with Lord George Murray, whom Charles wanted arrested for treason.

Amongst Stuart supporters, the shock of Henry's move was extreme. Even James' illegitimate first cousin, Francis FitzJames, the Catholic Bishop of Soissons and 3rd Duke of FitzJames, pleaded with him to reverse the decision, arguing that it was not only the worst thing possible for the Stuarts, but that its repercussions would be damaging for Catholicism. Similarly, the Catholic priest Father Myles MacDonell wrote to James from Paris describing Henry's move as 'a mortal deadly stroke to the Cause'. Back at the Palazzo del Re, the new cardinal started a career of party-giving for friends who were described by his father as 'low company'. Before long, he scandalised the Romans and still more so his father, by introducing a suspiciously attractive young priest into his household. Yet, when his father insisted on the latter's dismissal, according to Horace Walpole, 'instead of parting with his favourite, the young cardinal with his minion left Rome abruptly, and with little regard to the dignity of his purple'.

Charles was incredulous and turned to his maternal aunt's family of de Bouillon for support. In 1743, the duke's son, the Prince de Turenne, had married Princess Louise-Henriette of Lorraine, whilst his daughter, Louise, had married Prince Jules-Hercule de Rohan, the future Duke de Montbazon and Prince de Guéméné – all interrelated families with blood ties to the Stuarts and Bourbons. Both Turenne and Rohan had been Henry Stuart's enthusiastic *aides de camp* at the time of the French invasion preparations. But in the Summer of 1747, both were away campaigning. And it was that August when Charles found support and understanding through his uncle's criticism of Henry, James, and even Louis.

Following the Battle of Lawfeld, when the 'Butcher' Cumberland had to flee for his life, Charles' optimistic vitality was briefly rekindled, and his bitterness vanished in joyful letters dashed off to the French king and his minister of war. He hoped their superb victory might bring about a positive change regarding the Stuart Cause. But it didn't. His mood turned to defiance. Having been given Louis' permission to hunt at La Plaine Saint-Denis, Charles deliberately offended him by doing so in an area strictly reserved for the king. Then, whilst Turenne and Rohan were away winning the military honours in which he badly wanted to share, Charles fell desperately in love for the first time. Towards the end of that summer, at Navarre, Charles and his first cousin, Louise de Rohan, became lovers. Their affair reached almost insane heights of intensity, during which Charles astounded his father by writing to him about the way in which the Sobieski inheritance had been divided between Louise's mother and his own. The love-stricken Charles said that Louise had been 'extremely wronged' and, referring to the Sobieski jewels, he was 'entirely resolved to yield my share if your Majesty thinks it reasonable'. His amazed father did not and bluntly said that he and Henry would be more appropriate recipients.

Charles swept Louise away in an unrestrained flood of the most passionate love, both physical and emotional, reminiscent of the red-blooded passion his great-grandfather King John Sobieski displayed towards his French wife and whose letters to her are one of the masterpieces of the Baroque. Then, when Louise became pregnant, Charles' ardour increased to fever pitch. But towards the end of the year, her husband Jules-Hercule returned from campaigning with the Marshal de Saxe and Charles became insanely jealous. For Louise now had to share a bed with her husband so that he would think the child his own. Careless of any problems he was causing, Charles became more and more demanding of proofs of Louise's adoration. Furthermore, they were nightly making love in the Rohans' Paris mansion on the place Royale (since 1800, the place des Vosges), the Hôtel de Guéméné, where Charles once became so enraged that he fired his pistols off in hysterical anger. Discreet it was not, especially as Louise's far-from-naive mother-in-law was lady of the house.

In January 1748, when the heroically unaware Jules-Hercule returned to the front, Louise's father and mother-in-law confronted the devastated girl shortly after she had written to Charles: 'I will never leave you ... only death can separate us ... be sure that your faithful mistress will never cease to adore you. You will see when I am in your arms if I love you. I love you insanely!' Her words then changed to panic:

> Remember, I am bearing your child and that I am suffering because of you. If you stop loving me, it will be more than I can endure. But if you still love me, we will somehow keep in touch ... one day, I swear, we will be happy again.

The child, whom Louise called Charles, was born weak and died on 18 January 1749 aged five months and twenty-one days. He was buried as the Rohan son of Jules-Hercule in the crypt of St Louis in the Convent of the Feuillants, which was destroyed in the early nineteenth century.

The exposure of their illicit romance not only destroyed the affair, but more than soured Charles' relationship with the previously supportive de Bouillon, who, though no angel himself when young, now stung his nephew to the quick with all-too-justified accusations of ingratitude and worse. Charles consigned his uncle to the same dustbin as James, Henry, Louis, and George Murray. Another set of relationships lay in ruins.

Yet more knives of falsely perceived rejection were being sharpened. France and England were moving towards peace. And with that would come the self-pitying prince's expulsion from France, as once had happened to his stoical father. It was against this background, peppered with Louise's tragic letters pleading with him to stay in love with her and the alienation of his immensely influential de Bouillon and Rohan relations, that Charles fell in love again. It was April 1748.

He turned now to an older woman. Once more the object of his passion was a cousin on his Polish mother's side. As Louise de Rohan sat in the opera on Sunday 28 April, having begged Charles in a note written the day before to 'look at me with the eyes I adore', she found herself tormented by the appearance of a new woman at her lover's side – their mutual cousin, Marie-Anne de la Trémoille, Princess de Talmont. At forty-seven, twice Louise's age, this notorious woman was from the princely family of Jabłonowski, whose grandfather had been one of King John Sobieski's field marshals at Vienna, whose mother was Prince James Sobieski's first cousin, whose brother Anthony was the Stuarts' plenipotentiary for the Sobieski inheritance in 1739, and whose father was the uncle of Stanislas Leszczyński, the deposed King of Poland and father-in-law of Louis XV, who now held his exiled court at Lunéville as Duke of the Lorraine ... and with whom both she and her sister had been lovers. Not only was Marie-Anne beautiful, she was brilliant, quick-witted, and held convention in contempt. She made her own rules. No one ordered her around. People feared her. In Charles' frustrated, embittered state, she was irresistible.

At much the same time, the approaching peace between France and England as well as the need to offset his brother's damaging appointment as a Roman Catholic cardinal, pushed Charles into sending Sir John Graeme to Berlin on a secret mission to ask for the hand of the King of Prussia's sister, or any other Protestant princess of the king's recommendation. He also asked for a suitable residence in view of his inevitable expulsion from France. Frederick the Great was believed to be an admirer of Charles, but his hands were tied by recently established friendly relations with Hanover, which he wasn't prepared to risk. The next Protestant candidate was the daughter of the Prince von Darmstadt. This also failed. Hanover's tentacles appeared to embrace all the German principalities.

Yet pressure on Charles was increasing as the peace talks of Aix-la-Chapelle[14] progressed. It was now June 1748 and the French government was pushing for clarification of the prince's plans. The Hanoverian negotiator, John Montagu, 4th Earl of Sandwich, was categorical in his insistence that Charles' expulsion from French territory was a *sine qua non* for peace. Upon the treaty's terms becoming public on 18 October, both James and his son formally protested. But Charles printed his with the place of writing ostentatiously given as Paris, where he was officially required to be incognito. Louis could no longer deny knowledge of his whereabouts to the English. And such was the prince's phenomenal popularity in France that his protest became a best-seller. In it he laid out all that the 'Forty-Five had achieved for France by way of diverting Hanoverian attention from the Continental theatre and the appalling cost that his supporters had suffered as a result of French inaction. The defiant but futile note of the people's hero could change nothing. In fact, it was an insult, but this time not to a private family such as the de Bouillons and Rohans. It was a public challenge to Louis XV himself, and it cut no ice that men such as Montesquieu admired the manifesto for its 'nobility and eloquence'.

From then on, Charles conducted an unwinnable war with the French authorities, in which they progressively hardened their methods by which to enforce his departure. For his part, the prince used every technique possible to whip up popular feeling. But whilst he couldn't succeed in overturning an international treaty in an authoritarian state not ripe for the Revolution, nevertheless, the ground was fertile for mischief. His heroic reputation amongst the citizenry of Paris was of legendary proportions, and his appearances at the Comédie, the opera, the Tuilleries, and even church generated mass adulation. Moreover, the French people were deeply unhappy about a peace agreement that seemed unnecessarily generous to the despised Hanoverian regime. If it was Charles' intention to capture the public's imagination by presenting himself as the innocent victim of a treacherous state that rewards those who have helped it by brutal eviction, then he certainly succeeded.

Realising that Charles' public threats of armed resistance and suicide were way beyond even her exceptionally elastic conception of acceptable behaviour, Marie-Anne de Talmont distanced herself from events. Yet this only provoked her lover to explode in rage at the very doors of the Talmont residence. Meanwhile, at Louis' request, James wrote Charles a long letter condemning his son's refusal to leave France. In it, he told him:

> I see you at the very edge of a precipice, ready to fall in, and I would be an abnormal father if I didn't at least do the little I can so as to save you, and that is why I find myself obliged to order you, as your father and your king, to conform without delay to the intentions of His Most Christian Majesty.

Louis then took advantage of the opportunity to 'enforce a son's obedience to his father's wishes'. He not only published James' letter but, fearing public rioting in support of Charles, outraged Paris by sending an armed force of 1,200 troops under Louis-Antoine, Duke de Biron, to arrest him on 10 December as he walked with three Highland officers to his nightly adulation at the opera. Biron's men tied Charles hand and foot and threw him into a coach as he mockingly asked, 'Where are we going? Are you taking me to Hanover?' They imprisoned him in the tower of the Château de Vincennes, holding him under permanent armed guard in a cramped cell. His officers were locked up in the infamous Bastille.

The number of men used in the operation exceeded the total Highland Army that had rallied at Glenfinnan in 1745. It was only three years since Charles had stayed at Exeter House in Derby, expecting to commence the final leg of his victorious campaign as the French were putting the finishing touches to an invasion force of 12,000. He had reached that high point of success against all the odds and with unimaginable speed. Yet now, locked up by his former French ally and cousin, who had made peace with their mutual enemy of Hanover, the turn of events seemed no less incredible. Vicious satire circulated in Paris, inspired by Marie-Anne and Charles' supporters, accusing Louis of being in the pay of Hanover:

> George, you say, forced you to refuse shelter
> To the valiant Edward;
> And if he had demanded of you,
> Faithless King, to exile your whore,
> Tell me, miserable creature, would you have done that too?[15]

Amongst those disgusted at the arrest was Voltaire. The Dauphin publicly wept in shame. The Marquis d'Argenson commented, 'We shall be placed, without doubt, alongside Cromwell, who decapitated his king, and we, we have uselessly strung up the legitimate heir presumptive of that Crown!' Such was the groundswell of sympathy for Charles and universal condemnation of Louis that the government even made a ludicrous attempt to outlaw public conversation about the prince.

Yet, however much of a storm Charles had provoked, he had no choice but to leave France. For good measure, Louis exiled Marie-Anne to Leszczyński's Lorraine and refused her permission to bid farewell to her lover as he passed through Fontainebleau on his way to the Papal state of Avignon. He arrived there at seven in the morning on 27 December and was announced at James Murray's house as an Irish officer. His host said, 'I was never more surprised to see him at my bedside.' He had come with Sheridan, one officer, and three servants. Soon after, he was joined by the indomitable Marie-Anne and got in touch with John Hay. With them, he saw in the New Year of 1749 and celebrated his twenty-ninth birthday, writing to his father in Rome: 'I arrived here on Friday last, and am in perfect good health, notwithstanding the unheard of barbarous and inhuman treatment I met with.'

Another person who wrote to King James that New Year was his niece and the woman Charles had once adored and who loved him still. It was signed 'Louise de La Tour d'Auvergne, Princess de Rohan'. When she sent those greetings, her child by Charles was still at her side. Eighteen days into the New Year, the baby boy died. It is not known if, when he was at Avignon, the prince was informed. He left the city on 28 February accompanied only by his equerry Henry Goring and three servants – his every move observed, recorded, and relayed back to Westminster by the Hanoverian spy Walton.

Derby in 1745 had been the watershed, Culloden in 1746, the military defeat, but it was Charles' arrest in December 1748 that ended his desperate, frenzied struggle to rescue something from the 'Forty-Five, something of his dreams. Professor L. L. Bongie in *The Love of a Prince* writes, 'Afterwards, moral integrity and tranquillity of mind left him forever ... During the last forty years of his life, he who was once so ambitious to succeed, and who seemed in the beginning so richly deserving of success, attempted little that was commendable and accomplished even less.' Up until Charles' arrest, Bongie speaks of 'all his early promise, the hopes, prayers, and single-minded sacrifices, the high sense of purpose, the courage, the magnanimity and basic fairness of a true hero'. Thereafter, all those fine qualities 'rotted away'. It would not be too long before Charles would scribble

> To speke to ete
> To think to Drink

then cross it out and write instead

> To ete to think
> To Speke to drink.

His brother Henry referred to it as 'the nasty bottle'.

6

Flight from Carlsbourg: Plots & Parenthood 1749-1760

My life is done, yet all remains
The breath has gone, the image not
The furious shapes once forged in heat
Live on, though now no longer hot.

Edwin Muir

From Avignon, Charles travelled to Lunéville where Marie-Anne de Talmont had estates and her relation and former lover, Stanislas Leszczyński, ex-King of Poland and Duke of the Lorraine, held his bustling Franco-Polish court at his enormous château, which almost rivalled his son-in-law Louis' Versailles. Charles' destination was no accident. Because Lunéville was no ordinary court. It was a hotbed of potential contacts for Charles, related as he was to the French Bourbons, de Bouillons and Rohans, and through the Polish Sobieskis to the Radziwiłłs and Jabłonowskis.

Leszczyński was a highly enlightened man who attracted intellectuals such as Voltaire, who was staying at Lunéville when Charles' arrest in December 1748 was announced. At the very time, he was reading passages to a group including the ex-king himself from a manuscript describing the prince's 'noble exploits and heroic sufferings'.

To Lunéville flocked aristocrats and politicians from Poland's elite, opposed to Russia's suffocating hegemony over their country. Typical was Bishop Joseph Załuski, an enormously well-connected relation of the Sobieskis with significant influence not only at Leszczyński's court but also at those of the Pope, the King of France, King James, and others. On 18 May 1736, James and Charles made him the Stuarts' plenipotentiary for the Sobieski inheritance together with Marie-Anne de Talmont's brother, Prince Anthony Jabłonowski. Załuski prided himself on knowing everyone who was anyone throughout Europe.

Not by chance was Załuski a client of the 'Second Banker of Europe', or, as others put it, 'the Greatest Banker of the North', Peter Fergusson-Tepper. Such men executed currency and bill of exchange transactions, payments, held deposits, made investments, arranged loans, and acted as merchants for international commissions. They often owned large stores trading in expensive imported goods and were the trusted, discreet financiers and advisers who shadowed monarchs and nobles whose agricultural fortunes could not function smoothly without them in this credit-based environment. These were men like the Stuarts' bankers Waters (father and son) in Paris, or the Rohans' bankers Turnbull, Forbes & Co. in London and Pierre Riaucourt in Warsaw, or Fergusson-Tepper, also based in Warsaw but of Edinburgh origin and whose clients included Catherine the Great, King Stanislas Augustus Poniatowski of Poland, and Prince Charles Radziwiłł. Like today, these bankers formed an international network that knew no bounds.

Fergusson-Tepper's client, Radziwiłł, was not only the Stuarts' closest Polish cousin, he was also related to Marie-Anne de Talmont and was the leading pro-French opponent of Russian hegemony over Poland. Governor of Vilnius and Duke of Nieśwież, Radziwiłł was one of Europe's richest men and the son of Prince Michael, who as a young man used to hunt with the future Louis XV and future Duke de Bouillon. It was this Michael Radziwiłł who in 1739 bought the seven towns and 140 villages comprising the Żółkiew estate from the Stuart princes' Sobieska aunt. And it was these Radziwiłłs whom Charles had in mind when he wrote to his father in 1746 urging a bride for his younger brother Henry.

One Lunéville regular deeply sympathetic to Radziwiłł's pro-French anti-Russian politics was the brother-in-law of Charles' cousin and ex-lover, Louise de Rohan. That man was Cardinal Louis de Rohan, French Ambassador to Vienna and coadjutor of the bishopric of Strasbourg, the richest in France and a sovereign principality, which would pass into his hands shortly before he would scandalise all Europe as the hero of Marie-Antoinette's *Affaire du Collier de la Reine*.

Another web of powerful connections at Lunéville lay in the *Secret du Roi*. This was the personal secret service of the French king, which for decades infiltrated and influenced every meaningful Polish political centre and court, especially Radziwiłł's, as well as the banking community, in pursuit of the Bourbons' interest in placing their candidate on the only elective throne in Europe – that of the Polish-Lithuanian Commonwealth. The Count de Broglie was its director, succeeded by the Bourbon Prince de Conti. Amongst their agents were the banker Tepper and Cardinal de Rohan.

Lunéville was also thick with Freemasons. Probably from the early 1690s, but certainly by the 1720s, Freemasonry had become firmly established at the Stuart court of St Germain. From 1715, the Hanoverians had tried to infiltrate and take over the Masonic lodges of England and France, until then firmly loyal to the Stuarts. But though they succeeded in London, they failed in France and by mid-century had given up. At that time, French and Polish Freemasonry was an aristocratic and Catholic organisation whose secrecy was highly attractive, as it bypassed the centralised oppressive French and Russian states, of which the French populace had had enough, as their Revolution would soon demonstrate, whilst the Poles had every reason to circumvent the machinery of Russian hegemony. Paradoxically, even Louis XV held a *Loge du Roi* at Versailles, whilst the Bourbon Duke d'Orléans stood at the head of the French lodges, which included the *Grand Orient de Bouillon* presided over by Charles' uncle, who was succeeded by his son, Turenne. Leszczyński, Radziwiłł, most

Previous page: 1. King James VIII & III (1688-1766), Prince Charles Edward's father. This portrait hung in his wife's bedroom in the Palazzo del Re in Rome, the original of which was painted by Martin van Meytens in 1725 to celebrate the birth of Prince Henry. The original is lost but this 1730 copy by the Stuarts' court painter Antonio David is the only known version by that artist, who also painted the 1729 portraits of Charles and Henry at the Scottish National Portrait Gallery.

Opposite: 2. Queen Clementina (1702-35), née Princess Sobieska, granddaughter of King John III of Poland, and Prince Charles Edward's mother. This painting hung in her husband's bedroom at the Palazzo del Re and is a pendant by Antonio David to the portrait of James. They were the couple's favourite portraits and they ordered a number of copies in 1727-28 from the English artist E. Gill but resigned from the commission because they were unhappy with the quality.

Above: 3. Prince Charles Edward Stuart (1720-1788), miniature by Jean Daniel Kamm (1748), after the lost original by Louis Tocqué completed in January 1748 and then given by the prince to the first great love of his life, his maternal first cousin, Princess Louise de Rohan, Duchess de Montbazon.

Next page: 4. Charlotte Stuart, Duchess of Albany (1753-89), by Hugh Douglas Hamilton, the daughter and heiress of Prince Charles by Clementina Walkinshaw. Legitimised by her father and granted the rank of Royal Highness with the right of succession, she was recognised by the Pope, the King and Parliament of France, as well as the Grand Duke of Tuscany, but survived Prince Charles by only a year, dying from cancer of the liver just weeks after the outbreak of the French Revolution.

5. Prince Henry Stuart (1725-1807) by Maurice Quentin de La Tour. Until 2009, this portrait was believed to be of Prince Charles Edward. It was started in January 1746 and finished in February 1747, before Henry's appointment as Cardinal in June 1747. It was commissioned whilst Henry was in Paris during the winter of 1745/46, when he believed he would soon be sailing with the French fleet to join his victorious brother in Britain prior to a glorious Stuart restoration.

6. Marie-Victoire, the Demoiselle de Thorigny (1779-1836), the daughter of Charlotte Stuart and Ferdinand de Rohan. Legitimised at baptism by her uncle, Jules-Hercule, Duke de Moutbazon and head of the sovereign Princes de Rohan, she alone kept the bloodline going. This portrait of *c.* 1800 shows her just prior to her marriage to Paul Anthony, Chevalier de Nikorowicz, the rich, discreet merchant banker to the Stuarts' closest Polish cousins, the Princes Radziwiłł, from which family Prince Charles suggested finding a bride for his younger brother Henry in November 1746.

7. General Prince Louis de Rohan (1768-1836), painted in 1830 by Alexis Valbrun. Louis was the grandson of Prince Jules-Hercule, Duke de Montbazon and Marie-Victoire's long-standing confidant. Of their intimate Parisian correspondence from 1815/16 to 1825 some twenty-three of her letters survive in the Rohan archive from their estate of Sychrov in the Czech Republic. Of the many links between Marie-Victoire's cousin, Prince Louis, and Sir Charles Stuart (ill. 9), who helped her brother in 1817 and son in 1822, the most intimate was via the vastly rich, very beautiful but extraordinarily eccentric Wilhelmina de Biron, Princess of Courland, Duchess de Sagan, who was Louis' ex-wife and Sir Charles' ex-lover.

8. Bonnie Prince Charlie's unique great-grandchild, Marie-Victoire's son, Antime, Chevalier de Nikorowicz (1804-52), painted *c.* 1823 when he became an officer of the elite 4th Cuirassiers of the Habsburg Crown Prince Ferdinand, arranged in 1822 by the British Ambassador in Paris, Sir Charles Stuart. Because his mother never told him her 'Secret', Antime's was the first generation not to know that Marie-Victoire was the heir of the last Stuarts.

9. Sir Charles Stuart (1779-1845), Lord Stuart de Rothesay, painted in 1830 by Sir George Hayter. Seen wearing the robes of his 1828 peerage and the chain of a Knight Grand Cross of the Bath, he was British Ambassador to France from 1815-24 and 1828-30. In Paris, he not only knew Marie-Victoire and her brother, but also their 'Secret' thanks to the Coutts family of his aunt Frances, Lady Bute, who had been chaperoned for a year in Paris by Clementina Walkinshaw. It was Sir Charles who found a position for Antime in the Habsburg Crown Prince's 4th Cuirassiers through his friend, Lord Clanwilliam, whose brother-in-law, Count Karl Clam-Martinitz, commanded the regiment.

10. Antime, Chevalier de Nikorowicz, *c.* 1828, painted by Leopold Fertbauer, shortly after he left the Crown Prince's 4th Cuirassiers and prior to his marriage in 1829. Antime fought in the Polish Rising of 1831 and, during the Spring of the Nations in 1848, was unanimously elected commanding officer of the 1,200-strong Academic Legion.

11. Antime's eldest son, *c.* 1836, who was given the ill-fated Stuart name of Charles, never before used in his father's family. He joined the Spring of the Nations in 1848 but, ten years later, lost an 'American duel', whereby he had to commit suicide, which he did on 31 August 1859 in Versailles.

12. Antime's daughter, Julia Thérèse, Countess Pinińska (1833-93). Of the family's daughters, she was the only one who bore her husband a male heir, whose line survives unbroken to the present day. She also succeeded her brother Charles as the heiress of Grzymałów Castle, which remained her descendants main home until 1939.

of the Rohans, and Fergusson-Tepper were all Freemasons. Soon, Charles himself would become the *Soleil d'Or, Milete de Bretagne* and describe himself as head of the Order of the Temple and Grand Master of the *Ecossaise et Anglaise de la Constance*, part of a European-wide Jacobite Catholic Freemasonry movement of the *Rite Ecossais Ancien et Accepté* that supported the Stuarts. Charles' lodge included such influential Poles as Prince Sapieha and Count Szembek as well as the son of Count Brühl, the penultimate Polish king's all-powerful minister.

Thus, at Lunéville, through his relations, the bankers, members of the *Secret du Roi*, and Freemasons (many in more than one category) Charles had access to an extraordinarily extensive, close-knit, transcontinental network of the most powerful contacts. Small wonder his biographer Frank McLynn would describe him as being 'always at least one step ahead of those who sought him'.

And it was at Lunéville in April 1749 that Prince Charles planned his return to Paris to see his banker, George Waters, and stay a week, hidden by his lover, Marie-Anne de Talmont. In so doing, Charles broke his word to Louis XV never to return to France. But of that he cared little. He was not the only one who thought that Louis had been the first to prove faithless.

Once in the French capital, the prince's presence was soon noticed by the authorities, who put their internal security forces on nationwide alert. They issued standing orders to arrest Charles on sight, distributed 'wanted' posters bearing his likeness, and later carried out regular police searches for him both in Paris and Lunéville. By the end of April, he had returned with Marie-Anne to the Lorraine, whence he left via Strasbourg for Venice, from which he was promptly expelled after just a week, despite a personal appeal to the Empress Maria-Theresa. By early June, he was back in Paris and, on Marie-Anne's recommendation, approached her friend, Mademoiselle Elisabeth Ferrand, asking if she would agree to act as recipient for letters to be sent to him by Waters, addressed to Mr John Douglas, Charles' pseudonym.

Yet things developed further than that. For Mademoiselle Ferrand and Countess Antoinette de Vassé had rooms in the Convent of St Joseph on the rue Ste Dominique. Such guesthouses of convents were dwelling places for ladies and their children. It was there that Charles installed himself, secretly enjoying the company of these two women and his lover as well as their intellectual friends. At night, a secret staircase led him directly to Marie-Anne's rooms. But it could not be a permanent arrangement for several reasons. Firstly, Charles was in France illegally and had to remain on the move so as not to be caught by the French authorities – by November 1749, he was back again at Lunéville. Secondly, he was still obsessed by the Stuart Cause, which he could not effectively advance whilst in hiding. Thirdly, his paranoia was deepening and he felt the threat of assassins ever more frequently. Nor without reason. For Sir Charles Hanbury Williams in Dresden and the Earl of Hyndford in Moscow had both enthusiastically offered to organise his murder, and it would only be two years before the Whig fanatic Grossart actually tried to do so. Not that killing the Stuarts was a new idea for the London government. For example, in 1715, the British Ambassador in Paris, John Dalrymple, 2nd Earl of Stair, employed assassins to kill Charles' father, then in 1717 sent another to try again in Avignon, and one more was discovered at Urbino a year later, etc. Fourthly, Charles' passionate affair with Marie-Anne was degenerating. Ultimately, the lovers came to blows and their violent fights became so noisy that Madame de Vassé asked them to leave. However, their stormy relationship had more than a year to run until ended abruptly by Charles.

Up until this time, the prince had been financed by credit from Waters against the money that had arrived at Loch nan Uamh after Charles' escape from Culloden to the Outer Isles. It was known as the Loch Arkaig treasure and was being looked after in the Highlands by Cluny Macpherson. Now, in 1749, he received some £6,000 of it via Major Kennedy as well as £15,000 through Henry Goring from English Jacobites who made it conditional upon Charles removing the worst of his drinking companions from his household. At the same time, there were promising signs of renewed Jacobite activity in England, where Dr William King of St Mary's Hall, Oxford, claimed that 275 English supporters were ready to present signed testimonies, and one or two public pro-Stuart demonstrations had occurred. Charles resolved to go on a reconnaissance mission to London in 1750, writing that he 'is determined to go over at any rate' and 'will expose nobody but himself, supposing the worst'. He asked Sir Charles Goring to send a ship to Antwerp in mid-August, deposited 186,000 livres with Waters and, through a merchant, Mr Dormer, his 'chief medium of intelligence with England', ordered '20,000 guns, bayonets, ammunition proportioned, with 4,000 swords and pistols for horses in one ship which is to be the first, and in the second, 6,000 guns without bayonets but sufficient ammunition, and 6,000 broadswords'.

He wrote to his father in July, asking in an encoded message for a renewal of his commission of 1745. James' weary reply makes a stark contrast to his son's feverish activity. He felt Charles to be 'a continual heartbreak'. Nevertheless, he agreed:

> for I am sensible that should I have refused to send it, it might happen to be of great inconvenience to you. But let me recommend to you not to use other people as you do me, by expecting friendship and favours from them while you do all that is necessary to disgust them, for you must not expect that anybody else will make you the return I do.

The journey to London achieved nothing except that he went to the 'New Church in the Strand' and became a Protestant. Just as Charles had been in 1747 when Henry became a cardinal, so now were his father and brother 'ill with grief' when they heard of his conversion. His supporters rued the fact that he had not done the same thing in 1745. In London, Charles probably stayed at the house of Anne, dowager Viscountess Primrose on Essex street off the Strand. Upon appearing there unannounced, his astonished hostess immediately sent for Dr King, who wrote:

> If I was surprised to find him there, I was still more astonished when he acquainted me with the motives which had induced him to hazard a journey to England at this juncture. The impatience of our friends in exile had formed a scheme which was impractible ... No preparations had been made ... He was soon convinced that he had been deceived.

Charles also met about fifty English Jacobites, including the Duke of Beaufort and the Earl of Westmoreland. But nothing came of it and he left on 2 September, deeply disillusioned, arriving in Paris via Antwerp on the 24th, where he described his existence as 'sad loneliness'.

Staying only a short time, he left again for Lunéville where he took his frustration out on Marie-Anne, who wrote, 'I love you too much and you love me too little ... I see clearly, and with extreme grief, that you want to pick a lover's quarrel and set yourself at variance with me.' Next he hid in a château described as 'a lonely and solitary place', moved on to Boulogne-sur-Mer by January 1751, and then to Germany a month later, where he was received by Frederick the Great 'with great civility'. Having admired Charles' bravery in the 'Forty-Five, the Prussian King could do little for him now, though the arch-cynic continued to stay in touch through Henry Goring and the Earl Marischal. The thirty-two-year-old Charles returned to Paris.

Most of that year was spent between Paris and Lunéville. Yet, once again, his optimistic nature picked up. For the Elibank Plot was being hatched by Alexander Murray and his brother Patrick, Lord Elibank. Both were ardent Jacobites, though neither had been out in the 'Forty-Five. Murray's plan was to enlist some officers of Lord Ogilvy's regiment, cross over to England, and raise a body of several hundred supporters who would then storm St James' Palace and assassinate George II and his family on 10 November 1752. Murray had promised to find 500 loyal men in and around Westminster. Charles had become convinced he was about to form a strong alliance with Frederick the Great, or so he wanted the conspirators to believe. And they hoped that General James Keith, brother of the Earl Marischal, now Prussian Ambassador to Versailles, would agree to land in Scotland with some Swedish troops just prior to the outbreak of a rising led by Lochiel's brothers John Cameron of Fassiefern and Dr Archie Cameron, as well as Cameron of Glen Nevis, Ewen Macpherson of Cluny, MacDonell of Lochgarry, Forbes of Skellater, Robertson of Woodsheal, and Robertson of Blairfettie. Amongst the Scottish leaders was Alastair Ruadh MacDonell, Younger of Glengarry, who promised to have 'above 400 brave Highlanders ready at my call'.

Prince Charles briefed the Cameron brothers as well as Lochgarry and the others at Menin in Flanders and, two days later, was joined by Young Glengarry. But the man who had promised 400 men was a traitor, a Hanoverian spy code-named 'Pickle' who was relaying details of the plot back to Westminster. Perhaps the Jacobites got wind of it, for the plan was postponed and never revived. However, the still-unpopular Hanoverian regime, not wanting to publicise the existence of significant Jacobite activity, decided to make an example of one conspirator, whom they charged under the seven-year-old Act of Attainder for the 'Forty-Five. In March, following the collapse of the plot, Dr Archie Cameron failed to escape back to the Continent and was hiding at Brenachyle on Loch Katrineside at the home of David Stewart of Glenbuckie. Another Hanoverian spy, Samuel Cameron, brother of Glen Nevis and known as Crookshanks, told the commander of the garrison at Inversnaid about Dr Archie's whereabouts. Redcoats surrounded the house and arrested him, despite the fact that some children tried to warn him. He was taken to the Tower of London and, at Tyburn, on 7 June 1753, hanged, drawn and quartered, without trial.

During his imprisonment, Dr Archie had not been allowed pen, ink, nor paper. But with an overlooked, blunt pencil, he wrote a testimony on five scraps, the last of which read:

> I pray to God to hasten the restoration of the Royal Family, without which these miserably divided nations can never enjoy peace and happiness, and that it may please Him to preserve the King, the Prince of Wales, and the Duke of York from the power and malice of their enemies, to prosper and reward all my friends and benefactors, and to forgive all my enemies, murderers, and false accusers, from the Elector of Hanover and his bloody son down to Samuel Cameron, the basest of their spies, as I freely do from the bottom of my heart.
>
> Archibald Cameron

Elsewhere, Charles wrote: '*De vivre et pas de vivre, c'est beaucoup pis que de mourir*'.

What is striking about the Elibank plot is the treachery by a member of the family of a Highland chieftain. Likewise, Dr Archie's death was the result of betrayal by one of his own clansmen. Though France's military and political situation had not been conducive, perhaps Charles had been right when pleading with Louis XV for military intervention in 1746 before, as he had pointed out, the demoralising policies of Westminster could take effect.

Regular and large amounts of alcohol as well as his violent tormented affairs with Louise de Rohan and Marie-Anne de Talmont had exhausted much of the emotion that had engulfed Charles since Culloden. The Elibank Plot raised and dashed his hopes. Another loyal supporter, the brother of his faithful Lochiel, had been horribly executed – another wife widowed – another eight children left fatherless. Such intense guilt, disappointment, fear of the assassin's knife, drink, and the life of an outlaw constituted a level of stress that was unsustainable. Charles began to seek refuge in domesticity. Even prior to the Elibank Plot, some signs of this had appeared, as he had started to collect books, paintings, marble busts, and fine wines, despite the fact he had no home in which to put them. Waters the banker had to house them all and would receive detailed and meticulous instructions from the prince. Even more telling was Charles' acquisition of a house in mid-1751. Soon he would write:

> Be pleased, dear Sir, to give a distinct address how to find Mrs Clemi in writing to the bearer as he is an absolutely trusty servant. Also a letter to the bearer by which you are to say to the said Mrs Clemi that she may give entire credit to my servant (he will deliver the letter) as to anything whatsoever he may say to her. All this must be an inviolable secret betwixt us and you may be assured of my sincere friendship.
>
> John Douglas

This was followed by two from John O'Sullivan:

> Cambrai, 29 May 1752
>
> Sir,
> Nothing in life could have surprised me more than the sight of Your Royal Highness' letter. I kissed it a hundred times ... As to the person Your Royal Higness speaks of, I can assure Your Highness, upon my word of honour, I don't know what directions to give the bearer about her ... Her letter to me was from Dunkirk where she gave me to understand that if she had no account from you, that her intention was to go into a convent, and expressed to me that she wasn't very opulent ... As soon as I am informed of anything about her, I'll take the liberty to write by the way of Mr Wolf, to inform Your Highness of what comes to my knowledge.
> Champville

> Cambrai, 31 May 1752
>
> Mademoiselle,
> Since your last letter I have received a reply to yours sent to me without an address. This is entirely to your satisfaction, being that which you desire, and worthy of the person who has sent it. The matter at present is that you should be by this person's side, as the person absolutely desires.
> J. O'Sullivan

O'Sullivan had been devoted to Charles during the 'Forty-Five, escaped with him after Culloden, shared the first half of those five punitive months skulking in the Outer Isles, and then helped send the ships from France that rescued him. Mrs Clemi is Clementina Walkinshaw, whom Charles met at the Bannockburn home of her grandfather, Sir Hugh Paterson, where she nursed him through his illness after the Jacobite victory at Falkirk. There exists no evidence that proves that Clementina and Charles had been in touch since that time. Indeed, Charles had been too involved with Louise de Rohan and Marie-Anne de Talmont. Yet something now stirred both to seek each other out, and the desire seems to have been spontaneous and mutual.

Perhaps Charles' need for tranquillity recalled the gentle Jacobite nurse from the land of his beloved Highlanders, and for whom he was perhaps still a hero. For it was she who had tended to his fever during his ten day convalescence at Bannockburn House when his dreams seemed within grasp. That for her he might still be a knight in shining armour brings to mind the fairy-tale Italian chivalry that pervaded the atmosphere of his innocent Roman childhood when his mother was still alive. Charles knew that Clementina's father had been out in the 'Fifteen, a Jabobite Ambassador in Vienna, and involved in the arrangement of his parents' marriage. Moreover, Clementina was his mother's namesake and, some believe, her god-daughter. Had she not been linked to him since childhood?

Given Charles' exhaustion and disillusionment, the presence of some role he expected Clementina to act out is almost palpable. Maybe he hoped she might help him find a way forward. But if so, she had no chance to fulfil it. As for her, it seems she might have believed some platonic love or mutual attraction had sprung up between them. Though Lord Elcho claimed the two became lovers in 1746, his views are of little value, as he tried to make his peace with the Hanoverians after Culloden and was a man of cruel and vindictive character who had grown to despise Charles. And whilst it seems even probable that a man suffering from high fever should feel tenderness for his nurse, it seems less likely that he should attempt his first sexual conquest whilst ill. Furthermore, Charles' lack of interest in women was widely commented upon by contemporary observers during the 'Forty-Five. In Balhaldy's words, it was not until his affair with Louise de Rohan that he abandoned 'the resolution he had taken of being singular in that virtue'. His valet also confirmed that previously he had been 'given to no vice'.

Clementina later spoke of a promise she had made in 1746 'to follow the prince anywhere in the world' – something, however, many Jacobite girls must have said. And that between 1744 and 1747 she was 'undone' – which, in the language of the time, can be made to mean almost anything. It is also said that, about this time, she refused the marriage proposals of Archibald Stuart, Provost of Edinburgh, and John Campbell, 5th Duke of Argyll. What is certain is that her grandfather arranged a place for her as a canoness of a Noble Chapter at Douai. Having arrived at Dunkirk, she wrote to O'Sullivan in what presumably constituted her last chance to avoid that fate and see her prince again. In any case, the couple met in Paris in the summer of 1752 and went to Liège, where they lived together openly as husband and wife, using the name Count and Countess Johnson. According to Young Glengarry, Prince Charles 'keeps her well and seems to be very fond of her'. This was more than can be said of the English Jacobites who feared she was a spy because her sister Catherine was a lady-in-waiting to the Hanoverian Princess of Wales. Nor was Clementina approved of by James, Henry, or many of the more ardent Jacobites, all of whom felt that her presence would stand in the way of an advantageous political marriage for Charles, which might further the Stuart Cause. Each, over the next few years, would do everything possible to influence Charles against her, either by way of parental pressure, insults, insinuations that she was a spy, or straightforward bribery.

Nevertheless, the couple were very happy at first, and when Clementina appeared in public, Charles was always at her side, courteous, attentive, making no secret of their relationship, even when she was pregnant a year later. Clementina's sole motive for being with Charles seems to have been selfless love. For she made no apparent attempt to persuade him to marry her, even in 1753 when she gave birth to a baby girl who was christened on 29 October in the Church of Notre Dame des Fonts at Liège. Their happiness may even be reflected in the baptismal entry: 'Charlotte, daughter of the noble Seigneur William Johnson and the noble Dame Charlotte Pitt'. It is hard to believe they were not laughing when they chose the surname of that contemporary English statesman for her alias – William Pitt being at that time Paymaster of the Armed Forces!

It was Clementina's unswerving loyalty that seems to have appealed so much to Charles. But as his paranoid suspicion towards ever more people grew, so too was she doomed to become a victim. An indication of the prince's unbalanced state of mind appears in a letter to his father dated 18 November 1756:

> Allow me to take the liberty to mention some persons you should have guard against and not trust, Tencin, O'Brien and his Lady, Warren, Lord Clare, MacGregor, Sir J. Harrington, Aeneas MacDonald, O'Sullivan, the two Glengarries ...

The significance of this black-list was that it named most of Charles' remaining friends.

But his relationship with Clementina began to deteriorate not long after the daughter was born whom he adored, with whom he loved to play, and whom he affectionately called 'Pouponne' – meaning a little girl with a plump face. In the aftermath of Dr Archie's execution and the collapse of the Elibank Plot, his view of the future was bleak. For the present, wherever he went, he was followed by Hanoverian and French Government spies. Haunting him also was the fear of assassination, which would cause him to rush off and spend weeks hiding in German towns. To make matters worse, his finances were in a dreadful state and he had to sell his two jade-handled pistols. When he called at the house of the Duke and Duchess d'Aiguillon, he was almost turned away as 'an ill-dressed stranger'.

In these circumstances, Charles began to drink even more heavily, suffer black depressions, take offence at the drop of a hat, and fly into rages. For Clementina, the stress of such an atmosphere and worry about the future of their young child whilst living in ever more straightened circumstances was unbearable. Inevitably, the couple quarrelled – frequently and publicly. In November 1753, Charles wrote to Henry Goring telling him, with regard to the household he was still maintaining there, 'I have written to Avignon to discard all my Papist servants ... My Mistress has behaved so unworthily that she has put me out of all patience and as she is a Papist too, I discard her also!' Clementina was sent away to some friends of hers in Paris, but Charles immediately regretted it and the couple were reconciled.

Thereafter, they lived for a while in the French capital, but the problem didn't go away. O'Sullivan described one quarrel in the Bois de Boulogne as 'a devilish warm dispute'. Charles was also plagued by English Jacobites who came to try and persuade him to get rid of Clementina, describing her as 'a harlot'. But he would not hear of it. He described France as an 'abominable country' in which he was 'not able to breathe as much as the fresh air without the greatest apprehension'. Communication with James in Rome ceased completely, and his father wrote, 'I should not so much know he were alive did I not hear from second and third hands that those who have the same share in his confidence say he is in good health; for it is now more than two years since he has writ here at all.' The ever-faithful Henry Goring could take no more and resigned, pleading, 'For God's sake, Sir, have compassion on yourself.' But the prince flew into a rage and, despite Goring's long years of service and hardship, turned him out with nothing but insults. Charles was foolish enough to complain of the incident to George Keith. But Keith knew better and, taking Goring with him to Berlin in 1754, permanently broke off relations with Charles, who fell into despair. He wrote to Keith: 'My heart is broke enough, without that you should finish it.' The heroic Ewen Macpherson of Cluny, finally authorised to leave his decade of hiding in the Highlands and come over with the remnants of the Loch Arkaig treasure, tried to get Charles to drink tea instead of beer when thirsty and raise him from his depression. But he just met with hostility. Cluny must have wondered whether this was the same person as the dynamic, optimistic prince with whom he had once hidden in the Cage, who, when he had tried to kneel, had stopped him and embraced him instead.

Towards the end of 1755 until 1756, Charles, Clementina and Charlotte lived in Basle in the guise of Dr and Mrs Thompson and daughter. In the words of the Hanoverian minister in Berne, they lived as 'persons of easy fortune, but without the least affectation of show or magnificence'. Still their life continued to be dogged by financial difficulties. Charles was reduced to begging from Louis XV, whose pension he had once refused. Waters the banker wrote to James that 'as to the supplies from England, they have apparently stopped for good'. The English Jacobites cut off Charles' funding because of their unjustified suspicion of Clementina and a growing abhorrence of the prince's behaviour.

The couple's life was unstable for other reasons. In a letter dated 28 May 1756, the British minister in Berne wrote that 'though the Young Chevalier was often backward and forward, Basle was still his abode, and that his family continued there at this time'. It was this relentless coming and going, sometimes with his family, sometimes without, usually under a pseudonym, which was so unsettling. No doubt associated with Charles' fear of assassination, it was also prompted by his association with the pan-European Jacobite Masonic lodges and the multiplicity of plots and schemes they were incessantly inventing.

Such was the dismal psychological and financial condition of the *de jure* heir to the thrones of Scotland, England and Ireland when, in 1755, France and Hanoverian England once again found themselves at war. And with war came renewed interest in the Stuart Cause. Prospects seemed so good that even Lord George Murray, who had been so bitter in 1746, declared his readiness to fight once more. Charles' prospects for a politically advantageous marriage were also in the ascendant for the same reason. This was something about which his father had been becoming progressively more anxious. On 28 March 1756, he wrote to Charles that, with regard to the courts of Europe, 'I have never been abandoned by them, and they have so much at heart the preservation of our family'. However, concerning the French court's proposal to arrange a marriage with a lady 'who would not have been at all unbecoming to me to accept of', James reproached Charles that nothing would come of this because his son had 'taken care to let it be known that he would not enter into such proposals'. James was desperate and wrote to Louis as well as to Cardinal Pierre de Tencin asking them to help. He also sent Sir John Graeme to his son. But to no avail. Finally, James wrote to his son in October, trying to persuade him to come to Rome in the hope that he could somehow bring him to his senses: 'You will not grudge this one journey to see your old father that he may embrace you, bless you, and give you his best advice once more before his death ... I shall keep you here but a few days and as privately as you please.' At first, Charles agreed and, leaving Clementina and Charlotte in Liège, left for Paris. Then he changed his mind.

In 1757, the French asked Charles if he would like to lead their attack on Minorca. But he refused. There then followed meetings with Louis XV's ministers, the Duke de Richelieu and the Duke de Choiseul. Such was the prince's attitude that they concluded it was impossible to work with him. So long had Charles been consumed by bitter cynicism towards French ministers, so long had that cynicism been magnified by drink, that the thought of gathering his remaining strength and raising his hopes once more was more than he could manage. His father wrote, 'Act at least your part as a true Patriot, a dutiful son and a man of honour and sense; if you are in lethargy rise out of it, if you are not show it by your action.' Charles was burnt out. Yet there was no other Stuart the French could harness to their plans. James was too old, Henry had disqualified himself by becoming a cardinal, and Charles' daughter, Charlotte, was still a child and anyway a girl.

Later that year, the French began preparations to launch an attack on Ireland. Again, Charles was offered a role. Again he refused. Several months later, in February 1759, he was invited to discuss matters with de Choiseul, now foreign minister. He turned up drunk. Yet such was the political importance of even an alcoholic Stuart prince that the French carried on with the talks, mainly through Alexander Murray and Lord Clancarty. But Charles kept upping his demands and conditions – all of which Pickle the spy was relaying back to the Hanoverians, who must have been rubbing their hands with glee.

When large-scale naval preparations had finally been built up, the French asked Charles to ready himself and come to Brest. He even went so far as to write a proclamation in which he was to publicly announce his renunciation of Roman Catholicism. But the invasion under the Count de Conflans sailed without him, which was fortunate, because it was destroyed in Quiberon Bay by Admiral Hawke in November 1759. Writing in January 1760, Sir Richard Warren reveals the optimism for a Stuart restoration which had been felt by the Jacobites just prior to embarkation:

> This last sea fight has suspended for some time the execution of a scheme that could not but be advantageous to the Cause. Once landed we were sure to bring our neighbourhood to a better understanding. Never troops could show such impatience to be at the other side of the water nor could anything express the confidence they had in the Duke d'Aiguillon, our general.

With the French fleet destroyed, there was now no power in Europe with the naval potential to launch a successful invasion of England. No hope remained. A few months later, George III ascended the Stuarts' throne with neither worry nor hindrance.

Charles returned to the Château de Carlsbourg on the Bouillon estate of his uncle, with whom he was back on better terms. There, besides Clementina and Charlotte, he had the company of his uncle's plenipotentiary, Monsieur Thibault. With him, he would shoot or fish by day and drink himself into oblivion by night. One day, deep in his cups, Charles wrote:

> Thinking not Drinking
> Drinking not Thinking
> Can not be a Tool
> Or like a fool.

In Rome, James was more worried than ever about his son. In March 1760, he begged him to come and see him, pitifully telling him he could do so in complete secrecy and sending money for the trip. Perhaps realising he was in no fit state to be seen, Charles wrote back claiming to be 'suffering from nerves'. Someone genuinely in that condition was Clementina, with whom Charles argued incessantly, not least about Charlotte, whom her mother wanted to send away to be educated in a Parisian convent. But Charles doted on her and was categoric that his little Pouponne should always be beside him. According to the lurid description of the vindictive Lord Elcho, Charles would beat Clementina as often as fifty times a day and at night construct a defense system of chairs, tables and bells around their bed for fear of assassins. Whatever truth there was in this, Charles was obviously violent when drunk and deluded when sober.

The prince now contrasted women with men, writing of them as 'being so much more wicked and impenetrable'. It was more than Clementina could bear, deeply concerned about the effect on Charlotte. They had lived as a family for eight years, and later, when writing of this period, she would say that she had been pushed 'to the greatest extremity, and even despair, and I was always in perpetual dread of my life from your violent passions'. Consequently, at the end of July 1760, when the family was still at Bouillon, Clementina hired a coach and, taking Charlotte with her, drove to Paris. She wrote, 'There is not one woman in the world who would have suffered so long as what I have done ... I quit my dearest prince with the deepest regret and shall always be miserable if I don't hear of his welfare and happiness.' She showed her toughness in the fact that she had undertaken the whole thing herself so as to prevent any member of their household becoming victim to Charles' inevitable fury: 'You may not put the blame on innocent people, that there is not one soul either in the house or out of it that knew or has given me the smallest help in this undertaking.'

Grief-stricken over the loss of his beloved Pouponne, Charles wrote to Abbé John Gordon of the Scots College in Paris, whom he asked to help his servant John Stewart try and find Clementina and Charlotte: 'I shall be in the greatest affliction until I get back the child which was my only comfort in my misfortunes.' But on 31 July, Stewart wrote of his meeting with Clementina: 'I reasoned the matter with her, but all to no purpose. She told me that she would sooner make away with herself than go back, and as for the child, she would be cut to pieces sooner than give her up.' Charles tried frantically to find out where they were living, and on 6 September, Gordon wrote, 'Of all the places you mentioned there was only Mr Stak and Sir John O'Sullivan of whom as yet I have not got sufficient information. I can assure you she is not at St Germains, Lord Nairn's, Gasks's, Lady Ramsay's and not at the Convent of Conflans, nor rue Cassette.' Charles was beside himself and threatened to set fire to the nunneries of Paris until he found his daughter. Thanks to the Hanoverian spies who relentlessly reported back to London, we know that the search for Charlotte lasted a full month.

Prior to her flight from Bouillon, Clementina had been in correspondence with James, who helped organise her escape and granted her an annual allowance of 6,000 livres. Louis XV also took her under his protection, and she and Charlotte were placed in the care of Christophe de Beaumont, Archbishop of Paris, at the Convent of the Nuns of the Visitation. To Charles at Bouillon, she wrote, 'Nothing can be more sensible to me than this fatal separation. I can't express to you, my dearest prince, how much my heart suffers on this account.' She went on to explain that her 'one principal object was the child's education' and that Charlotte 'has a vast desire to see her dear Papa'. Louis replied to Charles' letter of protest with the blunt words, 'I cannot force the inclination of anybody in that situation.' Charles' father told him:

> It was many months before I had undoubted information of her desire to leave you, to satisfy her own conscience in the first place, and to stop the mouths of those to whom she knew herself to be obnoxious and suspected, and lastly to be able to give her daughter in a convent a Christian and good education ... You cannot but be sensible that I could not do otherways than grant her request not only on her own account, but even on yours, that her child might have a decent education, which you could not give her in the situation you are; and in reality it would be ruining that poor child if you were to keep her with you in the uncertain and ambulatory life you lead, and if you have a true love and tenderness for her, you should prefer her good education to all other considerations ... Oh my dear child, could I but once have the satisfaction of seeing you before I die, I flatter myself that I might soon be able to convince you that you never could have had a truer friend.

Clementina wrote to Charles about Charlotte:

> I will make it the study of my life to neglect nothing to have her well and virtuously brought up and to make her worthy of you and of the blood she has the honour to come of. I never intend to break the tie that unites her to you. She will always be yours, but my ambition is that she should do you honour.

Charles' recourse was to the bottle. Alexander Murray wrote, 'Your Royal Highness is resolved to destroy yourself to all intents and purposes. Everyone here talks of your conduct with horror, and, from once being the admiration of Europe, you are become the reverse.' A report from the British embassy in mid-1761 states that Charles 'is drunk as soon as he rises, and is always senselessly so at night, when his servants carry him to bed'. He hadn't seen his father since 1743, when he rode off into the night to stand at the head of what was to have been the 1744 French-led restoration of the

Stuart birthright. He had gone bursting with faith and energy. To return now to his father's dark eyes, which had known him since birth, would have been to see reflected in them the true extent of his failure and degeneracy. With Clementina, Charlotte, and all hope of military help from France gone, Charles cut himself off from the world in his uncle's Château de Carlsbourg, hidden from view amid the hills and misty forests of the Ardennes at Bouillon. He refused all contact, with the exception of one or two of his very closest friends. He replied to no one, neither the French Court, nor his Jacobite supporters, nor his father. In early 1762, James wrote, 'If you make no reply to this letter, I shall take it for granted that in your present situation you are not only buried alive, as you really are, but in effect you are dead and insensible for everything.' Clementina continued to write. So did Charlotte. She addressed her letters to 'Mon Auguste Papa' and signed them 'Pouponne'.

7

Lochaber No More: Marriage, Separation, Reconciliation 1760-1789

This lovely maid's of royal blood
That ruled Albion's kingdoms three
But oh, Alas, for her bonnie face
They've wranged the Lass of Albany.
We'll daily pray, we'll nightly pray
On bended knee most fervently
The time will come, with pipe and drum
We'll welcome hame fair Albany.

Robert Burns

In 1760, the seventy-two-year-old King James had fallen seriously ill, and though it did not kill him, he never fully recovered. In 1764, illness struck again, this time heralding the end. James' secretary, Andrew Lumsden, wrote to Prince Charles in February spelling out the seriousness of his father's condition. The months passed by and the old king hung on. No word came from his eldest son.

Henry wrote to his elder brother asking for an end to their near two decades of silence. The reply came through a secretary telling him that His Royal Highness neither wished to see nor write to anyone. In February 1765, Henry wrote once more, encouraging Charles by telling him that Marie-Anne de Talmont was in Rome and 'really seems sincerely attached to you. She complains she never can hear of you, and thinks she deserves a share in your remembrance'. It seems she also had a share in Louis XV's remembrance. In 1754, either by coincidence or deliberate irony, he had granted her an apartment in the Château de St Germain, still mainly inhabited by Jacobite families who had remained there after 1718. And the one she was given was the Royal Apartment where Charles' grandfather, King James VII & II had spent his final years.

One of the main reasons for Henry becoming a cardinal in 1747 was to secure the Stuarts' financial future, and in the intervening years, he had built up a position of great wealth and influence. He now not only described the terms of James' will but volunteered to pass on to his brother any bequests granted him by their father, adding, 'Among the misfortunes of our family I cannot but consider as the greatest of them all the fatal at least apparent disunion of two brothers.' But he got no reply. So he wrote again. In October, he received a curt note telling him to ensure the Pope recognise Charles as king when the time came. At least it was written by Charles himself, but it was out of touch with reality. Not only was Charles formally a Protestant but Westminster had been putting pressure on the courts of Europe not to recognise the Stuart succession. And the Vatican was indicating it would give in.

Henry carefully explained to his brother that though their family would always be extremely well regarded in Rome, it was nonetheless imperative to come in person, find a way to become quietly accepted back into the religion of his birth and re-establish relations with the Pope. Otherwise, there was no chance of being formally acknowledged as the *de jure* King Charles III. And if there was a sense of urgency about Henry's advice, it was because, if his elder brother was not recognised, then it would rule out his own succession later. For Henry felt keenly his family's right to their royal titles and support from the Vatican. Was it not in defence of equal rights for Roman Catholics that those thrones had been sacrificed in the first place?

Despite his illness, the dying king had been writing to Charles with words such as, 'Is it possible that you would rather be a vagabond on the face of the earth than return to a father who is all love and tenderness for you?' Finally, his son forced himself away from the bottle and isolation at Carlsbourg and, on 30 December 1765, set out for Rome. He left it too late. A life begun on 10 June 1688 in the Palace of St James in London, lived under a perpetually evil star, yet borne with grace, ended on the night of New Year's day 1766. Though neither of his sons were by his side, Lumsden wrote that James died 'without the least convulsion or agony, but with his usual mild serenity in his countenance', outliving all the usurpers – William of Orange (†1702), Anne (†1714), George I (†1727), George II (†1760), and even the 'Butcher' Cumberland (†1765).

The next day, Lumsden wrote to Charles: 'I most humbly beg to condole with you on the death of your Royal Father of blessed memory, and at the same time to congratulate you on your accession to the throne.' The Hanoverian spy, Sir Horace Mann, commented that 'the Romans were vastly impatient to bury him, that their theatres might be opened'. In fact, James' body lay in state on a cloth of gold for a full five days, after which, it was carried to St Peter's in a procession led by twenty cardinals along a route illuminated by 1,000 candles and thronged with large crowds. In the great basilica, the sermon was preached by Clement XIII himself.

The Pope, who continued the Vatican's lease of the Palazzo del Re for the Stuarts, ordered that the royal arms of Great Britain be taken down from the building's façade. It was an act done with indecent haste and behind Charles' back when he was away at Albano. Prior to this, Clement shied away from recognising Charles as heir to his father's rights by passing the decision over to the College of Cardinals, knowing they had already made up their mind. Mann wrote back to London in triumph.

Only his younger brother came to greet Charles when he arrived in Rome on 23 January. Once there, he spoke to Henry about his unhappy memories from childhood. Almost at once, he wrote to his drinking companion at Carlsbourg that he wished he had his 'dear Thibault to amuse and comfort' him. The only moral support he received was from Henry, who seated him on his right when driving in his cardinal's carriage – a mark of respect extended to reigning monarchs – and from the Scots, English and Irish Colleges in Rome who defied the Pope by receiving him with royal honours and singing a *Te Deum* for his restoration as King Charles III. Henry also helped him financially, passing over his inheritance from their father and annual Papal pension.

The first year back at the Palazzo del Re was a bitter period, because Charles was shunned by Roman Society, which took its lead from its Papal arbiter. So he passed his time hunting in the *Campagna* ... and drinking, which shocked Henry now that he saw it at first hand. Unable to go out and enjoy the music, which had been the principal childhood happiness he shared with his mother, Charles was introduced to the musician Domenico Corri by Cardinal Lorenzo Ganganelli. He even lived with Charles from 1767-69, and in his autobiography[16], Corri wrote that Charles

> kept entirely private, not seeing anyone ... In his retired life he employed his hours in exercise and music, of which he was remarkably fond. I usually remained alone with him every evening, the prince playing the violoncello and I the harpsichord, also composing together little pieces of music; yet these tête-à- têtes were of a sombre cast, the apartment in which we sat was hung with old red damask with two candles only and on the table a pair of loaded pistols (instruments not at all congenial to my fancy) which he would often take up, examine and again replace on the table, yet the manners of the prince were always mild, affable and pleasing.

Occasionally, Charles received visits from Jacobite supporters and sympathisers. One Englishwoman wrote:

> His person it is rather handsome, his face ruddy and full of pimples. He looks good-natured and was overjoyed to see me; nothing could be more affectionately gracious. I cannot answer for his cleverness, for he appeared to be absorbed in melancholy thoughts, a good deal of distraction in his conversation, and frequent brown studies. I had time to examine him for he kept me hours. He has all the reason in the world to be melancholy, for there is not a soul that goes near him, not knowing what to call him. He told me time lay heavy upon him. I said I supposed he read a great deal. He made no answer.

A little later, another described him as:

> Above middle size, but stoops excessively; he appears bloated and red in the face; his countenance heavy and sleepy, which is attributed to his having been given in to an excess of drinking; but when a young man he must have been esteemed handsome ... He is by no means thin, has a noble person and a graceful manner ... On the whole he has a melancholy, mortified appearance.

However, Prince Charles slowly began to lift himself out of this trough. Henry pressurised the Pope into receiving him, though this was conditional upon being in private audience and announced anonymously as 'the brother of the Cardinal York'. Primed by Hanoverian propaganda to expect some drunken brawler, the Pope was delighted to find that Charles knelt before him, kissed his ring and spoke with friendship and respect for about a quarter of an hour. Afterwards the clerics informed Horace Mann of the meeting, stressing its insignificance. Yet whatever the dubious loyalty of Clement XIII to the Stuarts, the visit opened the doors of Roman Society and Charles was able to breathe more freely. His young musical friend Corri even organised public concerts at which he and Charles performed together. Furthermore, the fresh air when hunting in the Italian countryside improved the prince's health and a period of sobriety began which restored his natural kindness. An English traveller noted:

> His person is tall and rather lusty. His complexion has a redness in it, not unlike the effects of drinking ... He talked very rationally, reads much and is fond of music. The Romans had conceived him to be a debauchee, but his behaviour in Rome has been perfectly sober and affable.

Charles began to send letters to former friends, even his old lover, Marie-Anne de Talmont, to whom he wrote of feelings that 'will always be engraved on my heart'. For her part, she wore a bracelet until her death in 1776 with a hidden spring which caused a tiny portrait of Christ to appear alongside that of Charles. Clementina Walkinshaw in Paris, on the other hand, remained out in the cold. As Lumsden wrote, 'His passion must still greatly cool.' It was typical of Charles that he could only cope with the loss of his daughter Charlotte by shutting out all thought of her.

But the improvement evaporated when, as a contemporary witness put it, 'he was met with things that vexed him'. In 1767, Charles wrote to Henry, 'What is in my breast cannot be divulged until I have occasion. God alone is judge.' Henry could only

> deplore the continuance of the bottle ... It is impossible for my brother to live if he continues in this strain ... I am severely afflicted on his account when I reflect on the dismal situation he puts himself under, which is a thousand times worse than the situation his enemies have endeavoured to place him in, but there is no remedy except for a miracle.

Until 1771, Charles' life was characterised by such dips into and out of drunkenness, typical of an alcoholic. They were punctuated only by trips to the spa at Pisa, during which he tried in vain to buy a home in Florence to escape from Rome. But the Hapsburg Grand Duke Leopold of Tuscany gave in to Hanoverian pressure and issued orders to ignore the exiled Stuart king. Henry succeeded in persuading his brother to rent a villa in Pisa for the winter months instead.

Then came a surprise initiated by Charles' cousins, Charles, 4th Duke of FitzJames, and Louis XV, as well as his old friend the Duke d'Aiguillon. In the aftermath of the Seven Years War, it was time for France to play the Stuart card one last time. A bride would be found to keep alive the prospect of a male heir to the Stuarts' rights. Hanoverian Westminster now became seriously alarmed – the surviving exchanges are panic-stricken – when they heard of the prince's arrival in Paris in late August 1771. The British Ambassador demanded an explanation from d'Aiguillon, who fobbed him off with calculated vagueness. Charles' two ducal cousins, FitzJames and Berwick, were both illegitimately descended from James VII & II by Arabella Churchill, and Berwick's heir, Charles, the future 4th Duke, was engaged to be married to the impoverished but well-born Princess Caroline zu Stolberg-Gedern. Given the hostility of the Hanoverians as well as the disastrous state of the Jacobite Cause, it was no small success to gain the hand of Caroline's younger sister, the teenage Princess Louise Maximiliana, who proclaimed herself 'very impatient to assume her position'. Delighted, the French Government provided the penniless bride-to-be with a substantial dowry, and Louise and Charles were formally married by proxy on 28 March 1772.

Louise was an attractive spirited girl, one of four sisters whose father had been killed fifteen years earlier at the Battle of Leuthen as a colonel in the Imperial Army. She had been placed from the age of six in a convent at Mons in Belgium in which she experienced little maternal love and had been anxious to escape. She was intelligent though manipulative, and whilst aware of Charles' exiled status, only partly realised the extent of his alcoholism. However, it was not obvious at first, for his regenerated optimism had made him considerably fitter by the time he travelled to meet his young bride at Macerata, where they were married in a small ceremony conducted by the local bishop. The marriage was even consummated the same day in satisfaction of a condition laid down by Louise's mother. Charles, pleased as Punch, reported to his younger brother that 'the marriage was made in all the forms'.

Receptions followed, alms were distributed, and on 19 April, the nineteen-year-old bride and fifty-two-year-old groom left for Rome in high spirits. Charles was anxious to arrive in the hope that France's public support for his marriage would trigger Papal recognition of the Stuart rights. Their arrival was commented upon by an eye-witness:

> First four couriers, the chevalier's post-chaise, then the princess's coach-and-six, followed by two other post-chaises, the chevalier and the princess in their coach, followed by the coaches-and-six with his attendants. The confluence of people at the cavalcade was surprising ... She is pretty and young, he strong and vigorous. They may produce a race of pretenders that will never finish, which the French will be always playing upon every quarrel. May they increase fruitfully!

But the new Pope, Clement XIV, though described by Domenico Corri as a friend of Charles when still Cardinal Ganganelli, continued to refuse recognition, despite French, Spanish and Maltese support. Notwithstanding, the newly-wed couple were invited everywhere. They attended the opera and concerts, receptions at ambassadorial residences, held open house at the Palazzo del Re, and went out for long drives in the *Campagna*. Charles drank less and his natural warmth remained in the ascendant. He wrote to Marie-Anne de Talmont and Louise de Rohan as well as to his mother-in-law, telling everyone how happy he was – a happiness, however, inextricably linked to his hope for a male heir. The months went by, and though rumours spread excitement throughout the Highlands, no pregnancy occurred. It turned out Louise could not have children. When that realisation sunk in, Charles reached for the bottle. On 11 December 1773, Sir Horace Mann informed London that 'he is seldom quite sober, and frequently causes the greatest disorders in his family'.

Bitterly hurt by the Vatican's refusal to acknowledge his family's rights, Charles and Louise left Rome in August 1774 and took a villa between Parma and Pisa, moving that autumn to Florence, where they lived in a palace offered them by Prince Bartolomeo Corsini – a family long friendly to the Stuarts. Corsini's generosity was all the greater in that it was in opposition to the Grand Duke, who again collapsed under Hanoverian pressure and ordered that no official recognition be given to Charles. The rest of the Florentine nobility sheepishly followed their duke's shabby example. It was worse than wounding: it made life utterly dull. This, the continued lack of an heir, financial problems, and the sheer pointlessness of his existence pushed Charles deep into the well of drunkenness. 'Poor man, behaves well when he is not drunk,' observed Horace Mann. Most evenings, Charles would sit alone in his box at the theatre and drink himself unconscious, the sordid details of which Mann reported back to Westminster.

Charles and Louise's relationship could only deteriorate. In 1775, she acidly wrote:

> If Your Majesty goes on sulking, I shall be obliged to justify myself before the world and make it clear why the royal countenance is not quite so dazzlingly glorious as usual and its beautiful eyes not quite so radiant. I shall send all my friends a copy of the enclosed memorandum I have already sent to Your Majesty in which I set out the facts as best I can in the belief that I am in the right and that people will realise this.

In her letters, Louise wrote of her hope that her husband would die and she might 'become mistress of my own destiny'. In 1775, she described how she and Charles 'go out walking and get bored, and that is no relief'.

With the couple living emotionally separate existences, the prince bought the Palazzo Guadagni in 1777 in the quiet, north-eastern outskirts of Florence. Though little more than a very large villa, it had beautiful views over the surrounding countryside. To Charles, it was more than a building; it was the only home that ever belonged to his family during their century of exile. He displayed immense pride in it, devoting all his energy to overseeing every detail of the building and garden's decoration. It is said there was one small room with the Stuart tartan frescoed on its walls. There was also a weathervane decorated with a royal crown, cipher and date, 'C.R.1777'[17], whilst over the main doors in the entrance hall was painted the Stuart version of the British royal arms together with a small thistle, white rose and the inscription 'CAROLUS III M.BRIT.ET HIBERNIAE REX'. In public, however, Charles continued to use the more modest title of the Count of Albany.

It was at this time that Louise acquired a lover – the twenty-eight-year-old Italian playboy Count Vittorio Alfieri, a talented poet with whom Louise shared an interest in literature and the arts. At first, Alfieri's animated conversation also won Charles' friendship, until the latter realised what was going on, became intensely jealous, and sank back down to the worst depths of alcoholism. As he had done twenty years before to Clementina Walkinshaw, so now did the seriously ill prince begin to physically abuse Louise when drunk and construct a mad system of alarm bells around her bed at night. Horace Mann wrote:

> He has a declared fistula, great sores in his legs and is insupportable in stench and temper, neither of which he takes the least pains to disguise to his wife.

Returning home drunk from celebrating St Andrew's Day on 30 November 1780, Charles burst into his wife's room, accused her of being unfaithful and assaulted her. That was what she had been waiting for and coldly made the pretext to end their relationship. She had carefully ensured that those who mattered were unaware of her affair with Alfieri. Mann exceeded himself, describing the sixty-year-old prince as having performed, almost acrobatically, 'the most nauseous and filthy indecencies from above and below upon her'.

Louise wasted not a second in contacting the Grand Duke and soliciting his protection. She and Alfieri then put into action a scheme devised with their young Irish friend Gehegan and his mistress, Signora Orlandini – ex-mistress of the French Minister in Florence. Whilst out driving with Charles, Louise and Signora Orlandini disappeared into a convent and behind the protection of the Grand Duke. The outraged Charles immediately realised what was going on. But his all-too-accurate accusations were met with Gehegan and Alfieri's theatrical poses of moral indignation. No one of any consequence was prepared to accept the word of an aging alcoholic against an intelligent, attractive young woman skilled in deception. So successfully did Louise plead the virtuous innocent to Henry that she forgot he was a cardinal who could and immediately did arrange her removal from Florence to a Roman convent. Horrified, she realised this would be a far greater obstacle to her affair with Alfieri than Charles had ever been.

The prince frantically tried to get his wife back, but to no avail. She departed in secret for Rome in late December with her lover in disguise, travelling on the box of her carriage. Mann reported:

> The mould for any more casts of the Royal Stuarts has been broken, or, what is equivalent to it, is now shut up under the double lock and key of the Pope and Cardinal York, out of reach of any dabbler who might foister in any spurious copy.

The Pope received Louise in private audience and promptly cut Charles' pension in half. Protesting illness, she persuaded Henry to lend her his seldom-used official residence, the Cancelleria. Alfieri then moved into the nearby Villa Strozzi and the two of them took promiscuous advantage of the Vatican residence and Papal protection. The news drove Charles wild. Even Corsini failed to open the eyes of the Pope and Henry. So badly did Charles want Louise back that those close to him became convinced he would die from apoplexy. Even Mann observed, 'He has totally altered his way of living and behaves in every respect with proper decency.'

Louise pushed her luck further. Having asked Henry to write to Charles for some books which he was refusing to release, she completely forgot herself: 'Your letter to the king is admirable, and if you will excuse the expression, it is full of malice; I think on reading it he will be at his wits end.' Henry still didn't see through her, unaware of her description of him as belonging 'to a race of amphibious creatures who are intended to be seen from a distance but whom an evil chance has brought close to our eyes'. On one occasion, she created a sensation by turning up to a theatrical performance at the Spanish embassy adorned with the magnificent Sobieski and Stuart jewels. The playwright and her partner for the evening was Alfieri. Rumours now began in earnest.

In late March 1783, Mann informed London that Charles was extremely ill and had received the Last Sacrament. So Henry hurried to spend most of each day by his brother's side. Once there, the truth about Louise and Alfieri was finally brought home to him. Mortified, he immediately informed the Pope and the playboy-poet was expelled from Papal territories, ridiculously protesting his innocence and confessing himself 'stupefied'. On the other hand, Louise kept her nerve and behaved with humility and dignity to avoid disgrace and ruin. The point was not lost on her mother, who arrived to try and convince her daughter to return to Charles. Mann lamented: 'The cat, at last, is out of the bag. The Cardinal of York's visit to his brother gave the latter an opportunity to undeceive him, proving to him that the complaints laid to his charge of ill-using her were invented to cover a plot formed by Count Alfieri.' Of Charles, Louise wrote to a friend, 'Reassure me, that he cannot last long ... Of course, he may at any moment succumb to the gout in his chest. What a brutal thing it is to expect one's happiness through another's death! ... His legs are become useless, yet he survives despite this malady'.

The Hanoverians also wanted him dead. But just as they hadn't been able to finish him off after Culloden, so now did he prove unaccommodating. Although the sixty-three-year-old had suffered a punishing illness, nevertheless, he more or less recovered, had won a battle and now detoxified himself sufficiently that his old self began to resurface. So much so that he spent much of the summer of 1783 convalescing, attending race meetings, fêtes, festivals, and travelling around Tuscany. But Charles was no longer in his twenties. He collapsed in exhaustion and was 'decrepit and bent; he walks with great difficulty, and is so impaired in his memory that he repeats himself every quarter of an hour'.

Later that year, King Gustav III of Sweden arrived in Italy and spent the winter there. He and Charles had become linked by Freemasonry and corresponded since 1776. Now they became personal friends and nothing could have been more welcome, for Gustav had great diplomatic skills and undertook to arrange a settlement between the royal couple. He travelled to Rome, conferred with Henry and finally agreed between the parties that they would sign a formal document of separation and that Louise would return the Sobieski and Stuart jewels as well as her share of Charles' Papal pension. He even arranged new pensions from the French and Spanish. Charles' separation declaration was signed on 3 April 1784:

> Our common misfortunes have rendered this event useful and necessary for us both, and in consideration of all the arguments she has adduced to us, we declare by these presents that we freely and voluntarily give our consent to this separation.

Both Louise and Charles wrote letters of gratitude to Gustav. The prince told him, 'I cannot sufficiently express my thanks ... It would be impossible to find anyone to whom I could better confide my honour and interests.' Charles' thanks didn't stop at that. He pledged Gustav the hereditary right of succession as Grand Master of the Masonic Order of the Temple.

Part of the separation agreement was that Louise would reside within the Papal states under the formal care of the Pope. It proved a flexible enough arrangement. Having learnt her lesson once, Louise was careful not to throw caution to the wind when reunited with Alfieri at the Inn of the Two Keys at Colmar in Alsace on 17 August. For as long as Charles was still alive, she remained his legal wife, her delicate but precious freedom resulting only from a formal separation overseen by a Pope whom she was not willing to anger again for mere weakness of the heart. In 1793, Louise and Alfieri returned to Florence, where they lived together until his death in 1803, when he was interred in the city's Basilica di Sante Croce – next to the tomb of Machiavelli. Louise would join him there in 1829, though she was buried in the more tasteful company of the Castellani Chapel. One epitaph for her came from the usually sensitive pen of Sir Compton Mackenzie:

> She was entirely without religion. She had no faith in humanity. She was mercenary. She was a liar. She was cold to the very core of her being. She was pretentious. She was self-complacent. Such humour as she had was of the privy. She began life as a chatter-box with good teeth and a pretty complexion. She ended as a dowdy, interminable old bore in a red shawl.

It seems harsh, but whatever she was like, the twelve years of the French Court's scheme to produce a male Stuart heir had come to an end, its sole aim unrealised.

Charles lived on alone in Florence, amongst his servants and the portraits of his ancestors. Mann observed that he lived decently, his drinking more or less under control. To pass the time, he would play the violoncello, French horn, flageolet or Highland pipes. It is said he had a piper who would play him *Lochaber No More*, the air for which Allan Ramsay had written words some fifty years earlier, including lines from before 1704 by Alexander Drummond of Balhaldy for his wife, Margaret

Cameron of Lochiel. The melody was of Irish origin, adopted by Charles' grandfather as a slow march when he landed in Ireland in 1689, which is why the Scots called it *King James' March to Dublin*. It was often sung by Jacobite prisoners awaiting execution. The last verse reads:

> I gae then, my lass, to win honour and fame
> And if I should chance to come gloriously home
> I'll bring a heart to thee with love running o'er
> And then I'll leave thee and Lochaber no more.

The prince's lonely evenings were spent in his Palazzo Guadagni on the Via Gino Capponi. Today, it is called the Palazzo di San Clemente and sometimes the Palazzo del Pretendente. It is Florence's most haunted building.

According to tradition, Clementina Walkinshaw was created Countess of Albestroff in 1760 by Emperor Francis I, Duke of the Lorraine and husband of Maria Theresa of Austria. But the title did nothing to improve her modest circumstances. For the first six years after Clementina's flight with Charlotte from the Château de Carlsbourg, both lived at the Convent of the Visitation in Paris, paid for out of the pension granted by King James. But its value had declined significantly, because in the meantime, the French capital had become the world's most expensive city.

After James' death in January 1766, Charles refused to support Clementina. He passed the responsibility on to Henry, who carried on paying the allowance, though he had always disapproved of his brother's relationship. However, the cardinal did two things. Firstly he reduced the pension from 6,000 to 5,000 livres. Secondly, having heard a rumour in 1767 that Charles had secretly married Clementina and fearing this might dissuade any prospective bride who might yet produce a Stuart male heir, Henry threatened to stop Clementina's allowance altogether unless she signed a formal declaration that she had never been married to his brother. Whatever the truth was, Clementina had no option and, no longer able to afford to live in Paris, left for cheaper lodgings at the Convent of Notre Dame de la Miséricorde in Meaux-en-Brie. From there, she wrote to Charles:

> Although I have been continually told that my letters weary you and it would be wisdom on my part to discontinue them, I should think myself guilty of ingratitude to Your Royal Highness if I did not express to you at the beginning of the New Year all the affection I have for you.
>
> Meaux, 16 December 1768

Half a year later, Charlotte's letter to her father from the same place mentions that her previous three had gone unanswered:

> Oh my King, it is from you that I derive life, you fondled me at my birth, the tenderest and most worthy of mothers thought it her duty to remove me from your love to give me the best masters to direct my education and make me worthy of Your Majesty ... That I may have the consolation of weeping one day, one day only, on the breast of my august Papa ... this affectionate Pouponne, who was once so dear to you, see her fly, or rather throw herself into your arms.

By the same post, Clementina added,

> This charming creature whom you brought into the world and who surely has never done anything to deserve to be abandoned by Your Majesty, because she is, I venture to say, worthy of you, of all you could do for her, this unfortunate child only claims the rights of her blood from you who are her king and father. And what will become of her if you refuse her this justice? ... She is now at an age when thought begins to become serious and she already feels only too keenly and with the greatest grief Your Majesty's neglect and indifference. The unhappy child repeatedly says to me: 'What will become of me if my Papa abandons me?' ... These sayings pierce me to the heart, and she also very often says to me: 'I am fit, Mama, to share the misfortunes of my king and father, but at least let him recognise me as his daughter' ... Can it be possible that you resolve to abandon a child who belongs to you and who has loved you? ... She is charming as regards all the qualities of heart and mind ... If we had been a little more affluent, her education would have been finished and completed, but we have retrenched in everything for that since the death of the king, who spared nothing to render this child worthy of Your Majesty ... She is a very good musician. She has a very beautiful voice, she has begun the harpsichord ... I could not give you, Sire, a greater proof of my attachment and respect than that of forming a creature worthy of you. I hope one day you will do me justice and I will die content ... These are the wishes which the unhappy mother of your child will always make, who will be faithfully and inviolably attached to you until her last sigh.

Yet such was Charles' fury at Clementina that Waters the banker was told by Henry to mention her existence only when absolutely necessary and only in letters marked with an **X**, 'for she must never be mentioned to His Majesty'. Then, horrified by the implications of the unexpected news of her father's marriage to Louise zu Stolberg-Gedern, the eighteen-year-old Charlotte wrote to her father from Meaux on 27 April 1772:

> Having exhausted all the sentiments of my heart in the infinite number of letters that I have had the honour to write to you, none of which have made any impression upon you, my august Papa, which is a very clear proof to me of your total abandonment which I have never merited ... I can only share in the honour of being your daughter, as one without hope, because I am without future and portion and consequently condemned to lead the most wretched and miserable life in the world.

She even came with her mother to Rome to appeal for recognition, refusing to see her father unless her mother was there too. But their visit infuriated Charles, who let it be known through a third party that his daughter could stay, but Clementina never. The teenager bravely refused the offer and returned with her mother to their simple existence at Meaux after Henry let them know he would cut off their income if they did not do so immediately. The cardinal added that he would also do this if Charlotte lived anywhere but in a convent. During their stay in Rome, her mediator was Monsignor Lascaris, Henry's acting treasurer. In thanking him, Charlotte hoped 'that His Eminence will not refuse my demand for exchanging my convent in Meaux for one in Paris'. Yet despite Charles' anger, it was after this episode that his interest in Charlotte was rekindled. This is also hinted at in the 'Memorial' that Charlotte sent to the French Court appealing for material assistance:

> The Lady Charlotte, daughter of Prince Charles Edward ... baptised under the name he was then bearing, brought up as his daughter in his household until seven years old, and presented in that quality to all ... Her mother, of one of the first Scottish families, allied to the House of Stuart, for which many of her relatives have shed their blood and lost their lives, and at that time treated by the prince as his wife, and known on his different journeys by the same name as himself ... The news of the marriage of the prince has altered the condition of both [mother and daughter] ... The Lady Charlotte, his daughter, is fully persuaded of his [Charles'] tenderness for her; she has received recent proofs of his attachment ... She reminds the king that she is the last scion of a sovereign house, allied to the House of France, celebrated for its misfortunes and which has sacrificed its dominions for the sake of religion ... The services rendered to his father [Louis XV] by the Scottish gentlemen have gained for them an annual subsistence. She dares to hope that the same assistance will not be refused to the daughter of him who fought at their head.

But despite Charlotte and Louis' shared descent from the great King Henry IV of France, as well as support from the Dukes de Bourbon and de Richelieu, Horace Walpole observed that 'the House of FitzJames, fearing their becoming a burden to themselves, prevented the acknowledgement of the daughter'. Despite being shunned by her father, Charlotte continued to write to him, even though when she was at her most eligible age he made her promise never to marry nor become a nun. These cruel orders were communicated to her by Abbé John Gordon, Principal of the Scots College in Paris, who wrote back to Charles on 27 February 1775:

> I communicated to the young lady in question the contents of your letter of the 10th, it touched her to such a degree that I was sorry that I had spoken to her so freely ... The doctor says that her grief has given her an obstruction of the liver ... She was only six years old when she was carried off, so that she ought not to be entirely ruined for a fault of which her age hindered her to be anybody's partner. I am heartily sorry for her misfortunate situation and think she deserves better, being esteemed by all who know her as one of the most accomplished women in this town.

Charlotte was twenty-two, outgoing, full of common sense, heroically patient and, though stubborn as her father, had a charm which won her some extraordinary victories. She had dark-blond hair and bright-blue eyes. Horace Mann described her as having 'a good figure, tall and well made, but the features of her face resemble too much those of her father to be handsome'. Another Englishman commented, 'She was a tall, robust woman of a very dark complexion and a coarse-grained skin with more of a masculine boldness than feminine modesty or grace, but easy and unassuming in her manners.' Placed in the most impossible financial, political and social situation, she decided in early 1776 to apply to become an honorary canoness of the Noble Chapter of Migette, a convent near Besançon in Franche-Comté. On her way there, she was invited to a reception and dinner given by Lord Elcho. And whom should Charlotte meet there but the handsome, blue-eyed, thirty-seven-year-old Archbishop of Bordeaux with whom she had more than a little in common. For he was Prince Ferdinand, the youngest brother of Prince Jules-Hercule de Rohan, now head of the family as Duke de Montbazon and Prince de Guéméné, who had been *aide de camp* to Charlotte's uncle, Henry Stuart, in 1745 and husband of the Stuarts' cousin Louise, with whom her father had had such a passionate affair nearly thirty years earlier.

Even the origins of the families were similar: the Stuarts' progenitor was Flaald, eleventh-century hereditary High Steward of Dol in Brittany, whereas the Rohans descended from another great Breton noble, Guethenoc, Viscount de Chateautro en Porhoët, who built the massive fortress of Josselin in 1008. The Rohans, whose name came from an estate fifty miles south-west of Dol, were sovereign princes as descendants of Brittany's ruling family, recognised by the Dukes of Brittany in 1088, 1420, and 1457, and by the Kings of France in 1549, 1626, 1667, and 1692. Of them, Louis XIV declared, 'the House of Rohan should be treated in all matters equally with the Houses of Savoy and Lorraine' and as such were acknowledged by the Vatican, the Kings of Sweden and Spain, and the ruling Houses of Saxony, Hesse and Württemberg. It was because they were many times related by blood that Ferdinand's ancestor invited Mary Queen of Scots to his Château de Montbazon near Tours in May 1560, and Duke Henri de Rohan became godfather to the future King Charles I at Holyrood in December 1600 – the same Duke Henri who was heir presumptive of his cousin – and the Stuarts' ancestor – King Henry IV of France, with regard to the Kingdom of Navarre, until the birth of the future Louis XIII. The Rohans had several family mottoes, but the two most frequently used were: *Sooner Death than Disgrace* – how painful that must have sounded to Stuart ears – and *Roi ne puis, Duc ne daigne, Rohan suis,* which perfectly articulated their intense family pride.[18]

As for pedigrees, though certainly inbred, Ferdinand was hard to outclass. His father had been head of the Rohans and Duke de Montbazon, his mother was the daughter of the Duke de Rohan-Rohan, his grandmother was the daughter of the Duke de Ventadour, and another generation back two marshals of France had wielded their batons.[19]

Of Ferdinand's three brothers, Jules-Hercule was the oldest and, apart from having been cuckolded by Charlotte's father and acted as *aide de camp* to Henry Stuart in

1745, was a lieutenant general, duke, and now head of the family. Then came Armand, an admiral who was guillotined in 1794 and died childless. And third was Louis, a cardinal, Prince-Bishop of Strasbourg, and French Ambassador to Vienna.

It must have seemed as if Charlotte had known Ferdinand's family all her life. Were the Rohans not regulars of Leszczyński's Franco-Polish court at Lunéville where Prince Charles had spent so much time? Was it not from the Château de Carlsbourg of their mutual relation, the Duke de Bouillon, that Charlotte had been separated from her father as a little girl? And after that traumatic event, was it not the Rohans who had proved the most loyal of friends, inviting her and her mother to Paris even when forced to move to Meaux by Henry?

If they didn't know each other before that dinner at Lord Elcho's, Charlotte and Ferdinand soon discovered how much they had in common. All would have been perfect were it not that this was pre-revolutionary France where many great aristocratic families pushed younger sons into church careers for the considerable income it could bring – about which Ferdinand would later write with bitter regret. Highly intelligent, he had a doctorate of theology from the Sorbonne and by the age of twenty-one had become grand prior of the chapter of Strasbourg, Abbé of Mouzon, and a canon of Liège. Then, at the age of thirty-one, Louis XV had nominated him Archbishop of Bordeaux.

Charlotte's situation when she met Ferdinand was acutely difficult. For years, she had been ignored by her father and remained formally unrecognised. She had seen her mother's modest pension cut by Henry as well as her appeal for a pension from the French Court blocked by her FitzJames cousins, and she was without dowry. Yet she was the only member of the last generation of the ancient royal Stuart dynasty and at twenty-two was in her prime. But, held in reserve in case of political need, Charles had forbidden her to either marry or become a nun. A more impossible social position in the eighteenth century is hard to imagine. That was how things looked when Charlotte fell in love with Ferdinand – her relation for whom marriage and family life had also been ruled out.

Needless to say, Charlotte changed her plan to become a canoness and returned to Paris, where she and her mother were lady pensioners at the Convent of the Visitation on the rue St Jacques. Meanwhile, Ferdinand took a lease on a house in the same street and acquired a country home for them at Anthony, a few miles south of Paris.

During the remaining years of the 1770s, Ferdinand completed a magnificent palace in Bordeaux[20] and, in 1781, was elevated to the Archbishopric of Cambrai, where he instructed Bishop d'Amycles to act as his deputy so as to be able to spend more time in Paris with Charlotte, who soon began to move in court circles at Versailles. In such a gossipy milieu, it was no surprise that her close friendship with Ferdinand and the Rohans quickly became public knowledge. But not even the all-seeing eyes of the Hanoverian spy, Sir Horace Mann, discovered the fact that between 1778 and 1784 Charlotte Stuart and Ferdinand de Rohan became parents to two little girls and a baby boy.

In March 1783, fate played the cruellest of tricks on Charlotte. She was almost thirty years old and, since 1775, had given up hope of being recognised by her father

– hence her secret family. At that time, Charles was so ill that he had been given the Last Rites and was convinced he was dying. Yet without warning, he suddenly decided to make Charlotte his heiress under the terms of his last will and testament dated 23 March with a codicil of 25 March. Never one to do things by halves, he also made a solemn declaration that he had no other children and created her Duchess of Albany, the traditional title for the heir of a King of Scots. Then, by an act dated 30 March, he granted her the additional title of Her Royal Highness and raised her to the status of legitimate child, which was recognised by the Vatican, the King and Parliament of France, as well as the Grand Duke of Tuscany.

Ten months later, between 24 January and 14 February 1784, Charles was again struck down, this time with a suspected stroke. For two days, he lay unconscious and once more received the Extreme Unction. Again he rallied. But it was only when he recovered that he sent word to Charlotte in Paris, telling her of his decisions and asking if she would come to Florence and live with him. Nothing could have been more unexpected. Nothing could have been more badly timed. She had just given birth to her third child.

On 10 July 1784, Mann wrote from Florence to London that Charles

> acknowledges his natural daughter who with her mother resides in a convent at Paris in the quality of pensioners by the name of Lady Charlotte Stuart. She is about thirty years of age and as she is not obliged to conform to any of the rules of the convent she is often absent from it and frequents the Prince of Rohan, Archbishop of Bordeaux. Count Albany says that he will send for her to live with him here.

A week later, Mann's next report to London reads:

> He often talked of sending for his natural daughter from Paris, to live with him here, though nobody then believed he would so soon put it into execution, but two days ago only, he took the resolution to send his old servant Stuart who has attended him in all his excursions for that purpose to Paris ... He has wrote to his daughter ... to inform her that he had acknowledged her by a public deed, and by his will had appointed her his sole heiress ... He has wrote likewise to the Count de Vergennes[21] to desire that he will get the deed of acknowledgement of his daughter registered in the Parliament of Paris.

That Act of Parliament was signed on 7 September by Louis XVI, who also granted Charlotte the right of tabouret.[22] Soon after, he granted Charles a pension of 60,000 livres a year with a reversionary payment to Charlotte of 10,000 livres a year upon her father's death. Mann wrote again on 18 September:

> Count Albany has received notice from Paris that his natural daughter whom he calls Lady Charlotte Stuart, to which name in the act to acknowledge her he added the title of Duchess of Albany, was on the point of setting out on her journey hither ... He is very busily employed in making preparations and furnishing his house ... He received a large

> quantity of plate and his share of the jewels which belonged to his mother, except the two large rubies which were pawned by the Republic of Poland to his grandfather, Sobieski ... Count Albany's health continues daily to decline, of which he is very sensible, and it makes him the more impatient for his daughter's arrival.

On 9 October, he continued:

> On the 5th instant Count Albany's daughter arrived here ... She has appeared every evening since with her father at the theatre very richly adorned with the jewels that the pretender had lately received from Rome ... All the ladies and gentlemen of the country leave tickets of visits at her door ... The pretender has wrote letters to the Pope, to the cardinal his brother, to the Courts of France and Spain and probably to many others, to announce the arrival of his daughter here.

Then, on 7 December:

> Though Count Albany is extremely infirm nevertheless ... he has private balls three times a week at his own house ... On the 30th of last month being St Andrew's Day ... he performed the mock ceremony of investing his daughter with the order of St Andrew ... Your Lordship will perceive ... how weak the understanding of the pretender is grown.

This last was a curious conclusion given that the Order of the Thistle with its Cross of St Andrew had been revived by Charles' grandfather in 1687, from whom Mann's Hanoverian masters were not descended.

Yet so it was that the prince began to enjoy life again and Charlotte took him on a tour of Tuscany no more than two weeks after her arrival. On their return father and daughter became such regular attendants at the theatre and opera that the Grand Duke had the Stuarts' boxes redecorated, the former in yellow and the latter in crimson damask. However, Charles' health continued to plague him. Mann wrote that at their soirées 'he drowses most part of the time', had high blood pressure, breathing difficulties and suffered badly from gout, his legs being so badly swollen that he had to be carried everywhere in his chair. As for the bottle, Charlotte kept this under control, dissuading her father with her '*ton de fermeté* '. In April 1785, when Charles had a terrible attack of gout, Charlotte told her mother, 'My father has been in continual rages ... wine is not the cause, he drinks almost none.' Senility was also now beginning to set in. Mann noticed that 'he is quite incapable of transacting his own business, and his mind seems to approach that of imbecility'. Charlotte wrote to her mother that 'Lord Nairne and my father dispute and quarrel all day long. He's quite gone in the mind'. Even Charles admitted to his brother, 'I am so bothered in the head'.

Also troubling were the financial problems from which Charles and his daughter sought relief by trying to obtain the capital and even greater amount of accrued interest relating to the dowry of his grandmother, Mary of Modena. This money had been owed to the Stuarts by the London government since 1685, voted through by Act of Parliament, confirmed by William of Orange at the time of the Treaty of Ryswick and by Queen Anne in the Treaty of Utrecht. In 1718, the arrears amounted to an incredible £2,500,000. By 1785, it would have been far greater. Nevertheless the London government never honoured the debt, even in part, and finally reneged in 1787.

Charlotte likewise had problems. She had become the mother of three children. Yet she could not reveal their existence to anyone, as the scandal would be seized upon by the Hanoverians to destroy what little was left of the Stuart Cause. Worse, Charlotte's own position as Stuart heiress would also be ruined and, by extension, that of her children and mother. She had waited more than twenty years before coming into her own. Hopefully, she would soon inherit, her father and uncle would be no more, and she would be free to help her family. In the interim, all she could do was to write letters to her mother and Ferdinand in Paris, rather naively encoded so that Hanoverian spies would not understand them. Ferdinand, whom she initially forbade to write back because of this danger, was referred to as 'my friend' who was 'jealous as a tiger'. Their children were 'my little flowers' which 'need to be watered and tended every day', which she and Ferdinand had 'planted together in the garden'. In her twice-weekly letters to her mother, Charlotte constantly wrote of hoping to see her flowers 'before they grow much higher' and of them 'not forgetting me'.

In January 1785, she wrote to Clementina, 'What I give you will serve for your comfort and for the upkeep of my garden. My worthy friend has so fair a soul that I don't doubt that he will attend to everything, but for myself I wish to have my little part, otherwise I should be jealous.' One letter, dated 25 March 1785, written several months after the birth of her youngest, contained instructions referring to his wet-nursing: 'He who is in the country will no doubt soon be returning to the city, and it is quite time that he did so. I count on you, dear Mama, to watch over his health and see that he wants for nothing'. Also from this period comes Charlotte's comment to her mother that she hopes 'my friend' will be pleased with his new child and love and cherish him tenderly. Later she wrote asking for the latest on the European-wide scandal of the *Collier de la Reine* of which Ferdinand's brother, Cardinal Louis, was a central figure; he had been famously arrested in the *Galerie des Glaces* at Versailles and imprisoned in the Bastille, where the legendarily loyal Rohans were lobbying vigorously for his release.

Another problem was Henry's attitude. On 2 November 1784, Charles wrote to his brother:

> I am very glad to tell you myself that my very dear daughter, having been recognised by me, by France, by the Pope, is Royal Highness for all, and everywhere. I do not dispute your rights. They are established, because you are my brother; but I beg of you also, not to dispute those of my very dear daughter.

But dispute he did, for Henry was still supportive of, and still being manipulated by Louise zu Stolberg-Gedern and was more than a little offended by his brother's recognition of Charlotte and her honours. So he issued a formal declaration, publicly protesting that his permission had not been asked, that what Charlotte had received constituted a slight to himself and his sister-in-law, and objecting to her elevation to the right of royal succession, which not even the FitzJames' had received – and that was what bothered him most. Undaunted and admirably equipped with her father's boldness and grandfather's patience Charlotte began to correspond with her uncle in Rome, writing him warm, courteous letters. At first, they went unanswered, yet slowly her star began to wax in Henry's eyes just as surely as her stepmother Louise's began to wane.

In addition to being Charles' permanent nurse, his daughter also began to bring order to the household's finances, finding in this another pretext to communicate with her uncle on matters of family 'business'. Her letters were largely concerned with her father's health, but they also became increasingly condemnatory of Louise and Alfieri's conduct. Henry began to reply.

Meanwhile, Charles' health remained dire. On 9 May, Charlotte told Henry, 'The leg is very bad; the swelling enormous.' And in July: 'He complains much of his stomach and is obliged to remain in bed a great part of the day.' At the same time, Charles pushed his daughter's cause as hard as possible, writing to Henry on 9 April 1785: 'My daughter is doubly dear to me when I see her occupied in recalling to me a way of thinking which I hope will not change again, and which I love to assure you of the endurance of.' On 9 July, he added, 'I cannot describe to you, my very dear brother, the happiness I feel in expecting that some day you will play the part of a father to a daughter I have every reason to love tenderly.'

At first Henry's rapprochement with his niece came on paper, accompanied by disgust for Louise's ongoing affair with Alfieri, which he described as 'a union so offensive to our family. It makes me furious ... she has deliberately broken her word to me.' On the other hand, 'I am greatly obliged to your daughter for interesting herself so with you on my behalf. It proves the kindness of her heart, to which everyone bears witness'. Even Pope Pius VI congratulated Henry on the improved spiritual condition of his brother, openly attributing it to Charlotte, whose title of Duchess of Albany he formally recognised. That summer's correspondence began to discuss when she and Henry might meet. Charlotte discovered her uncle would be visiting Perugia, so she persuaded her father to travel with her to Monte Freddo and see him. Their meeting was such a success that it removed any residual reluctance Henry had in acknowledging her rank and title. It also cemented his reconciliation with his brother, which then remained unbroken till the end, both declaring they had rediscovered their childhood love for each other, both now determined that Charlotte should not only be Charles' heir but Henry's too.

Charles, knowing nothing of his daughter's relationship with Ferdinand de Rohan, had ambitions to marry Charlotte into a reigning family. The Baroness de Castille commented, 'Many Italian princes have offered to her, and one of the brothers of the King of Sweden. Her father, who wished to see her on a throne, presses hard for the latter.' In 1785, Abbé Charles Dupaty wrote,

> If benevolence alone were necessary to entitle her to the throne of her ancestors she would soon ascend it ... Her attention to her father is extremely affecting. When this old man calls to mind that his family has reigned, his tears flow not alone.

Charlotte now succeeded in persuading Charles to leave Florence for Rome, telling him it was only for the winter, believing it to be essential for his health and the Stuart Cause. On 1 December 1785, they started off on the eight-day journey to the detested city of Charles' birth, bidding farewell to the Florentine nobility with a huge party. Henry came to meet them at Viterbo and saw to his surprise with what firmness yet tact his niece managed his notoriously difficult brother – that she was succeeding where all before had failed. Charles clearly trusted her completely. For Henry, too, she became unique as the only woman apart from his mother who not only won but retained his love. Of this, he gave his niece the ultimate symbolic proof:

> Cardinal York has given up to his niece all his own jewels ... including the great ruby, which was mortgaged by the Republic of Poland to the King Sobieski, which is supposed to be of very extraordinary value.
>
> Florence, 28 January 1786, Sir Horace Mann

In fact, there were two great rubies, one of which Henry kept and had set in his bishop's mitre that same year.

On 31 December 1785, Mann noted that Henry presented Charles 'to the Pope to whom likewise he had presented his niece some days before; and as she does not assume or pretend to any distinction, she has been received by the Roman ladies with great civility'. Furthermore, the Pope at last agreed to treat Charles with some of the dignity due to reigning monarchs. For although the Vatican would still not openly recognise him as a sovereign, nevertheless, he was granted the right to use the Royal Tribune at St Peter's, as previously granted to King James. The Pope also paid for the refurbishment of the Palazzo del Re.

Charles and Charlotte went out to parties, concerts, the theatre and opera, and lived for the moment, furiously making up for the lost years. It exhausted Charles. Local wags said that Charlotte was trying to kill him off. But living life to the hilt was what she intuitively knew her father wanted. When she gave musical parties for Rome's dignitaries and nobility, Charles sat quietly, radiant with happiness. In April 1787, the Tuscan envoy reported,

> The Count of Albany was openly insulted by the Marchese Vivaldi, owing to which the marchese was arrested by the troops in the Theatre of the Valle, and by order of the Pontiff was imprisoned in Castel Sant'Angelo; he was liberated through the request of the Count of Albany.

Ill, old, badly stooped, the man who once embraced Cluny Macpherson as an equal was back; who, after Prestonpans, when his prisoners broke parole, granted it a second time; who, after Falkirk, refused to let his officers cut the musket thumb off the right hand of the captured enemy – and who, in September 1745, wrote to his father about 'the errors and excesses of my grandfather's unhappy reign'.

Having won over Henry and brought the two brothers together again, Charlotte also returned Charles into the bosom of the Church. She then managed the unthinkable. Since 1785, Charlotte had been relaying back to her mother words of tenderness from Charles. On 3 January 1787, Charles wrote to Clementina:

> Although I have charged my dear daughter, the Duchess of Albany, to tell you how much I was moved by your letter of the 18th of the past month, I cannot refrain from indicating also my sincere gratitude. The prayers that you address to Heaven, the wishes that you make for my happiness and felicity I believe most sincere, and it seems that they may be realised since I enjoy perfect health, and hope in return that you may always be in the same state. My dear daughter, the Duchess of Albany, is also at this moment in the best of health. The sweetness of her nature, her good qualities, and her amiable companionship diminish greatly the pains and inconveniences that are indispensably joined to my aged condition. Rest assured that I love her, and that I shall love her with all my heart, and that I am and shall be your good friend,
>
> Charles R.

Charles and Charlotte spent the summer months at the Palazzo Savelli at Albano where a small theatre was opened for them. Visitors came in droves. Not all were tactful. The inaptly named dramatist Robert Greatheed pushed his reluctant host to tell him about the Rising:

> For a brief moment the prince was no longer the ruin of himself, but again the hero of the 'Forty-Five. His eyes brightened, he half rose from his chair, his face became lit up with unwonted animation, and he began the narrative of his campaign. He spoke with fiery energy of his marches, his victories, the loyalty of his Highland followers, his retreat from Derby, the defeat at Culloden, his escape, and then passionately entered upon the awful penalties so many had been called upon to pay for their devotion to his Cause. But the recollection of so much bitter suffering – the butchery around Inverness, the executions at Carlisle and London, the scenes on Kennington Common and Tower Hill – was stronger than his strength could bear. His voice died in his throat, his eyes became fixed, and he sank upon the floor in convulsions. Alarmed at the noise, his daughter rushed into the room, 'Oh Sir! What is this? You must have been speaking to my father about Scotland and the Highlanders! No one dares to mention those subjects in his presence.'

At last, Charles' strength began to ebb away. But at least he had the grim consolation of outliving the British minister who for decades had relentlessly monitored his every move. Sir Horace Mann died in Florence in November 1786, as James Lees-Milne put it, 'more than a year before the wretched victim of his acidulated pen'. Having been suffering from recurrent dropsy, Charles returned from Albano with Charlotte in the autumn of 1787, by which time, he was lapsing into unconsciousness and would pass the time lying on a couch with his favourite dog. On 7 January 1788, he suffered a major stroke, which paralyzed him down one side. It was the first of a series as he lay in semi-consciousness for the next three weeks. Finally, he could take no more. The Irish Franciscans of Saint Isidore gave him the Last Rites, and on the 30th of that month, he joined his comrades with whom the romantics regretted he had not fallen on Drummossie Moor on 16 April 1746.

During the Rising and after, Charles had always seemed curiously in tune with the ordinary people of Scotland. Perhaps it was fitting that the son of a Highland peddler, Uilleam Ros, the Gaelic poet from Skye, should write the last genuine Jacobite song.

It was called *An Suaithneas Bàn* or *Farewell to the White Cockade*[23]:

Bha mi seal am barail chruaidh	For a while I had firm faith
Gun cluinnte caismeachd mu'n cuairt,	That thy war-cry would be heard,
Càbhlach Thearlaich thighinn air chuan,	The fleet of Prince Charles coming o'er the seas,
Ach thréig an dàil mi gu Là Luain.	But now we'll ne'er meet till Doomsday.
'S lìonmhor laoch is mìlidh treun	Many a hero mighty, brave,
Tha an diu an Albainn as do dhéidh,	To-day in Scotland mourns for thee,
Iad os n-ìosal sileadh dheur,	In secret are they shedding tears
A rachadh dian leat anns an t-streup.	Who keenly would have followed thee.
Soraidh bhuan do'n t-Suaithneas Bhàn,	Farewell to the White Cockade
Gu Là-Luain cha ghluais o'n bhàs;	Till Doomsday he in death is laid,
Ghlac an uaigh an Suaithneas Bàn	The grave has taken the White Cockade,
Is leacan fuaraidh tuaim' a thàmh!	The cold tombstone is now his shade.

Six altars were erected in the antechamber and 200 Masses were said, a cast was made of his face and his body was embalmed and placed in a coffin of cypress wood. On his breast lay the Scottish Order of the Thistle with the Cross of St Andrew and the English Order of the Garter with the Cross of St George. Throughout the thirty hours before Charles' body was removed, the Irish Franciscans chanted the office of the dead. But the Pope, despite Henry's efforts, refused to bury him in the same style as his father. So Henry had his brother's body carried on a litter to Frascati where it lay in royal robes, sword by his side, crown on head, sceptre in hand and the great seal on his finger. On his coffin was the inscription 'Carolus III Magnae Britanniae Rex'. Henry celebrated High Mass in tears before 'a very great crowd of people, largely foreigners and the nobility, who when the service was over were in the Sacristy to cordially compliment the duchess who was found there with the Cardinal Carandini'. The entombment followed the next day – on the third, a requiem. The coffin was later removed and placed in the crypt of St Peter's with those of his mother and father.

In February, Gustav III of Sweden learnt of Charles' death and immediately sent a Masonic emissary to Rome who obtained from Charlotte the Latin document drawn up five years earlier in which Charles promised Gustav the formal transfer of the Grand Mastership of the Masonic Order of the Temple. It remains the prized possession of the Swedish Grand Lodge.

Charlotte's father was dead, but in his last three and half years, he had enjoyed greater peace, contentment and fulfilment than at any time since Derby in December 1745. His thirty-four-year-old daughter, who had been the architect of this happy twilight, who had suffered so much throughout her youth, surely deserved some measure of relief from the ill star that had hung over the Stuarts for so long. Yet during Charles' last months of life, her letters to Paris had grown steadily more anxious, and she longed to be reunited with her mother. Would her children recognise her? Did Ferdinand still love her? Had he found another? Would she see any of them again? Barely a soul knew she had malignant cancer of the liver. For, apart from to her mother, she hardly ever complained about it until she could hide it no longer.

In Florence, Charles had revealed his belief that the only hope for the Stuart Cause lay with his daughter, to whom he had granted the right of succession, which Henry had formally protested. Indeed, Charles had even designed four versions of a medal of honour, one side of which depicted Charlotte whilst for the other there were four possible versions. One portrayed the Figure of Hope pointing to a crown with the legend: '*Spem juvat amplecti, quae non juvat irrita semper*'.[24] The second was of Charlotte with one arm pointing towards the Stuart arms and her eyes gazing at an empty throne alongside the inscription '*Spem etsi infinitam persequar*'[25]. The remaining two were along the same lines.

Notwithstanding, as soon as his brother was dead, Henry transformed his ducal coronet into a royal crown, struck a commemorative medal as Henry IX, instructed his household to address him henceforth as 'Your Majesty' and signed his letters with the prefix *denominato*, signifying that he continued to call himself the Cardinal of York only for the sake of convenience. He even published a proclamation to underline that it was he who had inherited his brother's rights. Charlotte showed no sign of protest. At least the Pope granted her the right to use the Royal Tribune at St Peter's. In any case, she had far more serious problems. For her cancer was incurable and the pain was increasing every day. She also had to deal with the legal consequences of her father's death. And though she inherited her father's estate, nevertheless, it was not enormous. Furthermore, the French and Papal annuities had ceased with his death and the jointure under Charles' separation settlement with Louise zu Stolberg-Gedern had to be paid. What remained was an annual pension of 20,000 livres, which the French Court granted Charlotte, as well as the palace in Florence with all its contents. This she sold with all its furniture to the Duke di San Clemente, clearing all financial obligations to her stepmother by passing the proceeds over to her. All the family portraits, plate and jewels, valued at £26,740, were sent to Rome. Most had come from the Sobieskis and were described as 'many precious ornaments that belonged to King John of Poland, especially those acquired by him at the deliverance of Vienna from the Turks and the grand vizier who commanded them, being arms and armaments from his tent'.

With the Florentine Palace gone and the tenure of the Palazzo del Re terminated, Henry now made available to Charlotte a fine suite of rooms in the Cancellaria. To this, he added three rents from French properties amounting to 8,750 livres per annum from which Charles had previously benefitted, as well as his £2,200 cardinal's allowance. In return, she made over to him the Crown Jewels. With this much-needed income, Charlotte was able to continue supporting her mother and family in Paris as well as settle the various legacies her father had made, which, in total, exceeded the potential of the assets she had inherited.

In fact, Henry's generosity was not quite as great as would appear. In 1742, it had been decided that Charles had the absolute right to decide on any liquidation of the fabulous Sobieski jewels, which had been deposited in the financial institution known as the Monte di Pietà. On the other hand, to release them, Henry's co-signature was required, which, in 1784, he refused, fearing his brother would misspend the proceeds. Instead, although a very rich man thanks to his Church income and various other pensions, Henry set harsh conditions, as a result of which, in 1786, he had the great Sobieski ruby set in his bishop's mitre and a decade later sold another 'as large as a pigeon's egg' for the then gigantic amount of £60,000. At least he unquestioningly passed over to Charles the rest of the Sobieski jewels and, in 1786, gave Charlotte his own, all of which, of course, came back to him after their deaths.

Charlotte spent much of her time in Henry's company, as his diaries record, sometimes singing to him after dinner. She also became a godmother at Countess Mary Norton's confirmation at Frascati, the latter being a member of Charlotte's modest court, which also included her bright young cousin James FitzJames, who had just become the 5th Duke of Berwick and Liria[26]. Then there was the distinguished intellectual Cardinal Ercole Consalvi as well as Henry's old chaplain and now hers, Monsignor Christopher Stonor.

In March 1789, she sent a new portrait of herself to Ferdinand. But her feelings must have been deeply influenced by her health, which was continuing to deteriorate. As early as June 1786, she had written to her mother, 'I have a swelling on my side which pains me when I breathe.' Then, on 11 January 1788, during her father's last days, she was 'unable to leave her bed owing to her wretched state of health ... For the lady this was a cause of great affliction, the more so that until this morning her father's illness had been concealed from her'. A day later, she 'was in bed afflicted with the constant torment of hernicrania, the sharp pain being much worse at night than by day. Distress at her father's illness and being unable to help him sensibly increased her trouble.' On 29 November, 'the Duchess of Albany was suffering from fever and a cold, and pains about the waist and chest for which she had been bled, and again this morning. Doctor Mora feared it was the beginning of a serious illness'. In the summer of 1789, her doctors ordered her to take the waters at Nocera in Umbria. It did her little good. In early October, she moved to Bologna, the best centre of medicine and surgery in Italy. On the 10th, she wrote to Clementina, 'Don't worry. I am well; I love you and will send you news as soon as possible.' Referring to her three children, she also asked her mother to 'kiss my dear friends for me'.

Having been operated on, Charlotte remained in Bologna at the Palazzo Vizani belonging to her friend the Marchesa Giulia Lambertini-Bovio, who wrote to Henry,

> She has had a very serious relapse with terrible chills and a high fever. The doctors in treating the wound have drawn off a great quantity of matter of very bad colour and odour, whilst her pulse is very far above normal. I cannot sufficiently express my anxiety.

On 13 November, she wrote again:

> I must tell you the fever increases every moment, so that we fear to lose her very shortly. My Lord, the Cardinal Archbishop remains constantly with her, nor does he mean to leave her bedside so long as she is alive.

A day later:

> The doctors are confirmed in their opinion that this is a fever of re-absorption, and therefore of a fatal type. Her resignation continues unaltered in the face of imminent danger, and she has already put her will into the hands of the Cardinal Archbishop.

Three days later, on 17 November, the Marchesa informed Henry that Charlotte 'passed to the Other Life this evening at nine o'clock. So blessed was her death, that the tears I pour out from grief are tears of tenderness.'

Charlotte had made her will the same day. In it, she asked to be buried as simply as possible in Bologna's Church of San Biagio. She was thirty-six. Her friends called her 'the angel of peace' and 'her father's guardian angel'. Her detractors accused her of shallowness, resentful that she wrote to her mother of girlish things such as the latest fashions in Paris. How quickly they had forgotten her long years of denial. But though neither political nor military, none can deny her extraordinary achievements at the human level. Henry held a grand memorial service at Frascati and, in August 1790, came to pray at her graveside. Seven years later, the Church was closed by the revolutionary French Army and pulled down. In 1801, the bodies from San Biagio were reinterred in the Certosa. But Charlotte's name was not amongst them. Where her remains lie no one knows. Only her memorial stone was reset into the pavement of the adjoining Trinità. In her will, she remembered everyone, even her black page. But she still couldn't openly mention her three secret children. She left 50,000 francs to her mother and, significantly, 'any of her necessitous relatives'. The rest of her modest property went to Henry on condition that he continued to pay her mother's allowance. Amongst the objects he inherited from her was the garter jewel worn by Charles I at his execution.

At the time of Charlotte's death, the *de jure* King Henry IX was in his mid-sixties. And whilst there was no one to dispute his hereditary right to the triple throne of Scotland, England and Ireland, he was the first Stuart prince to make no attempt to regain it. A childless Roman Catholic cardinal was anathema to Protestant England. Henry lived between Rome and the Villa Muti in Frascati[27] until his declining years were interrupted by the French Revolution, which lost him his income from that country. Then the Spanish Court stopped their pension to him. Next, Henry squandered his part of the Sobieski and Stuart jewels in a forlorn bribe to help the Pope keep Napoleon out of the Papal States. And, in 1798, the invading French Army chased the elderly cardinal out of his rural home and forced him to leave behind everything he cherished, which they plundered.

In September 1799, Cardinal Stefano Borgia sent a letter to Sir John Cox Hippisley who from 1792-95 had semi-officially represented the British Government at the Court of Pope Pius VI, in which he said, 'It is very afflicting to me to see so great a personage, the last descendant of a royal house, reduced to such circumstances.' On 28 February 1800, *The Times* newspaper wrote,

> The malign influence of the star which had so strongly marked the fate of so many of his illustrious ancestors was not exhausted and it was peculiarly reserved for the Cardinal of York to be exposed to the shafts of adversity at a period of life when least able to struggle with misfortune. At the advanced age of seventy-five he is driven from his episcopal residence, his house sacked, his property confiscated, and constrained to seek his personal safety in flight, upon the seas, under every aggravated circumstance that could affect his health and fortune.

George III responded by granting Henry an allowance of £4,000 a year to be paid through Thomas Coutts, the banker. It was a pittance by comparison with the gigantic amount the London government had repeatedly contracted to repay the Stuarts for Mary of Modena's dowry and ultimately reneged upon thirteen years earlier. Nevertheless, Henry replied with exquisite manners through Lord Minto: 'I am, in reality, at a loss to express in writing all the sentiments of my heart; and for that reason leave it entirely to the interest you take in all that regards my person to make known in an energetic and convenient manner all I fain would say to express my thankfulness'.

Revolutionary France concluded a concordat with the Vatican in 1801, which permitted the titular King Henry, who became dean of the College of Cardinals in 1803, to return to his home, for which he commissioned frescoes by the Polish artist Thadée Kuntze. He lived out his last years quietly, dying peacefully on 13 July 1807 with his old friend Monsignor Angelo Cesarini, Bishop of Milevi, by his side, to whom he entrusted all his property for distribution. At last, Henry's body was placed alongside that of his parents and brother in the crypt of St Peter's.

During this final twilight period, with just a little of Charles' panache, Henry used to enjoy himself by galloping at full tilt in his coach and six across the Roman *Campagna*. But whereas his elder brother had cut off his means of escape in 1745 by sending Antoine Walsh's *du Teillay* back to France, Henry always made sure he was followed by a second empty coach in case of disaster.

8

The Prince's Heirs: Secret Family & Polish Exile 1776-1859

All that radiant kingdom lies forlorn
as if it never stirred
no human voice is heard amongst its meadows
but it speaks to itself alone
alone it flowers and shines
and blossoms for itself while time runs on.

Edwin Muir

When she went to live with Charles, Charlotte entrusted her three secret 'little flowers in the garden' to the care of their grandmother Clementina Walkinshaw and her 'worthy friend' Prince Ferdinand de Rohan. It was 1784 and the children barely knew their mother. The oldest was five and the youngest just a few weeks old. In one way, their situation was better than Charlotte's had been, for she regularly sent money from Italy and Ferdinand generously supported them. In another, it was not. Because for the first years of Charlotte's life, she had been brought up by Prince Charles and Clementina, and all three lived together openly as a family unit. Charlotte knew who she was. However, for the sake of the Stuart Cause, as well as her and Ferdinand's positions, their three children were worse off than orphans – their parents pretended to live apart, to be merely friends, the children themselves hidden from view, their very existence some unfathomably dark political secret. In a very real sense, they were the last and most innocent victims of the Stuart Cause. Until 1789, when the French Revolution destroyed their world, the single fixed point in their young lives was their devoted Scottish grandmother, the much-maligned unsung hero of their mother's upbringing.

But let us return to 1776 and that fateful dinner at Lord Elcho's where the twenty-two-year-old Charlotte met her relation Ferdinand, gave up her plan to become an honorary canoness at Besançon, and returned to Paris, where she and her mother had been lady pensioners at the convent on the rue St Jacques. Soon after, they moved into a house on the same street, near the south bank of the Seine opposite Notre Dame, rented for them by Ferdinand from the Abbé de la Villette. For greater privacy, he also acquired a country home for them all at Anthony, a few miles from Paris' prying eyes in the direction of Fontainebleau.

The gossipy court circles of Versailles in which they now moved soon got to know of Charlotte's friendship with Ferdinand, of which they made no secret, though acting with perfect discretion lest anyone should realise the full extent of their relationship. In this, they were completely successful. Even as late as 1784, Sir Horace Mann would only report back to London of a platonic link between them. When together, summer was spent between Versailles and Anthony, but Charlotte would be with her mother at the house on the rue St Jacques when Ferdinand was away completing the palace at Bordeaux, before becoming Archbishop of Cambrai in 1781, when he launched into another grand project: the creation of the superb gardens there. Winters were spent close to one another in Paris, where Ferdinand had a house on the rue du Regard, a short walk from Charlotte's rue St Jacques, or socialising at the magnificent Hôtel de Rohan on the rue Vieille du Temple just across the river.

One of their two daughters was given the unforgiving Stuart name of Charlotte, then Maximilienne after Ferdinand's second name, with Amèlie as her third. It is not known exactly when she was born. And whilst the choice of Charlotte might suggest she was the oldest, her parents may have been cautious with their first-born and only risked such a Stuart name with their second when they felt more confident. Young Charlotte's death certificate suggests she was born in Paris in late 1780. Furthermore, there is no evidence that she was formally recognised as a princess de Rohan – which was not the case with her sister – moreover, she was not the first to marry, implying that Charlotte was actually the younger daughter.

Regarding young Charlotte's sister, it was mentioned earlier that Ferdinand's eldest brother Jules-Hercule was Henry Stuart's *aide de camp* and the husband of his and Prince Charles' cousin Louise. Jules-Hercule was also the 7th Duke de Montbazon and head of the sovereign House of Rohan as Prince de Guéméné. The Château de Montbazon was in the Parish of Veigné just south of Tours and was where his ancestor had entertained Mary Queen of Scots in 1560. Nearby, another forebear had built the dukes' summer residence, the Château de Couzières, where, in 1619, he orchestrated the reconciliation between the Stuarts' ancestress Marie de Medici and her son Louis XIII. A mile or so down the road stood another of Jules-Hercule's castles, the Château de Thorigny. But it was in the private chapel of the Château de Couzières in 1779 that the aging duke, whose only son was already thirty-four, signed a most unusual certificate of baptism which read:

> On the nineteenth of June in the year 1779 was baptised ... Marie, born yesterday, the natural daughter of the very high and powerful and very excellent Prince Jules-Hercule, Prince de Rohan-Guéméné, Duke de Montbazon, Peer of France, Lieutenant-General of the King's armies, who has come in person to recognise her by the present act which he has signed with us, and by which he has named her the Demoiselle de Thorigny.

The baby Marie's second name of Victoire was after her godmother, Victoire Wallin, and her third name, Adélaïde was presumably after Ferdinand's cousin, the daughter of the Bourbon Prince de Condé by Princess Charlotte de Rohan.[28] The honours

13. King John III Sobieski (1629-96), Prince Charles Edward Stuart's great-grandfather, engraved in 1684, the year after his magnificent victory at Vienna over a Turkish army of almost 100,000, described by Lord d'Abernon as one of the eighteen battles that changed the course of world history. A brilliant warrior and passionate lover, his letters to his French wife are one of the great works of the Baroque.

14. Prince Charles Edward Stuart (1720-88), by Giles Hussey *c.* 1735, who became known as Bonnie Prince Charlie because his Christian name in Gaelic was *Thearlaich*, similar in pronunciation to Charlie.

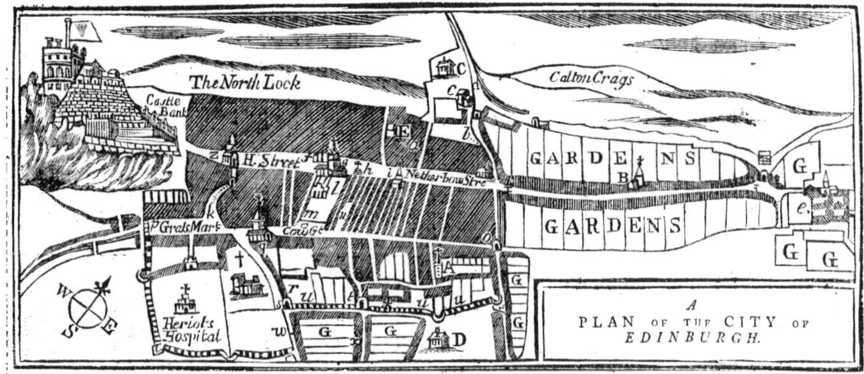

15. A plan of Edinburgh published in the 1745 edition of *The Gentleman's Magazine and Historical Chronicle*.

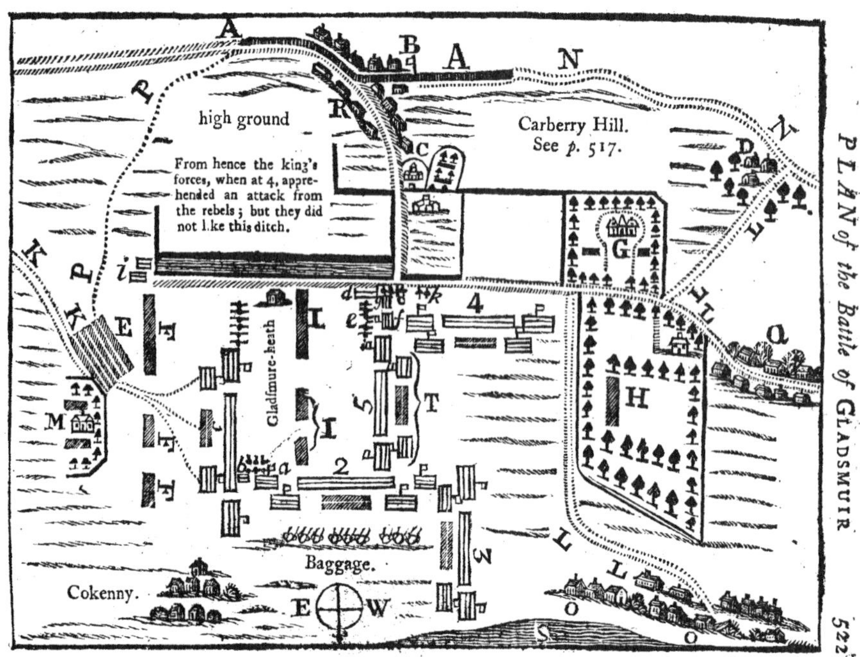

16. A plan of the Battle of Prestonpans, or Gladsmuir as it was originally known, fought on 21 September 1745, published shortly after in *The Gentleman's Magazine and Historical Chronicle*. A Jacobite officer, Lieutenant Anderson, was a local farmer's son who told Lord George Murray of a secret path through some marshland, enabling the Highland Army to start their move at 4 a.m. and launch a surprise attack at 6 a.m., which secured victory within minutes, inflicting heavy losses on the Hanoverians. Prince Charles Edward personally insisted on the best possible treatment being given to his enemy's wounded and prisoners.

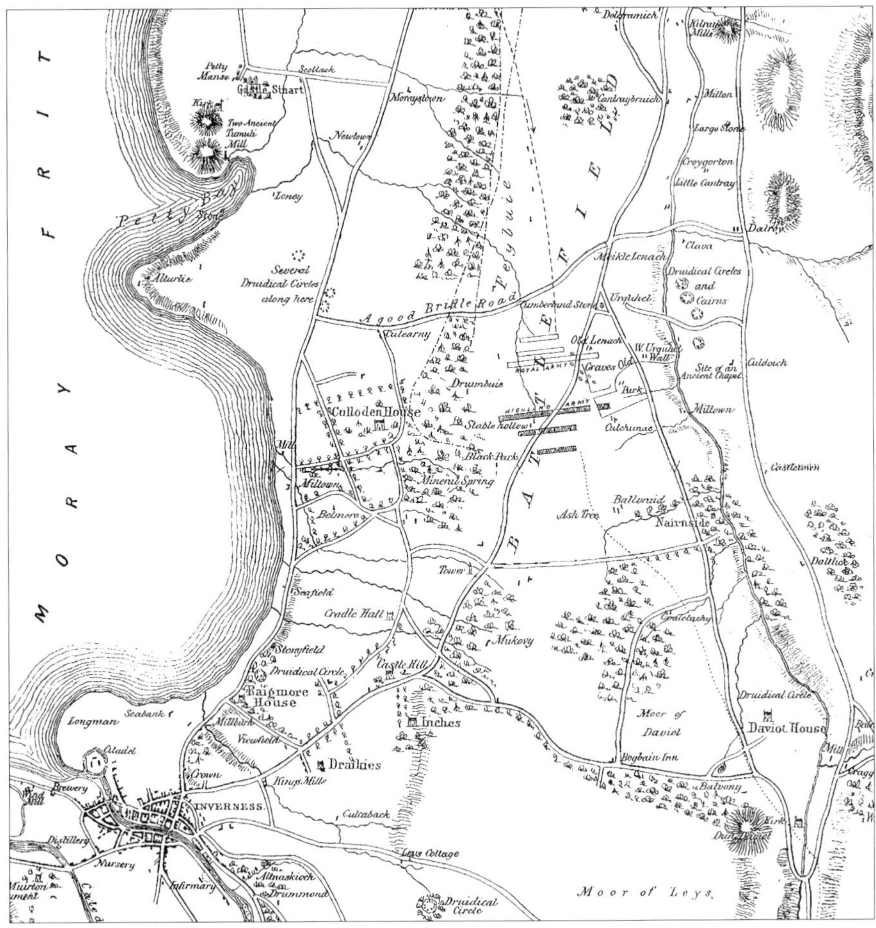

17. A map of Culloden or Drummossie Moor from the 1871 edition of *The Memoirs of the Chevalier de Johnstone*, showing the coastline and woods to the left (north), with the steep-sloped River Nairn and high moorland beyond to the right (south). It is clear from this how limited was the choice of battlefield given Prince Charles Edward's conviction that the Jacobite Army's provisions at Inverness had to be protected at all costs. Lord George Murray argued against giving battle, and for dispersal and a guerrilla campaign. But Sir John O'Sullivan saw the weakness of this and pointed out that the Highlands were at the end of a long, hard winter and so food was very scarce, the area left in their control was relatively small, and that half the army was non-Highland in origin. Lord George then argued for positioning the army on the higher ground and slopes of the River Nairn; however, this contained the fatal flaw of leaving the road to Inverness wide open.

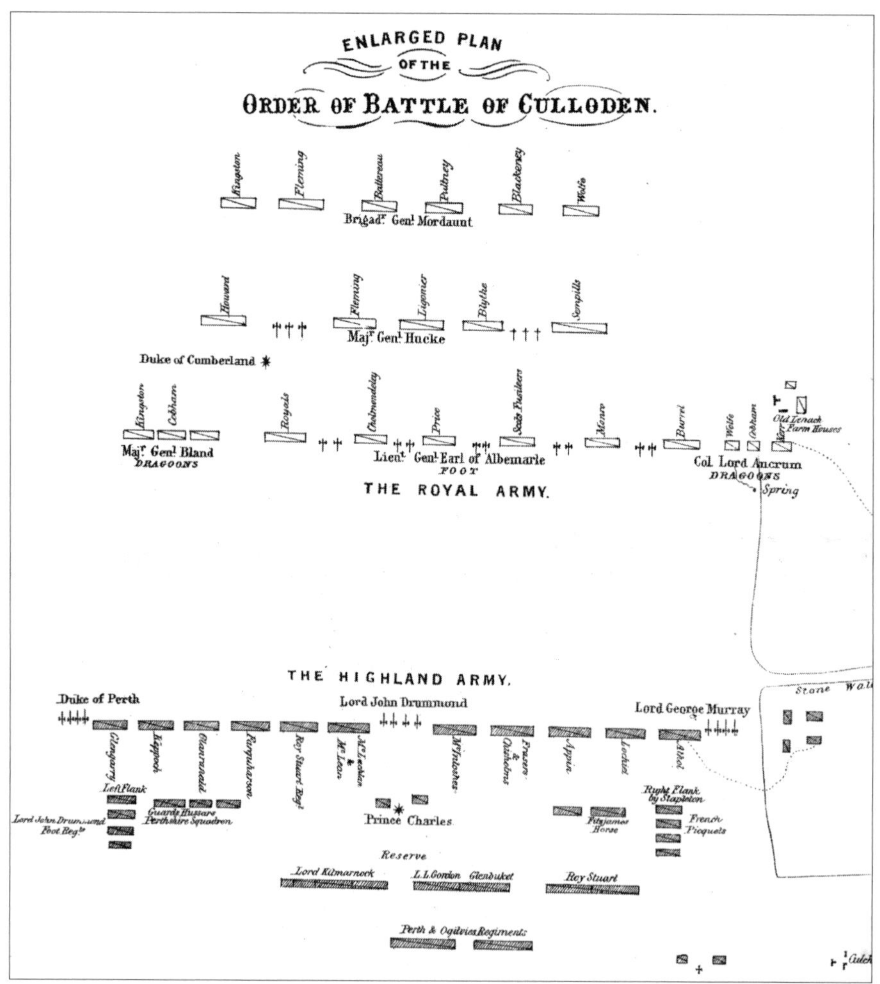

18. The Order of the Battle of Culloden, as illustrated in the 1871 edition of *The Memoirs of the Chevalier de Johnstone.* Apart from the various regiments, it also shows the gun placements. The Hanoverians stood to the east, with their backs to Nairn and the icy-cold wind and sleet, whilst the Jacobites were to the west with Inverness behind them.

Publiſhed by Authority,
Whitehall, April 26, 1746.

This afternoon a Meſſenger arrived from the Duke of Cumberland, *with the following* Particulars of the VICTORY *obtained by his* Royal Highneſs *over the Rebels, on* Wedneſday *the* 16*th inſtant near* Culloden.

Inverneſs, April 18.

ON *Tueſday* the 15th the rebels burnt fort *Auguſtus,* which convinced us of their reſolution to ſtand an engagement with the king's troops. We gave our men a day's halt at *Nairn,* and on the 16th marched from thence, between four and five, in four columns. The three lines of foot (reckoning the reſerve for one) were broken into three from the right, which made the three columns equal, and each of five battalions. The artillery and baggage follow'd the firſt column upon the right, and the cavalry made the fourth column on the left.

After we had marched about eight miles, our advanced guard, compoſed of about 40 of

Dd *King-*

19. An article in *The Gentleman's Magazine and Historical Chronicle* from late April 1746 announcing the outcome of the Battle of Culloden.

20. The *de jure* King Charles III in 1776 in Florence, an engraving after the original portrait by Ozias Humphrey, RA. One traveller wrote of him, 'When a young man he must have been esteemed handsome... he is by no means thin, has a noble person and a graceful manner ... on the whole he has a melancholy, mortified appearance'.

21. Clementina Walkinshaw (1720-1802), Prince Charles' third love after his cousins Princess Louise de Rohan and Princess Marie-Anne de Talmont. She was from a loyal Jacobite family and the mother of his daughter and heiress, Charlotte Stuart, Duchess of Albany. She was also the great niece of 'Bobbing John', 6th Earl of Mar (Duke of Mar in the Jacobite Peerage), who by his ineptitude snatched defeat from the jaws of victory during the 1715 Rising.

22. Prince Jules-Hercule de Rohan, Duke de Montbazon (1726-88), the 'dutiful' head of the Rohans, whose family solidarity was legendary. This 1780 likeness is the only image known and shows him as he was when he baptised his niece, Marie-Victoire.

B.
Marie
Thorigny
naturel

le dix neuf de juin de l'année mil sept cent soixante dix neuf
a été baptisée sous condition par nous vicaire soussigné marie victoire
fille naturelle de très hault très puissant et très excellent
prince jules hercules prince de rohan guémené duc de
montbazon pair de france lieutenant général des armées
du roy, lequel est venu en personne la reconnoitre par ce présent
acte qu'il a signé avec nous, et a laquelle il a donné le nom de demoiselle de thorigny, et de demoiselle marie grossot: le parrain
a été le sieur simon pierre corret de la demenchecrie, et la marraine
demoiselle victoire jeanne vallin épouse dudit sieur corret
secrétaire des commandements de mondit seigneur, qui
ont aussi signé avec nous.

Jules Hercules Prince De Rohan — femme Corret
Corret De la Chemandrie — venier vic.
un mot ajouté bon.

23. The 1779 baptismal entry for Marie-Victoire (1779-1836), Charlotte Stuart's daughter by Ferdinand de Rohan. From the Parish of Veigné near Tours, it is signed by Prince Jules-Hercule de Rohan, Duke de Montbazon, who legitimised her and granted her the title of the Demoiselle de Thorigny.

24. The Château de Couzières in the Parish of Veigné in whose chapel Marie-Victoire was baptised. Her title of the Demoiselle de Thorigny came from the neighbouring château which, like Couzières, was a fief of the Rohans' Duchy of Montbazon.

25. Prince Ferdinand de Rohan (1738-1813), Archbishop of Cambrai and Count of the Napoleonic Empire, the brother-in-law of the Stuart Princes' first cousin Princess Louise de La Tour d'Auvergne whose husband was Prince Jules-Hercule de Rohan, Duke de Montbazon, Henry Stuart's ADC in 1745.

de londres
Je rouvre ma lettre parceque je recois dans l'instant la reponse de mr. Thomas Coutts;
ce fameux banquier si riche et qui est lié avec tout ce qu'il y a de mieux, et de plus considerable
en angleterre; je l'ai connu à paris, et à liège; il me mande positivement qu'il y a très peu
d'assurance que les indes occidentales francaises et particulièrement St. domingue, restent sous la
domination anglaise même pendant la guerre. il m'ajoute, que les hommes les mieux informés de l'angleterre
regrettent que le gouvernement aie adopté la mesure de les subjuguer dans ces tems, où l'idée de les retenir
sous la protection de la gde. bretagne même quand il y auroit une paix... sa lettre est très récente, car
elle est datée du 24 mars; — il trouve aussi que le séjour d'angleterre peut devenir mauvais pour un
etranger surtout, et il voudroit lui même que ses affaires lui permissent de venir à Venise qu'il regarde
comme l'endroit le plus sûr. — il me mande du bien de mr. Turnbull qu'il dit être un négotiant, marchand,
de bonne réputation; il me semble qu'on vous avoit dit qu'ils etaient banquiers très riches, de la cour?..
je suis, mon cher frere, très faché d'apprendre d'aussi mauvaises nouvelles, mais elles viennent d'un
homme bien instruit, en consequence je ne compte presque plus sur St. domingue, ce ne sera encore
qu'un beau rêve, à moins que l'on ne fasse stipuler à la paix que les français laisseront jouir paisiblement +
1180

26. Part of a letter from Prince Ferdinand de Rohan to his brother, Cardinal Louis, dated 17 April 1795. Sent from Venice to Ettenheim, Ferdinand describes the help that Thomas Coutts the banker is providing.

27. Cardinal Louis de Rohan (1734-1803), Prince Ferdinand's elder brother and the hero of the scandalous *Affaire du Collier de la Reine*. After the French Revolution erupted, Louis, who was Prince-Bishop of Strasbourg, retreated to the safety of Ettenheim in the eastern part of his principality, where he helped his relation, the Bourbon Prince de Condé, form a counter-revolutionary army and where he looked after Charlotte Stuart's children.

L'an Dix huit Cent et six, Le Vingt huitieme 193
jour Du mois De novembre aux quatre heures
après midi,
Par devant Nous, Charles Hanotte maire adjoint
et officier de l'Etat Civil de La Ville de huy, chef
Lieu du troisième arrondissement du departement de l'Ourte
Sont Comparus joseph [illegible], Ecrivain agé de Vingt huit
ans, Domicilié En La Commune de [illegible] et Nicolas-
joseph [illegible] Employé dans Les droits réunis
agé de trente ans Domicilié En Cette Commune
tous deux amis de Charlotte maximilienne amelie
De Roehenstart, née à paris, Domiciliée En Cette Commune
agée De Vingt Six ans Epouse à jean Louis [illegible]
[illegible] Cousin de Lamortière receveur principal des
Droits reunis, fille de maximilien de Roehenstart
et de Clementine de [illegible], Lesquels nous ont
declarés que Ladite Charlotte maximilienne amelie
De Roehenstart est décédée Le Vingt Six du present
mois a trois heures après midi, En Son domicile
Section du [illegible] rue de l'[illegible],
et ont, Les Declarants Signé avec nous, Le present
acte de décès après Lecture.

28. The death certificate of Charlotte Maximilienne, daughter of Charlotte Stuart and Ferdinand de Rohan, who lost her baby and died in childbirth after her first pregnancy at Huy near Liège in 1806.

Recomendatus obsequijs Sacræ Regiæ Majestatis à Celsissimo Duce Radziwiłł Pro
sub tempus Comitiorum, mediante Patrocinio Illustrissimæ Excellent
obtinui literas favorabiles Secretariatûs et Commissoriatûs, dabam ope
per hoc spatium temporis; nè videar communi plurimis acquiescere desidere
ut possim particulare aliquod exequi obsequium, mittebam Famulos Consta
tinopolim et nihil indè singularis potui conducere, et sic pensatis pensandis
assumpsi propositum migrandi in Persiam, ubi speciosissimæ et singulares
res reperiuntur et fabricantur, quoniam verò ad illud Regnum ob magnam
stantiam loci difficilis et periculosus est aditus, constitui supplicare Illustrissi
Excellentiæ, quatenus possim ob securitatem tam vitæ, quam subtilis fortunæ m
in charactere Legati seu Missarij hoc iter conficere, sicuti practicavit piè def
Jacobus Murkiewicz à Serenissimo Divæ Memoriæ Augusto II ad
Regem Persiæ Missarius. Advolutus itaq plantis Illustrissimæ Exce
lentiæ Domini mei Clementissimi humillimè supplico ut similem expeditionem
à Serenissimo Rege feliciter nunc regnante, mediante interpositione Illustri
ssimæ Excellentiæ obtinere possim, non quæro indè privatum lucrum, sed solu
modò desidero alacris animi mei ad obsequia, exhibere documenta, prætereà om
possibilitate procurare studebo, ut consideratis maturè Regni Persici Incolarum neg
tionibus, correspondentiam constituere, et commercium cum Incolis Poloniæ et S
nia quam optimo modô stabilire possim, quoniam verò tam pro famulatu characte
adæquato, quam pro donariis Regi Persarum, et ejus Ministris spectantibus p
um impendam pecunium, quod debebit esse notabile, idcircò ut aliquod levame
in expensis habeam, humillimè supplico quatenus possim per Imperium Mos
viticum postiles equos sinè exactione solutionis ex Recomendatione Sacræ Regiæ
Majestatis pro commoditate mea et famulatûs mei habere, in felici verò re
in Poloniam ab exactione Te[illegible] meorum liber esse, quæ omnia Gratiæ, meq Patro
Illustrissimæ Excellentiæ in[illegible]

Illustrissimæ et Excellentissimæ Dominationis Vestræ Domini, Domini
mei Clementissimi

humillimus servus
Gregorius Nikorowicz
S. R. M. [illegible]

29. The 1744 letter of Gregory, Chevalier de Nikorowicz (1713-89), to King Augustus III of Poland, in which he refers to his patronage by the Stuarts' closest Polish cousins, the Princes Radziwiłł, and requests diplomatic protection and tax exemptions for his trade and espionage mission to the Court of Persia at Esfahan.

30. The Palace of Sychrov, north of Prague. Purchased in 1820, it was the Rohan family's main home until 1945. After their escape from the French Revolution, the Rohans never returned permanently to France, and it was here at Sychrov that Marie-Victoire's letters to Prince Louis de Rohan were kept.

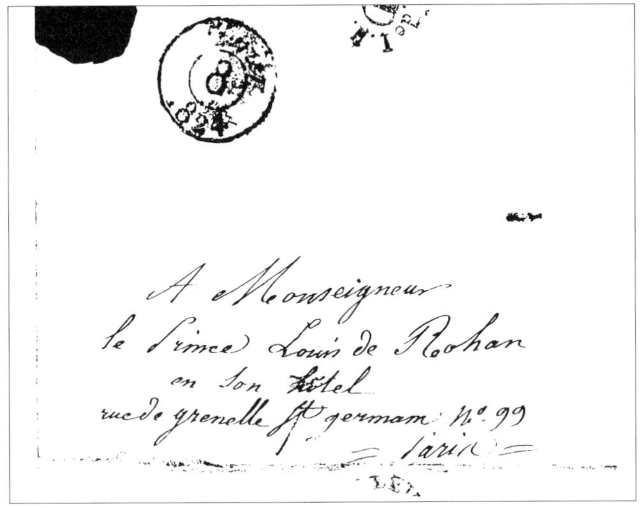

A Monseigneur
le Prince Louis de Rohan
en son hôtel
rue de grenelle St germain No. 99
Paris

31. An envelope written in 1824 by Marie-Victoire and addressed to Prince Louis at his mansion on the rue de Grenelle.

Rohan Stuard d'Overgne

32. The back of an envelope sent by Marie-Victoire to Prince Louis on which she calls herself 'Rohan Stuard d'Overgne'. In French and Italian, the letter 'd' is phonetically the same as 't' and Stuart is often spelt this way. For example, the old Bologna guide of *c.* 1793 describes Charlotte Stuart as 'Carlotta Stuardo' and the marble slab from her grave was spelt 'Stuarda'. Likewise, 'd'Overgne' is also phonetic, the correct spelling of her second husband's name being 'd'Auvergne'.

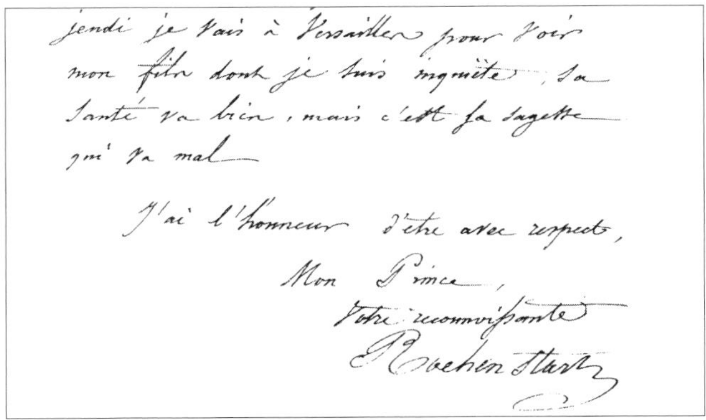

Jeudi je vais à Versailles pour voir mon fils dont je suis inquiète, sa santé va bien, mais c'est sa sagesse qui va mal

J'ai l'honneur d'être avec respect,
Mon Prince,
Votre reconnoissante
Roehen Start

33. One of Marie-Victoire's letters to Prince Louis, in which she refers to her son's education at Versailles. Though she describes herself as a widow and a mother, she uses the alias 'Roehenstart', a rebus of Rohan and Stuart, as a sort of maiden name. Her brother Charles and sister Charlotte also used the name at times.

mon Secret ..... combien de volumes
Sont remplis des histoires galantes, et des
amours des Stuarts et des Ro —
ce sang Breton qui coule dans mes veines
n'étoit pas très rassurant, Il fallut donc

34. One of Marie-Victoire's letters to Prince Louis, in which she refers to her 'Secret', to the 'romances of the Stuarts and Rohans' and to her 'Breton blood'. Both the Stuarts and the Rohans descended from ancient Celtic families of Brittany. The Stuarts' protoplast was Flaald, eleventh-century hereditary High Steward of Dol, whereas the Rohans' ancestor was Guethenoc, Viscount de Chateautro en Porhoët, who built the massive fortress of Josselin in 1008.

Mon premier bonjour est pour celui
à qui je le dois, c'est un bien heureux
accord que celui du plaisir et du devoir; j'ai
donc l'honneur de saluer mon Seigneur et
père et de lui offrir l'expression de ma reconnois-
=sance. — Je sais qu'il n'est pas
besoin de stimuler l'obligeance du Prince pour
rendre justice à une orpheline du pur sang
des R. et des S., mais je prie instamment
Monseigneur de ne point encore s'ennuyer, de
ne pas perdre courage ..... ce seroit s'arrêter
en trop beau chemin, la charité chrétienne
soutiendra votre bienveillance au moins jusqu'à
l'époque du mariage!! — Il est des services
qui valent cent fois plus que de l'or." J'ai
réfléchi qu'hier, en vous témoignant mon inquiétude
(qu'une certaine épithète lancée méchamment ne vînt
affecter la sensibilité du respectable;) vous avez
pu croire que je ne lui avois pas très franchement
parlé de ma naissance toute naturelle, il en sait
là-dessus autant que nous, il n'ignore pas que

35. One of Marie-Victoire's letters to Prince Louis in which she refers to herself as an 'orphan of the pure blood of the Rs and Ss' and writes of her 'natural birth'.

le brave Amiral Prince de M. n'a jamais été
marié avec la D.sse — J'ai cru nécessaire même, d'avertir
M. d'At qu'il pourroit peut être entendre dans le
monde répéter une calomnie affreuse qui a plané sur
la tête de mon respectable oncle et tuteur le P.ce J. —
Aussitôt que M. d'At. m'a parlé de ses espérances
d'union, je l'ai prévenu de tout franchement;
il sait que le P.ce J nommé tuteur après la mort
du P.ce de M. a seul veillé à mon éducation &&
et que par ce moyen ayant seul paru s'intéresser
à moi, la calomnie peut s'être exercée sur lui &&
— J'ai toujours l'honneur de prier de nouveau le
Prince d'être mon généreux Chevalier dans le monde, s'il
en est besoin, je lui promets de ne jamais deshonorer
l'illustre famille d'où je sors. M. d'At. m'a
dit souvent qu'il aimoit la noblesse de mes sentimens
(je ne suis pas trop modeste de répéter ce compliment;)
qu'il savoit bien qu'il me manquoit quelques
parchemins pour prouver d'autres titres de
noblesse, mais que cela lui étoit égal, que
j'étois toujours à ses yeux une Re et une S. p

36. The second page of the previous letter in which Marie-Victoire admits her mother 'the Duchess' was 'never married', and appeals to Prince Louis to help reassure her future second husband d'Auvergne with regard to any gossip 'he could perhaps hear repeated in Society'.

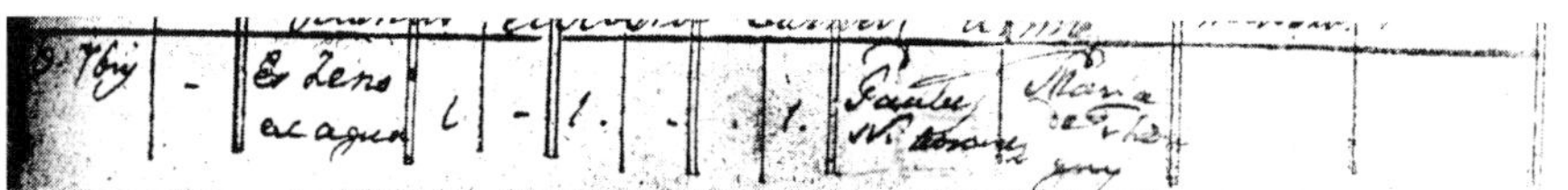

37. The 1804 '*ex aqua*' baptismal entry for Marie-Victoire's son by Paul Anthony, Chevalier de Nikorowicz, in the records of the Armenian Catholic cathedral of Lwów. Born prematurely, he was not expected to survive, was immediately anointed with the water of baptism, and temporarily given the name of the saint's day upon which he was born. That name was 'Zenon' from Zenodoros, meaning 'Gift of Zeus'. Careful of her Catholicism and 'bourgeois morality', Marie-Victoire preferred the Christian equivalent, 'Theodoros', meaning 'gift of God', which is why 'Theodore' became her pet-name for her son.

178 1806 Mensis	Nr. Domus	NOMEN	Religio: Catholica	Religio: Acatholica	Sexus: Puer	Sexus: Puella	Thori: Illegitimi	Thori: Legitimi	PARENTES: PARENS	PARENTES: MATER	PATRINI: NOMEN	PATRINI: CONDITIO
20a april 1806.	—	antimus in baptis. Marcus in confirm.	1.	—	1.	—	—	1.	Paulus de Nikorowicz	Victoria de Thorigny— Nikorowiczowa	Josephus de Botoz Antoniewicz; Kengardis Nikorowiczowa	advocat.; Virgo.

38. The 1806 record of the '*in baptismo et in confirmatione*' formal christening ceremony at the Armenian Catholic cathedral of Lwów. By this time, Marie-Victoire's son had become healthy. His temporary name of Zenon was now replaced by Antime and Mark and his godparents were appointed. As Marie-Victoire's only child, he was the unique great-grandchild of Prince Charles Edward Stuart.

39. The Castle of Grzymałów, *c.* 1900. Some 80 miles east of Lwów, the estate was bought in 1831 by Antime de Nikorowicz, and it was here that Prince Louis de Rohan's replies to Marie-Victoire were kept until the First World War, when the Russian Staff occupied the castle in 1914 and devastated its interiors.

40. One of the drawing rooms at Grzymałów Castle, *c.* 1900. The family's oldest documents were kept in a secretaire here, some of them dating back to the fourteenth century. Amongst them were the letters of Prince Louis de Rohan to Marie-Victoire, which were the key to unlocking the Stuarts' Last Secret.

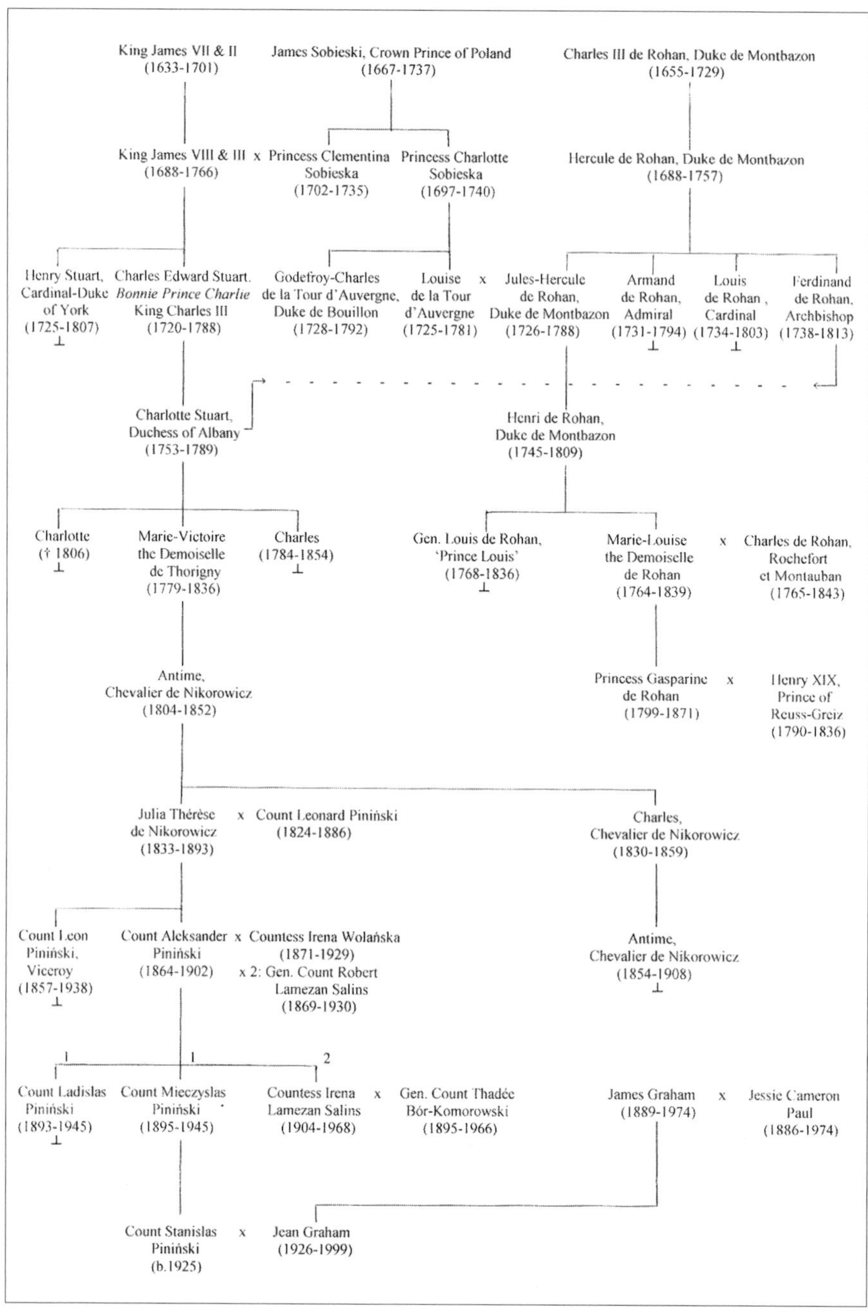

41. Genealogical table.

awarded this little girl were astonishing: she was the first natural daughter ever to be legitimised by a Duke de Montbazon; and of all the princesses de Rohan born in the eighteenth century, only three others were granted the title of '*la Demoiselle de …*'.

Illegitimate children of rich aristocrats having a good time were being born all the time, and not just in this period of French history. Their mothers were paid off and that was that. Unless circumstances were mighty special, their offspring certainly wouldn't be formally acknowledged, because that gave them the same rights of inheritance as legitimate children. Still less would they be granted a special title of honour. And the status of the person who played the role of mother at this particular christening definitely didn't warrant the extraordinary treatment shown to Marie-Victoire. Because that person was Marie Grosset, the simple daughter of Jules-Hercule's castellan at Couzières. The godfather was Jules-Hercule's steward and the godmother that man's wife – all people loyal and subservient, people who could be guaranteed to keep a secret. Not that a reward might not be in order. And sure enough, on 2 September 1782, Jules-Hercule signed a notarial deed at yet another of his Loire properties, the Château d'Ussé, in which he recognised 'the services that Mademoiselle Marie Grosset had rendered'. Tellingly, there is no mention whatsoever of any child – his castellan's daughter earned a life annuity for herself and herself alone. In the case of her death in those unhealthy and dangerous times, no one, no child, nor anyone else, was to inherit, whereupon the 'annuity will be extinct and amortised … which the said Mademoiselle Grosset has accepted, thanking very humbly his Highness for his benevolence and reward'.

Thus was Princess Marie-Victoire de Rohan, the Demoiselle de Thorigny, recognised at baptism by the head of the sovereign Princes de Rohan (of legendary family solidarity) and formally brought into the family of her real father, of course, Jules-Hercule's youngest brother Ferdinand who, as a Roman Catholic archbishop, could do no such thing himself. And the honour shown to Marie-Victoire was due to the person of her real mother, whom Marie-Victoire's private correspondence with her most trusted Rohan cousin will later reveal as Charlotte Stuart, daughter of the *de jure* King Charles III, who was the first cousin of Jules-Hercule's wife, Louise. According to Professor L. L. Bongie, the good Jules-Hercule was a man 'dutiful and tender … almost dripping with family sentimentality'. One wonders if he would have been quite so accommodating had he discovered that Charlotte's father had cuckolded him in 1747 and fathered his wife's little boy who died in infancy? Luckily for Charlotte and Ferdinand, he never did.

For his own services, Jules-Hercule was ill rewarded. His wife died in 1781, and in 1782, his only son and heir contrived a loss which was reported the length and breadth of Europe. That autumn, Henri de Rohan was declared bankrupt to the tune of a staggering 34 million livres. Mercifully, Henri was bailed out by yet another piece of strategic Rohan breeding, namely the vast fortune of his heiress wife, Princess Victoire de Rohan from the Soubise line of the family. Poor Jules-Hercule was not so lucky. Right up to his death in 1788, he was hounded by creditors and forced to sell all he owned. However, who should now come to his rescue but his brother-in-law and fellow *aide de camp* to Henry Stuart from 1745, Godefroy-Charles, since 1771, the new Duke de Bouillon. And where should he now park Jules-Hercule for the last years of his life if not at the same Château de Carlsbourg in the hills of the Ardennes in which Prince Charles, Clementina and Charlotte had lived during the 1750s and from which Clementina had fled with Charlotte to Paris leaving Charles in despair with only the 'nasty bottle' and his 'dear Thiboult to amuse and comfort' him.

The years 1783-84 brought with it Charles' successive health scares in Florence, which prompted his unexpected decision to make Charlotte his sole heir, legitimise her and create her HRH the Duchess of Albany, thus provoking Henry into formally protesting Charlotte's right to the royal succession. The astonished Charlotte was told of her father's decisions in Paris in July 1784, but didn't join him in Italy until October. Her delay was not without good reason.

On 13 May 1784, a little boy was baptised in Paris in the Parish of St Merry, whose church was on the rue St Martin. The baptismal acts of the Archives de Paris read:

> Auguste Maximilien, born the same day, the son of the noble Maximilien Roehenstart and the noble Clementine Ruthven, his wife, of this parish, the Cul de Sac des Anglois. The godfather Thibault Etienne Lauverjat, master in surgery, of the same house, the godmother Anne Victoire Lauverjat, under-age daughter of the godfather, of the same abode, the father absent on business.

This tells us that the baby was born so weak he was considered unlikely to survive and was therefore immediately baptised by sprinkling water on his brow for which no priest was needed, allowing the formal christening ceremony itself to take place at some later date if the child survived. This was baptism '*ex aqua*', as opposed to the christening ceremony's '*in baptismo et confirmatione*'. That is why the godfather was the doctor on hand to deliver the child and the godmother his young daughter. It is significant that Lauverjat was a master in surgery, because Charlotte would have feared complications given that, since 1775, she had been suffering the 'obstruction of the liver' which would kill her in 1789. And how conveniently located was the ironically named Cul de Sac des Anglois, just 350 yards from the Hôtel de Rohan. However, despite the baptismal entry claiming otherwise, the baby boy's fictitious parents did not live in that house. Because the Almanach Royal for 1784 reveals who did ... Lauverjat.[29]

Nor is there any record in the Paris archives of any family called Roehenstart or Ruthven. Nor was a noble family registered anywhere in Europe with the name Roehenstart. But then, that is scarcely surprising, because Roehenstart was a name invented by Charlotte and Ferdinand as a rebus of Rohan and Stuart. That is why this infant boy was given the same second name of Maximilien as his sister, young Charlotte, after Ferdinand's second name. That is why the mother's alias has the same Christian name as Charlotte's mother Clementina, and surname as Clementina's great grandmother (Lady Paterson née Barbara Ruthven). And that is why the father was so diplomatically 'absent on business' – and well he might have been, given that Ferdinand could no more reveal his identity in official records than Charlotte could.

Two months later, Charlotte would be told of her father's decisions and invitation to come and live with him in Florence, but for the moment, her little son had survived and was now strong enough to be sent to the country for wet-nursing. There he remained until late March 1785, when Charlotte wrote to her mother suggesting that 'he who is in the country will no doubt soon be returning to the city, and it is quite time that he did so. I count on you, dear Mama, to watch over his health and see that he wants for nothing.' And if Charlotte's little boy was now strong and healthy, he was also ready for the '*in baptismo et confirmatione*' christening ceremony. And there, 'in the country', just to the south of Tours, a familiar scene took place, once again involving the 'dutiful' Jules-Hercule. To quote the great-nephew of Abbé Barnabé, parish priest of Veigné, where Jules-Hercule's duchy of Montbazon was located and where Marie-Victoire had been baptised five years earlier:

> The Prince de Rohan arrived at the church in Veigné and presented the newly born boy as his natural son ... My great-uncle agreed to baptise the child, but absolutely refused to register him under the name of the prince ... he declared that 'there is no power in the world that can make him act against his conscience' and 'will never dirty one of the best and most ancient names of France, by a written proof of a relationship disapproved of by the Church ... As a priest, I must give the water of baptism to this child, but as a man of honour, I will never dirty such a great name with the fruit of debauchery – and perhaps intrigue!' These last words, said with such vehemence, produced an effect on the prince such as would lightning. He withdrew immediately with all his following.

This time round, the near sixty-year-old Jules-Hercule had a problem. He could no longer discreetly baptismally recognise Charlotte's son in the private chapel of the rural Château de Couzières as he had done with Marie-Victoire, because in the meantime, his son Henri had bankrupted, and Couzières, Thorigny, and a string of other Loire estates had had to be sold. Thus he went to the far more public parish church of Veigné in the town of Montbazon itself. Worse, the strong-willed Abbé Barnabé had obviously twigged that Jules-Hercule had lied in 1779 about Marie-Victoire's true parentage, and he wasn't going to stand for that a second time. His accusation of 'intrigue!' clearly hit home.

Thus do Charlotte Stuart's three children emerge from the mists of secrecy, disinformation and legend as Marie-Victoire, Charlotte Maximilienne and Auguste Maximilien, known familiarly as Charles Edward. They were the three little flowers whom their mother left in Paris with Ferdinand and their grandmother, Clementina, as well as the family's three dogs, Zemire, Jacquot and Moustache, when Charlotte went to live with Prince Charles in Florence in October 1784. There she hoped to take up her long-denied birthright and, upon surviving her father and uncle Henry, somehow bring her children out into the light of a day which would never dawn.

The winter of 1784-85 passed into history. Jules-Hercule returned to ward off his creditors at his brother-in-law's Château de Carlsbourg, Charlotte's infant son returned to Paris in the spring of 1785, and Clementina took all three grandchildren to Anthony for the summer. And it was there that Charlotte now addressed her letters, soon asking for details of that August's sensational arrest at Versailles by Louis XVI of Ferdinand's brother Cardinal Louis, who had foolishly become embroiled in the famous scandal of the *Collier de la Reine*. For the second time in three years, the Rohans shocked all Europe. Again, the clan flocked around their kinsman in solidarity.

Long months passed by and in 1788 Ferdinand, 'jealous as a tiger' as Charlotte put it, began to reveal his resentment of Charles' ambitious dynastic plans for his daughter. Not appreciating the financial and legal complications arising from her father's death, nor the delicate situation with her uncle Henry, nor the state of her declining health, he tried to provoke Charlotte with talk of courtesans and pressurise her into an early return to Paris, writing of their children's future and to 'remember her obligations'. Irritated, she told her mother what she thought of this: 'I have replied to him that I know the full extent of them, and that I will gladly, in that matter, walk in his footsteps.' They argued over the renewal of the lease for the house in the rue St Jacques because Ferdinand assumed Charlotte must now be rolling in money, which, of course, she wasn't. Just in case, she warned her mother not to let him know how much she had been receiving in Paris since 1786 from the Stuarts' bankers M. M. Busoni & Co. Eventually, the matter was agreed, and Charlotte told her mother that 'I am renewing the lease for only three years because I hope very much that before then we shall be reunited ... My friend has notified me that he has paid the rent. I replied that I hoped he would pay it as a good father'. Things were not that bad though. In March 1789 Charlotte sent Ferdinand a new portrait of herself and then helped him become Prince-Coadjutor of Liège by obtaining a recommendation from the King of Prussia, whose army had just driven the Austrians out of that principality.

Charlotte also kept in touch with the dutiful Jules-Hercule and his son Henri, who in late February 1788 told his father he would 'send you the letter of Madame the Duchess of Albany'. She also asked her mother to introduce a young English traveller she had met in Rome to the Princess de Rohan, apparently meaning Henri's daughter-in-law.

It was during this last year before the French Revolution exploded that another key relationship was formed. The wealthy and wonderfully well-connected London-based court banker of Scottish origin Thomas Coutts – who a decade later would organise Henry Stuart's pension from George III – was distantly related to the Walkinshaws, and Ferdinand invited him to come and stay. His three daughters were placed in a Parisian convent to improve their French, and Clementina acted as their chaperone. They were Susan – who would marry George North, 3rd Earl of Guilford; Sophia – who would marry Sir Francis Burdett; and Frances – who would marry John Stuart, 1st Marquess of Bute. In 1815, Frances would write of 'the unfortunate Duchess of Albany' and her mother Clementina, 'whom we all remember at Paris'. Charlotte's son would add that the three Coutts girls were 'practically brought up' by his grandmother.

Coutts also put Clementina in touch with a number of his international banking friends who could help her in his absence. And, in 1789, help was desperately needed. For in July, the Bastille was stormed by the Paris mob. The French Revolution had begun.

Poor Charlotte's last weeks of life were agonising. As the realisation that she was dying from cancer sunk in, she slowly understood she would never see Ferdinand or her children again. From the time her doctors ordered her to take the waters in the summer of 1789 until her death in November, she must have been worried out of her mind by the dramatic events unfolding in Paris. She wrote to her mother, 'Our friend must think up a refuge for our friends!' She then urged Clementina to take her children to Switzerland and, in despair, even bring them to Rome. But her strength was fading. Soon she would write hopelessly, 'Don't worry ... I love you ... Kiss my dear friends for me.' One month later, on 17 November, Giulia Lambertini-Bovio wrote from Bologna to Henry in Rome, telling him that his thirty-six-year-old niece was no more.

Events began to move fast. After the storming of the Bastille in 1789, Ferdinand left his Archbishopric of Cambrai and was named Regent of the Principality of Liège in 1790. Viewed as a liberal, he even swore an oath to 'the Nation of Liège to maintain the principles of the Revolution'. But a few months later, the tiny state was overrun, and by 1791, he was back in Cambrai, only to find things there even worse. So he withdrew to the Abbey of Saint Ghislain in the Austrian-controlled part of the diocese, where he refused to swear the revolutionary oath to the civil constitution for the clergy.

Ferdinand forgot neither Clementina nor the children, Marie-Victoire, Charlotte and Auguste – now called Charles – who were still together until late 1791. It was then that Ferdinand's right-hand man from Bordeaux, Cambrai and Liège, Abbé Henri-Gabriel de Montrichard evidently organised a refuge at Fribourg for Clementina and at Ettenheim for the children, where Ferdinand's brother Cardinal Louis had been since fleeing Paris in mid-1790. There, Louis could look after them in this eastern part of his principality of Strasbourg, protected by the might of the Holy Roman Empire. Louis would die peacefully at Ettenheim in 1803, but for the moment, the town was buzzing with life, for it had become a recruitment and organisational centre for the counter-revolutionary army of the Bourbon Prince Louis de Condé, a relation through his wife, Princess Charlotte de Rohan.[30] Another cousin sheltering there was a younger Princess Charlotte de Rohan, soon to be married to Condé's grandson, the Duke d'Enghien, who was later abducted by Napoleon and shot at Vincennes.

Clementina was safe at Fribourg, where Ferdinand's Montrichard remained to help refugees until 1798, but she was far from happy. She had been parted from her only daughter in 1784, then Charles had died in 1788, followed by Charlotte's illness and death in 1789, together with the anguish, terror and chaos of the French Revolution. And now she was separated from her beloved grandchildren. The poor woman, in her seventies, survived on irregular income from Charlotte's will, sent from Rome by Henry, but heavily devalued by punitive exchange rates and the financial turmoil caused by the Revolution. If that was not enough, Henry was not always co-operative. On 8 August 1793, Hyacinte Bruni wrote to Clementina from Florence saying that her pension had not been sent and advised her to put pressure on Henry. Then, in 1798, even these funds dried up when Henry had to flee Frascati

In January 1800, Thomas Coutts interceded on Clementina's behalf with the British Government; however, they refused help. Nevertheless, he proved a loyal friend. As Clementina's servant, Pierre Couppey wrote:

> In all her distresses the Countess of Albestroff[31] at times received some help from Mr Thomas Coutts, Esquire, banker in London who, having learned of her misery, had pity on it. He was indignant at the conduct of the cardinal. Madame knew him very well in Paris with his wife and three daughters.

In her shaky hand, Clementina wrote to Coutts in gratitude, describing him as a man of 'unending kindness'. By mid-1802, Henry was able to restart her pension, at which point, Coutts corresponded on Clementina's behalf with Abbé Waters, Charlotte's old *major domo* and executor, writing of her 'very difficult life', which had been the case 'for some time'.

Clementina died on 27 November 1802 and was buried two days later in the cemetery of the parish and collegiate Church of St Nicholas in Fribourg, close to her last home. Despite everything, she remained in love with Charles until the end, always speaking of him with great respect and affection – in her will, she made special mention of 'a gold box surmounted with a medallion showing a woman crying next to an urn'. Significantly, she also referred to a 'genealogical act made in Edinburgh and dated 4 October 1769 signed by Douglas and Stuart[32], which is in a tin box and locked in the secretaire'. She added that this, along with other papers and letters in her desk, should be sent to Thomas Coutts and given to her family together with a copy of her will.

By then, Ferdinand had made provision for Clementina's grandchildren, Marie-Victoire, young Charlotte, and Charles, so what little she left went to Couppey, who had been with her since 1784 and knew her grandchildren extremely well. Clementina's reference to 'her family' is revealing, because her own siblings had all predeceased her and their wills make no mention of her. Consequently, upon her death, Clementina had no close family – other than her three grandchildren. Couppey wrote,

> When the tribunal of the District of Fribourg lifted the seals from the effects of Madame d'Albestroff, there was found a tin box which contained a genealogy on parchment and some other papers which a clause in her will charged her executor, Mr Weck ... to have sent to Mr Coutts in London.

Weck sent six parcels of Clementina's papers to Coutts in 1804. But when he had earlier tried sending them, they had been returned and Weck kept them because

> I opened one, and seeing that different persons could be compromised if they became public, I thought it proper to retain them ... But the relatives of the Countess of Albestroff, being very desirous of having them, to whom they are destined by the will of the deceased, and I relying greatly on the intelligence and discretion of those relatives, I now decide to send them on in the manner indicated to me. I beg you then, Monsieur, to send them to Mr Coutts.

Amongst the surviving documents of Clementina's grandson Charles, there is a letter dated 5 September 1806 complaining of delays by Thomas Coutts in returning

Charlotte's letters and commenting, 'Various persons may be compromised if the letters become public ... but the relations of the Countess of Albestroff very much want to have them'.

This is not the last we shall hear of Thomas Coutts and his family ... but returning to Ferdinand: having made sure that Marie-Victoire, young Charlotte, and Charles were all safe from the Revolution, he now took off. In September 1794, he wrote from Mulheim near Cologne to his brother Louis at Ettenheim. By December, he was in Venice and, obviously referring to the three children, told him, 'I am so pleased that all our relations and you, my dear brother, are well. Assure them, I beg you, of my tender attachment.' And in another letter: 'A thousand and a thousand more tendernesses for my relations who have the good luck to be with you.' By contrast, other members of his family only received his 'compliments'.

From there, Ferdinand went to Rome and Naples, but by next April was back in Venice and then Rome by June. But life was no picnic. Cut off from all his income, he wrote to Louis in November from Venice that 'I live as cheaply as possible; for this business may last long, even if all is not lost'. He was worried sick about his financial situation and exchanged frantic notes with Louis about their attempt to sell a Rohan estate in San Domingo via their London bankers, Turnbull, Forbes & Co., which failed despite advice and help from Thomas Coutts.

Ferdinand raged at the 'monstrous regicides ... I have heard all the details concerning the death of the young king ... I hope that God will one day punish these monsters ... The Jacobins carry themselves with an air of triumph. Oh my God, without luck we are lost!' Nor had these two younger Rohan brothers discovered the fate of the second oldest when Ferdinand wrote to Louis, 'I am no wiser than you as to where our poor brother is.' In fact, the childless Admiral Armand de Rohan had been guillotined six weeks earlier on 23 July 1794.

Ferdinand's peregrinations now took him to Bologna where Charlotte was buried, thence to Waldeck near Kassel in Germany, and, by May 1799, to a Warsaw filled with French refugees drawn to Poland thanks to connections made through the émigré politicians, aristocrats, bankers, members of the *Secret du Roi* and Freemasons from the Lunéville court of Louis XV's father-in-law, Leszczyński. Foremost among the exiled French was the future Louis XVIII as well as Princess Louise-Adélaïde de Bourbon, daughter of Ferdinand's cousin Charlotte de Rohan and the Prince de Condé whose counter-revolutionary army had been organised out of Louis de Rohan's Ettenheim. In 1802, Louise-Adélaïde would take her Holy Vows as a novitiate at the Warsaw convent of the Holy Sacrament in the presence of the French royal family standing beside the tomb of the Stuarts' aunt, Princess Charlotte Sobieska, Duchess de Bouillon, whose grandfather had founded the church. But Warsaw would prove more than a refuge from the Revolution, because it was there that Ferdinand established another banking connection via those 'greatest bankers of the North', mentioned earlier in the context of Lunéville, the Warsaw-based financiers of Scottish origin, the Fergusson-Teppers, whose clients were the Stuarts' closest Polish cousins, the Princes Radziwiłł. As in the case of the Coutts family, we will hear more of the Fergusson-Teppers.

Not least for financial reasons, Ferdinand made his peace with Napoleon after the Concordat with the Vatican was signed in 1801. He returned to France but failed to get back his Archbishopric of Cambrai. However, Napoleon liked to have some of the great names of the *ancien régime* amongst his courtiers. Consequently, Ferdinand was appointed grand almoner to the Empress Josephine in 1804, then to the Empress Marie-Louise, was granted a pension of 12,000 francs, and, in 1808, given the title of count.

Ferdinand died in Paris on 30 October 1813 at the age of seventy-four, almost a quarter of a century after the love of his life and mother of his children, Charlotte Stuart. He was the last of the senior Guéméné line of the Princes de Rohan still living in France. His nephew Henri, the dutiful Jules-Hercule's bankrupt son, had died in 1809 and thus the centuries-old Breton-French chapter of Rohan history closed. But a new Austro-Hungarian one had begun. Of Jules-Hercule's three grandsons, two became Austrian field marshals and one a general called Jules-Armand Louis, known simply as 'Prince Louis'. Like Coutts and Fergusson-Tepper, he will reappear later. But neither he nor his brothers left a male heir. So, with that strategic breeding so typical of the Rohans, their sister Marie-Louise married her cousin Charles from the younger Rohan branch of Rochefort et Montauban and inherited from her eldest brother the beautiful estate of Sychrov, north of Prague, the family's main seat from 1820 to 1945. Yet neither the French Revolution nor exile severed the Rohans' connections with the Stuarts. In a letter dated 19 November 1803, sent to Prince Louis' brother from Frascati on behalf of Henry Stuart, Bishop Angelo Cesarini wrote,

> Your brother, the prince, has been informed of everything – a person very favourably perceived by His Royal Highness, and for whom he has great respect – and he will be able to come to a full understanding after his return to Vienna.[33]

A different letter was dated 1 January 1799 and addressed to Henry from Munich:

> My Lord,
> I avail myself of this New Year to present to Your Royal Highness the wishes which I form for You. Maman told me to love You and I do it very much. I shall be much happy if I can obtain your protection, for I am a good boy.
> Your respectful nephew, Charles
>
> P.S. Je prie toujours le Bon Dieu pour Your Royal Highness. C.

It was written by Charlotte and Ferdinand's son Charles, now fourteen – the draft is amongst his surviving documents at the Bodleian Library in Oxford. In another of his letters from Munich, this time to his grandmother Clementina and dated 4 January 1799, Charles tells her how she 'made up for my unhappy childhood' and encloses a copy of the letter to Henry, adding that it is 'to my great-uncle whom I don't love as much as you, because I believe him to be very bad' – a reference to Clementina's suspicion that Henry might have had a hand in Charlotte's untimely death. On 6 June 1800, Charles writes again from Munich, mentioning his 'uncle and protector', asking his 'Papa' to write him a letter, urging him to do so by telling him how happy he is 'each time we are reunited after so long a separation ... during this unhappy time'. But his '*Tendre Papa*' did not reply. So Charles wrote once more, asking, 'What am I to think of this silence?', before pleading for 'your letter which will give us so much pleasure and a joy, which, however, will not be perfect until we are all re-united'. Stressing that his Papa's 'kindness will be forever engraved upon our hearts', Charles finished with words more question than statement: 'You cannot doubt our sentiments for you.'

As Ferdinand had reconciled himself with Napoleon after the Concordat of 1801, nothing stood in the way of the three children returning to Paris. Much had changed since the Revolution, even the calendar. Thus, in the French capital on the 21st of Thermidor in the revolutionary year XII (9 August 1804), young Charlotte married the French nobleman Jean Louis Cousin de la Morlière, son of a *Conseiller du Roy* and former mayor of Montdidier where his family had lived since the fifteenth century. The groom's puritanical brother was so unhappy with the choice of bride that the two of them 'were never reconciled'. Because, just as with her brother's baptismal entry from 1784, 'Charlotte Maximilienne Amèlie' was

> said to be the daughter of the late Maximilien Roehenstart and of Clementina Ruthven; but in reality the natural daughter of Cardinal [*sic*] Ferdinand Maximilian Mériadec de Rohan, Archbishop of Cambrai ... and Charlotte Stuart ... The name Roehenstart but a rebus more or less recalling the two names Rohan and Stuart.

Ferdinand was not only present at the wedding but granted Charlotte a dowry of 20,000 francs – his relationship to the bride described by that familiar code-word, 'Friend'. Also 'on the side of the bride' were 'Monsieur Auguste Maximilien Roehenstart, brother' and 'Mademoiselle Victoire Adélaïde Roehenstart, sister'. Despite her baptismal recognition at Couzières in 1779, Marie-Victoire could obviously not appear under the name Rohan or as the Demoiselle de Thorigny given that she was the sister of the bride who was using the name 'Roehenstart', and Ferdinand was present but only termed a 'friend'.

For about a year, Charlotte remained in Paris, where she and Marie-Victoire were friends of the famous Parisian lawyer, Pierre-Nicholas Berryer, who lived in the cloister of the Church of St Merry where their brother's baptism was registered in 1784 and where Berryer married in 1789. Both he and his son, Antoine-Pierre, were fervent legitimists and would defend Marshal Ney in 1815 during his trial before the Court of Peers, as well as the former Bourbon agent Louis Fauche-Borel a year later.

As Charlotte's letters to the Berryers in the Archives de Paris show, marriage brought with it a new attitude visible in her assumption of the title, the 'Countess de la Morlière'. Marie-Victoire's were signed similarly, as the 'Countess de Thorigny'.

Soon Charlotte moved with her husband to the rue l'Apleit at Huy, just west of Liège. But their happiness did not last long. The ill star afflicting the Stuart name Charles or Charlotte shone its dark light throughout the night of 25/26 November 1806 as the young wife struggled in the throes of labour at the end of her first pregnancy. At five in the morning, the exhausted young woman gave birth to a stillborn baby boy. Later that day, at three o'clock in the afternoon, as the records of the Archives de l'Etat at Huy reveal,

> Charlotte Maximilienne Amèlie de Roehenstart, born in Paris, domiciled in this Commune, aged about twenty-six, the wife of Jean Louis Lugle Luglien Cousin de la Morlière, Receveur Principal des Droits Réunis, the daughter of Maximilien de Roehenstart and Clementina de Ruthven ... died on the 26th of the present month.

Her husband of just two years never remarried and died childless in Paris forty years later.

As for Charlotte's brother and sister, a hint of their early lives was described in two curiously accurate letters sent to the *Oban Times* in 1939. The first, from Iain Gordon, stated that two of Charlotte Stuart's children (Marie-Victoire and her brother) 'were secretly adopted by a family in Poland' and that, later, Charlotte's son wrote to Marie-Victoire in Warsaw asking her to send him their grandmother's genealogical papers, which she had received sometime after Clementina's death in Fribourg in 1802, according to whose will they were to be sent to Thomas Coutts and given to her family. The second, signed 'Morvern', read,

> Coleridge's Life of Coutts states that a certain 'R' wishes to repay a loan of two hundred and sixty two guineas lent by the banker to Countess d'Albestroff. The same 'R' states at the time: 'I have every reason to believe that more money has been paid to my grandmother.'

Morvern added that Marie-Victoire and her brother had been 'adopted by a family in Warsaw named Fergusson-Tepper'.

Both letters are slightly muddled, as usual with legend handed down over generations. But there can be no doubt this information originated from Charlotte's brother when he was in Scotland over a century before. Because Gordon and Morvern wrote those letters in Scotland in 1939 when even in Warsaw only specialists in the history of eighteenth-century Polish banking still knew who the long-gone but once fabulously rich and well-connected Fergusson-Teppers had been. Gordon and Morvern would certainly have said so had they realised the Fergusson-Teppers were the 'second bankers of Europe' behind Rothschild, whose clients were the Stuarts' closest Polish cousins, the Princes Radziwiłł, with whose financial affairs they were deeply involved when Ferdinand's exiled peregrinations took him to Warsaw in the 1790s. Such were the connections that the Fergusson-Teppers' palace on Długa Street[34] had been acquired from the Rohans' Warsaw banker, Pierre Riaucourt. And it almost goes without saying that these families were all Freemasons connected to Leszczyński's close-knit Franco-Polish court at Lunéville. Peter Fergusson-Tepper was even treasurer to the Order of Malta whose grand master was François-Emmanuel de Rohan, who for years had been in love with Ferdinand's niece.

Another major client of Fergusson-Tepper was Prince Louis of Württemberg, whose brother Ferdinand was a colleague of Charles de Rohan, Ferdinand de Rohan's great-nephew. There was also a third Württemberg brother, Alexander. And the Württemberg brothers' first cousin was the wife of the Stuarts' cousin, Prince Jerome Radziwiłł. The phrase 'it's a small world' seems completely inadequate.

When set against this background, the early career of Charlotte and Ferdinand's son Charles comes as no surprise. He was apparently tutored by the Protestant family of Korff in or near Munich whence, in 1799, he wrote to his great-uncle Henry and grandmother Clementina. Perhaps significant is the fact that, in the 1780s, one of the Barons Korff was a financial adviser to Fergusson-Tepper's clients, the brothers Charles and Jerome Radziwiłł. Around 1806, Charles joined the household of a general in the Russian service who had been appointed Governor of White Ruthenia. And who should that general be if not Prince Alexander of Württemberg, the brother of Fergusson-Tepper's client. Charles, his baptismal name quaintly russified as 'August Maximovitch Roehenstart', was treated as an exceptionally privileged member of the Württembergs' closest family circle, which included Alexander's elder sister Sophia Dorothea, who had become the Russian tsarina. This was alluded to in a letter to Charles sent from Paris in 1807 by a Monsieur de la Croix who knew Prince Alexander well:

> I received your letter from Coburg ... and am convinced you will not fail to have a career in a land in which justice rewards ability and in which you will also have the protection of Monsieur the Duke and his wife.

If the Fergusson-Teppers didn't adopt Charles, they most certainly were the key to his superb start in life with the Württembergs in St Petersburg and the former Polish town of Vitebsk. But what of his surviving sister, Marie-Victoire, Charlotte and Ferdinand's much honoured Demoiselle de Thorigny, who Morvern claimed had also been adopted by the Fergusson-Teppers?

By the end of the eighteenth century, Poland had been partitioned by Russia, Prussia, and Austria. To the south of Vitebsk lay the former Polish city of Lwów, now the capital of Austro-Hungary's largest province, Galicia. Lwów was a rich cosmopolitan city, strategically placed on one of Europe's great trade routes linking Warsaw, Kraków, and Lwów with Constantinople on the Black Sea. Apart from its Protestant and Orthodox churches as well as synagogues, Lwów boasted no less than three archbishoprics – Roman Catholic, Greek Catholic or Uniate, and Armenian Catholic. In 1782, the latter community comprised only thirty-seven families and 268 people, but was the city's richest. At its head stood the ancient noble family of Nikorowicz, hereditary chevaliers of the Holy Roman Empire[35]. In Lwów's old market square, there still stand three magnificent Renaissance houses: the Royal House, which belonged to the Stuarts' ancestor, King John Sobieski; to its right, the Bernatowicz House; to its left, the famous Black House. The latter two both belonged to the Chevaliers de Nikorowicz.

Until his death in 1789, the head of the family was Gregory de Nikorowicz, a man with a formidable career behind him. In 1744, he had been appointed honorary secretary to the penultimate Polish king, Augustus III, then president of the independent Armenian judicial system, director of the Lwów Trade Court, president of the Galician Bill of Exchange Court and president of the Bill of Exchange Tribunal. A merchant banker whose clients included the king himself, he owned retail houses in Warsaw, Lwów and Constantinople specialising in hugely popular Turkish and Persian fabrics and rugs. He was also Poland's biggest importer of the exquisite ornamental sashes prized by the nobility and of their no-less-cherished oriental sabres. Nikorowicz was not only a member of the Galician Parliament but a diplomat who, on behalf of Augustus III, led a large heavily armed trade and espionage mission in 1744 through the wild and dangerous Ukraine, all the way to the Court of Esfahan, where he delivered 'appropriate gifts for the King of Persia and his ministers', before coming back months later laden with riches for his clients and information for the king.

Two things are crucial: firstly, the Bill of Exchange Court and Tribunal over which Nikorowicz presided were absolutely vital to the eighteenth century banking system. To quote the Polish historian Anthony Magier: 'The bankers Fergusson-Tepper, Blank, Kabryt, Heyzler, Szulc (Fergusson-Tepper's son-in-law), Rafałowicz, Prot Potocki etc, would make out in each other's favour Bills of Exchange'. Even had he wanted to, Nikorowicz could not have possibly avoided Fergusson-Tepper. Furthermore, Fergusson-Tepper was a pioneer in opening up the Black Sea trade and a founding partner of the Black Sea Company together with Stanislas Augustus, the last King of Poland. Yet no one had better contacts in Constantinople than Nikorowicz, one of whose sons, John, was a *dragoman*[36] at the Polish embassy, in regular correspondence with the king, who, in 1790, appointed him a chamberlain, and where the young Nikorowicz knew 'quite a few of the Turkish lords'.

Which leads to the second crucial thing, that, in the 1760s, Nikorowicz had found and brought from Constantinople the designs as well as the future director and his family, essential for the establishment in Słupsk of Poland's greatest manufactory of the much-prized gold and silver woven ornamental sashes of which he was the country's biggest importer. Nikorowicz did this for the family to whom he had been a discreet and intimate financier, banker, adviser and importer of luxurious oriental goods for most of the eighteenth century. It was this family's patronage, openly referred to in Nikorowicz's letter of 1744 to Augustus III, which ensured the success of his request for diplomatic status, travelling expenses, and tax exemptions. And it was to this key client that Nikorowicz's son Mark, the future vicar-general of Lwów, wrote from Rome in 1775 of

> the grace and protection Your Highness has always extended to my whole family ... only I know how much I have benefitted thanks to you, and how many times I have had the honour of treating with you.

Another of Nikorowicz's sons, the Viennese-based Joseph, future privy councillor to Emperor Francis I, was so trusted by his family's foremost client that he even managed his divorce proceedings.

So who was this most important of the Lwów-based Nikorowicz family's clients? He was none other than that key client of the Fergusson-Teppers in Warsaw, Prince

Charles Radziwiłł. Not only that, he was the brother-in-law of the Württembergs' first cousin, he was the closest Polish cousin of the Stuarts, he was the brother of the sisters Charles had proposed as possible brides for Henry in 1746, and he was the son of Prince Michael, who in 1739 had bought the vast Żółkiew estate near Lwów from the Stuarts' Sobieska aunt – in other words, from the mother-in-law of Jules-Hercule de Rohan, Ferdinand's eldest brother.

Might Nikorowicz have even met the Stuart prince? Possibly, because on 24 May 1752, long after Nikorowicz had become the Radziwiłłs' trusted adviser, Pope Benedict XIV reported that Charles was in Poland staying with the Radziwiłłs on their country estate. The Russian Tsarina Elizabeth was so angry that she wrote to Augustus III and even George II, insisting they kick Charles out. Clearly she hadn't been much taken by his 1746 idea of marrying her.

Apart from those already mentioned, the Chevalier de Nikorowicz had one more son, Paul Anthony. Born in 1751, he followed in his father's financially talented footsteps and leased the lucrative Imperial Salt Mines in Pokucie from the Habsburgs during the 1780s. But when he died in 1810, he had mysteriously become far richer than either his father or any of his brothers. Not insignificantly, Paul's brother Joseph had married a prominent member of the royalist French émigré community in Vienna, Baroness Anne Bourguignon de Baumberg, a well-known singer and friend of Joseph Haydn. Furthermore, Paul's last wife wrote that he died in the unspecified service of the future King Louis XVIII, whose exile in Warsaw was financed by unrecorded Polish bankers. But by whom? The chaos surrounding the collapse of the Polish State in 1795 caused a run on the banking system, and all the financiers, even Fergusson-Tepper, went bankrupt. In Warsaw, only the Polish-Armenian Mathew Łyszkiewicz survived. But so too in Lwów did the Chevalier de Nikorowicz's son and successor, Paul Anthony.

Paul's property portfolio was also enlightening. Apart from Lyczaków, an entire district of Lwów stretching some kilometres right up to the boundary of his main estate of Krzywczyce, he owned no fewer than nineteen landed estates. Five had an eye-catching provenance. They had been part of the Żółkiew estate owned first by the Sobieskis, then by the Radziwiłłs, and now they belonged to Paul. Two he inherited from his father in 1789, who acquired them from Charles Radziwiłł as settlement for loans the latter couldn't repay. Three others Paul acquired directly from the Radziwiłłs during the 1790s. By the beginning of that decade, Żółkiew was overwhelmed by a massive burden of debt, a mess which took until 1803 to sort out. And who was the financial adviser to the Stuarts' Radziwiłł cousins? It was, of course, Peter Fergusson-Tepper.

Lucky with the number of his offspring, less so with the longevity of their mothers, Paul's third wife died in his palace at Krzywczyce in April 1801. Nevertheless, the chevalier was persuaded to marry for one last time. He even had another child – a son. But the baby was born weak and it was feared he would die. Therefore, he was immediately anointed '*ex aqua*' with the water of baptism, registered at Lwów's Armenian Catholic cathedral as having happened on 8 September 1804. His father was fifty-three, his mother less than half his age, barely twenty-five. But who was this fourth wife of Fergusson-Tepper's associate and Radziwiłł's trusted financier? With no 'friend' Ferdinand present, nor siblings 'Roehenstart', Charlotte Stuart's daughter was recorded in the baptismal register as 'Marie de Thorigny'. And when the full christening ceremony took place at the Cathedral in Lwów on 20 April 1806 and godparents were appointed, she was described as 'Victoire de Thorigny'.

How astonished Ferdinand's sister-in-law Louise de Rohan would have been in 1747 had she known then that fate would lead the granddaughter of her Stuart cousin and lover all the way back through the blood of the French Revolution to Poland to become the châtelaine of part of the Żółkiew estate that her Sobieska mother had once owned.

And whatever else Gordon and Morvern wrote in the *Oban Times* of 1939 about Marie-Victoire and her brother, they were not wrong to mention the once-great name of Fergusson-Tepper. In fact, they hadn't even begun to appreciate its significance in finding a superb start in life for the Duchess of Albany's two surviving children – one in the household of Prince Alexander of Württemberg, the other in the family of the rich, discreet banker to the Stuarts' closest Polish cousins, the Princes Radziwiłł. Charles was now in the former Polish town of Vitebsk, Marie-Victoire in the former Polish city of Lwów, both far removed from the potentially compromising gossip of Napoleon's Court to which Ferdinand had returned, his duty done, to resume the lucrative career he would not risk a second time.

Charles August Maximovitch Roehenstart's career began auspiciously. In St Petersburg, Prince Alexander of Württemberg recommended him freely, signed letters wishing him 'a thousand compliments', and took him into the bosom of his family. Charles' role embraced everything from managing the household expenses to choosing ribbons for the ladies and acting as a trusted and valued tutor. When plays were performed by the family, Charles always had a role. When Alexander was invited for dinner, Charles received an invitation. Count Golovkin invited Alexander to present Charles to the Russian tsarina, Sophia Dorothea – Alexander's elder sister. To quote his biographer, Professor George Sherburn, Charles was 'socially desirable in any gathering'. Furthermore, Alexander's wife Antoinette treated him with the interest of a loving sister. And whilst Charles was in St Petersburg, he became initiated as a Freemason into the *Les Amis Réunis* lodge.

In late 1810, Charles organised the removal of the Württembergs' court to Vitebsk where they spent 1811, just one year before Napoleon passed through with his *Grande Armée*. And there, midway between Moscow and Vilnius, within the borders of the old Polish-Lithuanian Commonwealth, rich prospects awaited him. For the Württembergs had become friends with an old Lithuanian family that had owned the nearby estate of Krynki since 1540. Like Alexander, its owner was a general in the Russian service. His name was Vladimir Romejko-Hurko.

Hurko had two daughters, Evelina and Marianna. Tsarina Sophia Dorothea had organised that the former be married to another of the Russian generals, whilst Charles' financial agent Kramer told him that the owner of Krynki 'desired nothing so sincerely as to see you his son-in-law'. Alexander's wife Antoinette, Kramer, and Hurko were all convinced the world lay at Charles' feet. However, three events ruined this prospect. The majority of the fortune that Ferdinand de Rohan made over to Charles had been placed with two companies. The greater part was with the Rohans' London bankers, Turnbull, Forbes & Co., recommended to Ferdinand in 1794 by Thomas Coutts for the sale of the Rohans' San Domingo estate. But, in 1803, the company went bankrupt and John Forbes departed for America with the remnants of Charles' inheritance. Another part of his wealth was placed with the Russian banker Sofniev. In 1811, he too went bankrupt and Kramer advised Charles that he could only expect to recover 5 per cent of his capital – 5,000 roubles out of an original 100,000. To make matters worse, Charles and Evelina Hurko fell in love. But this was not what the Tsarina had arranged. Marianna had been earmarked for Charles.

Perhaps he and Evelina had been indiscreet. Or perhaps Charles couldn't bear to marry the sister of the woman he loved. But the main reason was that with most of his fortune gone, he felt inadequate. Charles suddenly left Vitebsk for England via St Petersburg. Alexander couldn't understand it. Antoinette was bitterly upset. 'She is much annoyed with you for leaving,' wrote one friend, whilst Kramer told him, 'You have acted wrongly in leaving here without conferring with Her Royal Highness. She would have fixed everything for you; you know very well what she would have done with pleasure; and if she knew the motive for which you have left her, she would not forgive you'. Charles received four heart-broken letters from Evelina. As he set sail from Kronstadt in the autumn of 1811, with little besides two letters of recommendation from Alexander and Antoinette, he wrote,

> Father of Heaven! What have I done to deserve this misery? Why have I been, at one stroke, deprived of all that rendered existence estimable? Now I am bereft of all; I have neither father, mother, nor country.

By November, Charles was in London. From there, he sent a hostile article to *The Sunday Review* in May 1812. In it, he accused the Hanoverian Prince Regent of authoritarianism and reminded him that thrones can be taken away by man, just as happened to 'that race which by birth had a stronger claim to the British sceptre than any of your own family'. With that salvo, he left for America in pursuit of John Forbes. He was probably also interested in his father and uncle's San Domingo estate, which had been worth 1,500,000 livres before the Revolution. In their correspondence of 1794-95, Louis and Ferdinand doubted whether their bankrupt nephew Henri could inherit. Then, in 1803, Louis' share passed to Charlotte de Rohan. Therefore, of the original owners, only Charles' father was still alive at the time of his departure for America in 1812. As San Domingo had been the subject of contested political control, a feigned sale of the estate had been arranged with Turnbull, Forbes & Co., who passed on the revenue to the Rohans for a while, but stopped when the plantation was expropriated. So Charles went to Haiti, but got nowhere, and the estate was still out of reach and unsold in 1841.[37]

From there, he travelled to New York where he arrived in May 1813 and not only undertook a highly risky venture but evidently had enough capital left or recovered with which to finance it. It was his last throw of the dice, to judge by his later statement that he 'never knew before coming to this country how painful it is to have debts'. Having been encouraged to sail under the neutral and then prestigious Russian colours by Andrei Vassilovich Dashkov, the Russian Minister in Washington, Charles decided to buy a ship and do some provisions running from the American ports, which were being blockaded by the British. In August, he bought the *Betsy* in New Haven, which he renamed the *Alexander*, and loaded her with a cargo of corn, flour and other items that he declared were bound for Havana. Disaster struck. In September, the *Alexander* was intercepted by an American ship, the export of provisions having been declared illegal by President Madison. Such seized cargoes were often ransomed, and after a couple of months, Charles was trying to negotiate the sale of part of his failed enterprise. However, the ship herself seems to have been forfeited. According to Charles' estimate of 25 November 1813, his total loss was $17,900. Even allowing for his tendency to exaggerate, he had quite obviously suffered a third major financial loss. He was only twenty-nine.

Problems now began in earnest. Earlier that year, Charles had borrowed a few hundred dollars from his friend, Count Gabriel Sampigny d'Yssoncourt. At that time, such sums seemed small change. But now he couldn't repay, and Sampigny began to threaten lawsuits. The two men knew a French widow in New York called Madame Chapus whom Charles described as his 'good friend'. He wrote to her in late December 1813 telling her that

> Sampigny is a monster. I now have only $200 ... I can give only the half. If you are willing to lend me $200, remit to him the enclosed note ... I don't wish to tie myself by an uncertain promise; sooner than four months I shall not succeed in repaying, but I will, just in case, give you against all risks a letter of exchange on my sister in case I am not in a position to pay sooner.

This last statement is very revealing. For in all his letters, it was Charles' only explicit mention of his sister Marie-Victoire. He must have overlooked it, given his policy of erasing all trace of the one person who could reveal the secret of his natural birth, to which he never admitted. In his final will of 29 December 1853, he gave firm instructions that those documents not already destroyed 'are to be burnt, particularly the sealed parcels marked: *To be burnt at my death*'. Yet it proves something else – Charles could hardly have used Marie-Victoire as his financier of last resort had the two of them not been close.

Charles returned to Europe on 3 May 1814, seven months after Ferdinand had died in Paris. His return could scarcely have been less triumphant. The bitterness of his feelings was reflected in a startlingly accurate self-analysis:

> It is strange, but it is true, that those who have been thrust by misfortune to a state beneath their birth and expectations consider themselves the object of universal hostility. They see contempt in every eye. They suppose insult in every word. The slightest neglect is sufficient to set the sensitive pride of the unfortunate in a blaze; ... fancied ills which, however unfounded, keep the mind in a constant fever with itself, and warfare with the surrounding world.

Despite his losses, Charles still had modest funds from somewhere or someone upon which to live. For he did not work and travelled freely, though living modestly and spending carefully. His debts were never big and he always settled them sooner or later. Nonetheless, his return to Europe heralded a fundamental change. He set aside his solemn vow never to publicly mention his parentage and began to try and recover something of the Stuart fortune, which he wrongly presumed his mother to have left. He started to write of his '*reclamations*' – the word by which he always referred to his claims. In his search for funds, the Stuart route was the only one left open. For, by 1814, Marie-Victoire and he were the only living Stuart offspring. The same was not true of his father's family. In any case, he had already received an inheritance from the Rohans and could scarcely feel cheated. But to successfully press a Stuart claim, Charles was convinced he had to present himself as legitimate.

Not once did Charles show the slightest pretension to the Stuarts' thrones. He was solely concerned with trying to recover something of his late mother's wealth or obtaining a pension of state from the British or French. But it was a road to nowhere littered with forced lies and half-truths that would generate bitter frustration, disappointment, and emotional isolation. Only the bottle would have been required for his life to degenerate into a rerun of Prince Charles'.

And it was to his grandfather's estranged wife, Louise zu Stolberg-Gedern, in Florence that Charles first turned, whom he all too accurately described as 'a woman of great intelligence but she is malicious and vindictive to a superlative degree'. From his step-grandmother, he obtained nothing except the address of his mother's god-daughter and lady-in-waiting, Countess Mary Norton, to whom he wrote:

> I had taken the engagement never to break the silence which I have so strictly observed, but having been told that the Cardinal Duke of York repeatedly asked for me before his death, this reason alone could induce me to recover a part of my mother's fortune of which I have been so unjustly deprived.

Apart from the embroidery concerning Henry, he added,

> An unfortunate circumstance compelled me to go to America, whence I am returned since a few months ... I flatter myself that the remembrance of my poor mother will act upon your mind in favour of her unfortunate son who has constantly been the sport of fortune. Fate has indeed contrived to pour on my head such a torrent of combined evils that my fortitude has scarcely been proof against them.

But she died before he could meet her.

Another possibility was Fribourg. Charles knew of the tin box containing the genealogical act of 1769 signed by 'Douglas and Stuart', as well as other documents mentioned in his grandmother's will. He was given these details by Pierre Couppey, the faithful valet whom Clementina had made heir to the negligible residue of her estate. So, in late July 1815, Charles went to Fribourg to see his grandmother's executor, Councillor Weck. From him, he heard about the six parcels of his mother's letters which had been sent to the Coutts family along with the tin box. Thirty-one documents still in Weck's possession were handed over to Charles. During his time in Switzerland, he stayed in Berne. There too was his grandmother's former charge, Thomas Coutts' daughter Frances, now the dowager Marchioness of Bute. He visited her on 4 August and commented that the three sisters: 'Ladies Bute, Guilford and Burdett were practically brought up by the Countess of Albestroff' and that Lady Bute spoke very warmly of Clementina. She invited him to dine with her. Afterwards, he noted that amongst the guests was the wife of the famous Polish general Henry Dąbrowski. Charles and Lady Bute subsequently met several times, and she gave him letters of introduction to her father and sister. In the former, she wrote,

> This letter will be delivered to you by the Baron Roehenstart, the son of the unfortunate Duchess of Albany, daughter of our old acquaintance, Madame d'Albestroff, whom we all remember at Paris. He is the last of the Stuarts and his history is a very sad one ... He is a very well-bred, agreeable man and should he put his present intention into execution of going to England I hope you will see him and I need not say I am sure you will do him any kindness in your power.

In recording one of his other visits, it is curious to see that Dąbrowski was not the only Pole to catch Charles' eye. He noted down old signatures from the guestbook of a local auberge. They included: 'General Thadée Kościuszko, Princess Jabłonowska and Princess Lubomirska'.

Next, he was in Strasbourg in November, where he received a very friendly letter from Prince Hohenlohe, whom he had known in Russia, who wrote,

> I suppose you must await with much impatience the letter that will determine the direction you are to take ... for this wandering life cannot be agreeable ... I beg you not to forget that I take a considerable interest in anything that concerns you.

In his uncomfortable situation, Charles had asked if he could return to the Württembergs. But though he would appeal to Princess Antoinette more than once over the next year to accept him back, her offended door remained firmly closed.

The early months of 1816 were spent in Florence, Ascoli, and Venice. Afterwards, Charles spent quite a long time in Vienna, where he befriended Baron di Carnea, who was a chamberlain at the Habsburg Court. Interestingly, Charles seems to have had a source of income there, possibly from Marie-Victoire's brother-in-law, Joseph, the wealthy imperial privy councillor who had married Haydn's friend, Baroness Anne Bourguignan de Baumberg. She died in Vienna a year later, and when Charles' sister died, she was buried alongside her.

Finally, Charles arrived in London from Hamburg in September 1816, where he intended implementing two plans. The first was to use Lady Bute's letters of introduction to the Coutts family to try and get back his grandmother Clementina's tin box, its contents and the correspondence between her and his mother, Charlotte. However, the Coutts family had long been bankers to the Hanoverian Court and could harm their position if they returned documents that might be used to raise the ghost of Stuart claims. Though the ladies of the family claimed they searched high and low, only a few uninteresting documents were ever handed over. Enraged by the Coutts' behaviour, Charles considered prosecution. Worse, they had now scuppered his second plan based on the belief that amongst his grandmother's papers would be documents that proved him to be his mother's son. Foolishly, he had already appealed to the Prince Regent for recognition as the grandson of Prince Charles, which he now found himself embarrassingly unable to document. His 'Memorial' was comparable to his mother's to the French Court in 1772. Unfortunately, Charles was naive enough to believe that the Prince Regent would receive him privately and settle the matter chivalrously as one royal to another. Instead, he met with deliberate bureaucratic obfuscation. To make matters worse, his prose was exaggerated, and he invented a 'great-grandfather' in the Swedish 'Baron Roehenstart, Count of Korff, who came over to England in the year 1715 and served in the English Army; he afterwards ... married Miss Sophia Howard, by whom he had two daughters and a son'. Without doubt, this claim was quickly exposed, yet certain phrases cast light on his past. He wrote that his grandmother

> insisted on my being brought up in the Roman Catholic Church, and my father would never consent to it: she was for this reason much irritated against him ... I was on the point to make ... a marriage which answered all that I could wish. But adverse fortune seems to have brought me to a state of prosperity, merely to throw me into an abyss ... I received the news that a merchant, Mr Forbes, in whose hands was placed the greatest part of my fortune, had become bankrupt, and was gone to the United States of America. This was to me a thunderbolt. If I had not been so foolishly scrupulous, my marriage might still have taken place ... A short time after my arrival in Philadelphia, I had the satisfaction to recover a part of my money ... My earnest wish is not to give publicity to this very unfortunate business, out of respect for my grandfather's name. But by merely proving that the cardinal had no right to enjoy my mother's fortune, to show that I am the first creditor of his succession.[38]

In an accompanying letter, Charles added, not without justification, 'My whole history has been kept so strictly secret both by my father and grand-mother, that it appears indeed difficult to explain this enigma.' In a private letter to a friend dated 8 November 1816, he added,

> Not having any more money I could not muster courage enough to wait upon the Duke of Gloucester, to whom I have been strongly recommended five years ago by his particular friend, the Duke of Württemberg. One feels indeed very stupid 'sans argent' ... Having been several times to Carlton House my papers were sent by Mr Watson to Lord Sidmouth: this distresses me very much, as they were intended for the prince alone, and the idea of any publicity of my sad story makes me shudder ... I awake now after a long

> dream, and I must absolutely forget all my pompous claims; ... pray mind that I allude only to Frascati and the pension of Government ... All what I look for at this moment of wretchedness is not to get a crown, but to get my bread in Scotland. Water and a crust of bread in that country, so endeared to me by so many sad and tender recollections, the theme of my infancy ... Had I not lost my brig and all I possessed, I should have religiously kept my word and never said a thing about my claims.

Charles then travelled to Edinburgh. But his stay there only lasted a couple of months before he returned via London to Paris. He had intended to travel to Russia in the hope of picking up again with the Württembergs and perhaps recovering some of the second fortune he had lost there. But during his six months in Paris, an unbelievable event occurred. The British Government instructed their Paris-based agent, John Schrader, to spy on Charles and try to compromise him. An opportunity presented itself when, at Charles' instigation, a young Prussian officer called Augustus von Assig was arrested for theft. Schrader then persuaded von Assig to accuse Charles of trying to organise an army with which to invade England. This might seem incredible, but in 1817, not that much time had passed since the last period of Jacobite discontent. Furthermore, the Hanoverians had proved themselves capable of relentless persecution of the Stuarts. And Lord Sidmouth, to whom Charles' papers had been passed, had recently been responsible for brutally suppressing civil disturbances in Derby and elsewhere. Moreover, Sidmouth stood at the head of the British secret service at a time when the Hanoverian succession was in serious doubt. For out of the seven surviving sons of George III, none, in 1817, had any legitimate offspring and the future Queen Victoria had not yet been born. Even so, Westminster's initiative was astonishing.

On 3 July 1817, Charles was summoned by the *Ministère de Police Générale* on the basis of an unspecified charge against him. Appalled to discover that he was being accused of high treason, he appealed for help to the British Ambassador in Paris, saying, 'I am being made an instrument to destroy the peace of the country. To lay any weight upon this charge would be proof of insanity.' A fortnight later, in the presence of several French police officers, a friend of Charles, Edward Storr Haswell, managed to get von Assig to confess that he had acted under pressure from the British spy Schrader. His statement was immediately sent to the British Embassy. Further exoneration was sent by the French police to their ambassador in London in which the British agent's charges were described as a 'ridiculous exaggeration and culpable bad faith'. They described Charles' situation as 'cramped by financial losses. His behaviour, reserved and discreet, suits his condition. He sees few people and receives few letters.'

The fact that the British Government contrived this bizarre episode proves they knew precisely who Charles was. They would scarcely have gone to all that trouble if they had believed him to be an imposter. But why did Charles turn for help to the ambassador of the very country that was trying to frame him? Indeed, why would a British ambassador want to help the grandson of his Hanoverian masters' mortal enemy, Prince Charles Edward Stuart? On these points, the ambassador's background is more than a little illuminating.

Previously, he had been secretary of the British Legation in Vienna from 1801-04 and in charge of it from 1803-04. One of his main areas of interest were the activities of the émigré French royalist forces allied to Austria, for whom Vienna was a key political centre. Though he remained *chargé d'affaires* in Austria until 1806 and returned there informally in 1809, in between times, he became Secretary of the British Embassy in Russia from 1804-08, acting as minister *ad interim* from 1806-07. This was exactly when Charles was there with Prince Alexander of Württemberg and was 'socially desirable in any gathering' – and what gatherings they were, given that Alexander's sister was the Russian tsarina. The future ambassador could not have avoided Charles. Then followed the two ambassadorships to France: 1814-24 and 1828-31. But there was more.

Because the British ambassador to Paris was Sir Charles Stuart – created Lord Stuart de Rothesay in 1828. And he just happened to be the nephew of John Stuart, 1st Marquess of Bute. In other words, the ambassador's aunt was none other than Thomas Coutts' daughter, Frances, that same Lady Bute who had been chaperoned in Paris by Clementina Walkinshaw just before the French Revolution and who, when she met Charlotte Stuart's son Charles in Berne in 1815, gave him letters of recommendation to her sister and father in which she was 'sure you would do him any kindness in your power'. The ambassador could scarcely have been more closely related to the Coutts, who had been friends of the Rohans from before the Revolution, who tried to help them in 1794 with the sale of their San Domingo estate, who with 'unending kindness' helped Clementina Walkinshaw, whom they 'all remember in Paris' during the decade up to her death in 1802 in Fribourg, after which all her personal letters and documents were sent to them, and who from 1800 helped Henry Stuart with his pension of state.

Moreover, the ambassador was himself a Stuart, a romantic, and an individualist with a grudge against the Hanoverians because of George III's treatment of his grandfather, John Stuart, 3rd Earl of Bute, who was prime minister from 1762-63. In 1841, Sir Charles would even snub Queen Victoria by taking up his post as ambassador in St Petersburg without bothering to take official leave of her.

Thus, the British Ambassador in Paris, Sir Charles Stuart, a man who prided himself on knowing everything and everyone, was perfectly aware that the person who appealed to him for help in 1817 was the grandson of Prince Charles Edward Stuart. Indeed, the two men knew each other well. And that is why Charles turned to the ambassador for help. And that is why the latter was more than happy to oblige.

In July of that year, Charles had believed that 'no man could be more firmly attached or more sincerely devoted to England'. Not that he viewed himself as English. That same month he asked a friend, 'Why are all the English so partial to Geneva?' Bitterly disillusioned by the humiliating dismissal of his Memorial and the failed attempt to frame him, his attitude towards England turned cynical. He wrote that, by the Act of Union, Scotland had been 'cheated of her independence' and that

> the wrongs of my country shall be a sharp sword that will at once defend me against all opponents; ... that at this moment I could communicate to the heart of every Scot an

> equal ardour to that which burns in mine. Then should our haughty English foes flee as heretofore they died at Bannockburn.

In the end, Charles didn't go to Russia whence he received 'unsatisfactory news'. Instead, he spent the winter in Italy, which for over a decade became something of an annual migration. The next event of Charles' wandering existence was mentioned in a letter written to Louise zu Stolberg-Gedern in early 1820, after having come back from tutoring two young men around the Middle East. He informed her 'of my marriage with an Italian lady, brought up in Paris, of the Barbieri family. This house, though not rich, is distinguished and of rather ancient nobility.' It did not last long. His wife died childless in July 1821 aged thirty-one and was buried on the 20th of that month in the Parish of St Marylebone, Middlesex, as Maria Antoinetta Sophia, Countess of Roehenstart.

Two years later, on 15 September 1823, Charles received a letter from Sampigny d'Yssencourt in which he wrote, 'Mrs Bouchier Smith is the lady to whom you had the kindness to bring a letter for me last year, she has become a widow and thinks to settle in France.' It was a contact which led to Charles' second marriage, to Louisa Constance, the moderately wealthy daughter of Joseph Bouchier Smith, who had died earlier that year. Constance's family had belonged to the Oxfordshire landed gentry and had old university connections until her father sold his manor of Kidlington together with Garsington to the Earl of Peterborough. Thereafter, he lived in London as well as Godstone in Surrey.

Constance and Charles' wedding at St Pancras on 13 December 1826 was a far cry from the Imperial Court at St Petersburg, Prince Alexander of Württemberg, the estate of Krynki and the prospect of the generously endowed hand of Marianna Romejko-Hurko. But a lot had changed since then and none of it for the better.

After their marriage, Constance suffered the consequences of Charles' inability to commit himself to a trusting and intimate relationship. So she was left on her own for long periods while Charles meandered all over Europe and Asia Minor on one pretext or another. She lived for periods in France, where she struggled to learn the language, and also in London. But she hardly features in her husband's surviving papers. Travel seemed the only thing which brought Charles peace. His observations reveal an intelligent well-informed mind and natural kindness. He wrote with tenderness even about the stray dogs of Constantinople. And his relief is palpable when 'vaulting on my noble arabian I bounded over the desert'. His writings betray a special interest in Turkey. One wonders if this wasn't triggered by the connection with Constantinople and the family origins of his sister Marie-Victoire's first husband. For in writing about Turkey, Charles also referred to Armenia.

Another aspect of his personality was the identity complex evident in his membership of various orders of chivalry, fashionable again after the long years of the French Revolution. From 1825, he had been given permission by the King of France 'to wear the decoration of the Grand Cross of the Chapitral Order of Ancient Nobility and of the Four Emperors and that of the Grand Cross of the Order of the Lion of Holstein'. And like his sister Charlotte's use of the title of the Countess de la Morlière, and Marie-Victoire's of the Countess de Thorigny, so too did Charles progress from calling himself the Chevalier de Roehenstart to Baron de Roehenstart and finally Charles Edward Stuart, Count de Roehenstart, or occasionally Count Stuart. In public, he initially stuck to his formal baptismal names of Auguste Maximilien, but after his father's death in 1813, he gravitated towards his mother's family and began to use the names Charles Edward by which he had been known at home during childhood. There was even a transitional phase around 1816 when he used all four names, though the order was significant – Charles Edward came first.

He could also be terribly hurt and become enraged by the smallest offense. In 1833, having been badly treated by customs officials, he complained to the Prince of Monaco. But the latter's response seemed arrogant and he demanded satisfaction, contemptuously telling him that he was the 'heir of a House far superior to that of Monaco'. To ram the point home, he signed himself 'Stuart'.

Then, in 1838, he was turned away from the Paris home of Alexander of Württemberg's son to whom Charles sent a bitter letter saying, 'I used to know several members of your family' and called Württemberg 'the littlest kingdom in Europe, the dignity of which was only granted by the grace of Napoleon'.

The final insult came with the appearance of the notorious though exotic charlatans, John Carter Allen and Charles Manning Allen – two brothers who posed as the 'Sobieski-Stuarts'. Though long-since debunked, they gained tremendous notoriety during the gullible age of romanticism and conned a lot of people into believing they were Bonnie Prince Charlie's grandsons. Disgusted by their fabrications and publicity-mongering, Charles wrote to his wife in August 1836:

> My dear Constance,
> I saw in Galignani's a paragraph copied from a Scotch paper, giving an account of a visit paid to Scotland by two young men, brothers, one Charles Edward, the other John Sobieski, represented in glowing colours etc etc. I felt certainly ruffled, having made up my mind not to stir anymore in this melancholy business.

To Mrs Hamilton of Kames Castle, Edinburgh, he wrote from Wiesbaden,

> As heir to my unfortunate race, isolated, with nothing left but my name, it is not a little vexatious and annoying to see it so conspicuously and falsely assumed by these men.

He told her that he deeply regretted having put forward his Memorial, but was 'reconciled to my fate' having been 'the sport of a sad destiny and placed in a false position in the world'. Characterised by a defenceless innocence, people were often drawn to him. As Lady Bute said, 'He is very well-bred' and 'gentlemanlike'. He could also be disarmingly sincere, such as in his observation to Mrs Hamilton that, despite everything, he had 'known moments of happiness'.

According to her death certificate, Charles' second wife, Constance, had been born in London and was sixty when she died in central Paris on 20 October 1853 at their modern, comfortable, unpretentious, third-floor apartment at no. 9, rue de Notre Dame de Lorette, built in 1845.

Charles survived her by just one year. He was killed in a coaching accident near Dunkeld in Perthshire. A wheel broke off, the coach overturned, and he was thrown. Badly injured in the fall, he held on for a couple of days but died on 28 October 1854. He was seventy. Though twice married, he left no children. Nor is there a portrait of him. It is known only that he was not tall and had blue eyes like his mother and two sisters. Charles also shared the fair, ruddy complexion and oval face of his grandfather. At least he was buried in the soil of Scotland whence 'so many sad and tender recollections, the theme of my infancy'.

On his tombstone under the far wall of the ruined nave of Dunkeld Cathedral, friends added the words '*Sic Transit Gloria Mundi*'. The epitaph scarcely suited his life. Perhaps it referred to the long and blighted chain of events which had preceded his birth, darkened by the black light of the cold and unforgiving Stuart star – the sole inheritance Charlotte passed on to her children. Two had died childless. Only Marie-Victoire was left.

Bonnie Prince Charlie's grandchildren did not fit into any neat social, legal, or psychological category. Born of the complex politics of the exiled Stuarts in the fallout from the 'Forty-Five, their case calls to mind no obvious parallel and can scarcely be dismissed as some typical royal illegitimacy. Of the three, Marie-Victoire is unique. Because only in her case is there proof that she was formally recognised at baptism. And only she kept the bloodline going.

Ferdinand had found a rich husband for her through the Fergusson-Teppers in the person of the recently and thrice-widowed, aging landowner and discreet banker to the Stuarts' Radziwiłł cousins, namely Paul Anthony de Nikorowicz, hereditary chevalier of the Holy Roman Empire. A year or so after her marriage, Marie-Victoire was back in Paris with her father and brother for the marriage of her sister Charlotte to Jean Louis Cousin de la Morlière. At that time, Marie-Victoire was pregnant but not yet ready for her confinement. In what she would later describe as 'running around the world', she immediately left for Lwów. However, the strong-willed twenty-five-year-old misjudged her resilience, and the journey caused her child to be born prematurely at her husband's palace at Krzywczyce, his main estate just outside the city's eastern boundary.

On 8 September 1804, Marie-Victoire gave birth to a little boy who was so weak it was thought he would die. He was immediately baptised at home '*ex aqua*' – as his uncle Charles had been twenty years earlier in Paris. Caught unprepared, no godparents had been chosen, nor even a name. So the infant boy was registered at Lwów's Armenian Catholic cathedral with the name of the saint on whose feast day he was born – Zenon. Curious of the origin of her son's unusual and accidental name, Marie-Victoire discovered it came from the Greek 'Zenodoros', meaning 'gift of Zeus'. Careful of her Catholicism, even proud of what she called in her letters her 'bourgeois morality', she rejected the pagan for its Christian equivalent, 'Theodoros', meaning 'gift of God'. And Theodore remained Marie-Victoire's pet-name for her son long after she and her husband finally agreed the names their son would receive when he became strong enough for his formal christening ceremony. And what a 'gift of God' he must have seemed. Not only because he barely survived and Marie-Victoire would never have another, but especially when her sister Charlotte and stillborn baby both died two years later, whilst her twice-married brother Charles never had children.

Marie-Victoire soon recovered enough strength to categorically refuse her husband's choice of name, Nicodème, and the two were at loggerheads for over a year and a half. Eventually, she came up with the obscure but Armenian-associated name of Antime, with Mark as a second, whilst Nicodème scraped in third. The chevalier did what chevaliers should, and conceded, leaving the way open for the christening ceremony of Prince Charles Edward Stuart's unique great-grandchild at Lwów's Armenian Catholic cathedral on 20 April 1806, where he exchanged the name of Zenon *ex aqua* for Antime *in baptismo* and Mark *in confirmatione*, with godparents from his father's immediate family – a daughter and son-in-law – a level of discretion reminiscent of Marie-Victoire's own baptism at Couzières with no one present but the most intimate of Jules-Hercule de Rohan's household.

Just three years later, Antime's father died, on 21 April 1810, leaving Marie-Victoire a young widow with one child. But her husband hadn't made a will. Consequently, the Court of Nobility in Lwów had to decide how to divide his great wealth, which included the five ex-Sobieski/Radziwiłł estates. Yet there were two strange aspects of the case.

The first was that Marie-Victoire was absent from the list of beneficiaries, which comprised only her husband's six surviving children, even though she was the deceased's wife of seven years. Perhaps Marie-Victoire received some out-of-court settlement from the family. But she cannot have voluntarily resigned. Because, by law, her share would have been added to her son's. Yet his portion was no bigger than any other. That Paul's great fortune was split up between his heirs is no surprise – that was the Polish custom – though it does seem significant that the five-year-old Antime, despite being the youngest, received the primary palace and estate of Krzywczyce, his father's main residence.

The second odd thing was that even though Paul's eldest son Roman was appointed sole guardian of his two other under-age siblings apart from Antime, Marie-Victoire was not given sole guardianship of her own son. She was only nominated Antime's co-guardian along with Paul's sixty-four-year-old brother, John. The result was that, without the co-operation of her brother-in-law, Krzywczyce's income could not be accessed by Marie-Victoire, but was reserved exclusively for Antime. Furthermore, whilst a guardian's allowance, payable out of Krzywczyce's income, was granted to Marie-Victoire, its amount was set by the joint beneficiaries of her husband's will in agreement with the court and would not have been more than a figure reasonable for Lwów's modest cost of living. Thus, Marie-Victoire's brother-in-law John, as co-guardian, held the purse strings. But whereas he was not short of income as the owner of three estates near Lwów, Marie-Victoire was apparently reliant on her joint-guardian's allowance. Worse – for her – John's career suggests an abstemious approach to life. He had pioneered two charitable foundations: for poor peasants on his estates, and another to help small-holders in difficulty pay their agricultural taxes. He had also helped set up the Institute for the Poor in Lwów and the city's Fund for Deserving Soldiers after losing his only son whilst he was still in his teens. He was clearly not a man to indulge extravagance.

Marie-Victoire remained in Lwów until at least July 1813, looking after her infant son and dealing with the legal consequences of her husband's death. During the same period, her brother Charles was with the Württembergs in St Petersburg and Vitebsk. A clue as to what happened next is contained in a letter postmarked 1820, which she wrote to the youngest of Jules-Hercule's exiled grandsons, Prince Louis, the Austrian general. She said she had been 'running around the world throughout the ten years during which I have conserved my liberty'. Like her sister Charlotte, she had probably received a dowry from Ferdinand, though Nikorowicz was incomparably richer than de la Morlière, and possibly some cash settlement from her in-laws in 1810, but 'running around the world' was a very quick way of getting through money, travelling being much more expensive than it is today. During this time, Marie-Victoire must have been in contact with her brother, otherwise Charles could not have written to Madame Chapus in late December 1813, when he was in New York, 'I will, just in case, give you against all risks a letter of exchange on my sister.'

Marie-Victoire's letter is one of the surviving twenty-three to Louis de Rohan, all of which were sent and received in Paris during the years 1815/16 to 1825. They are from the archive of the Rohans' neo-Gothic palace at Sychrov, north of Prague, bought in 1820 by Louis' eldest brother, Charles, who succeeded his father, the bankrupt Henri, and grandfather, the dutiful Jules-Hercule, as Duke de Montbazon. Louis' replies to her were kept in an antique secretaire together with her descendants' most valuable family documents, some from the fourteenth century, at the castle of Grzymałów, about eighty miles east of Lwów, an estate which Antime bought in 1831. Though Sychrov and Grzymałów were both in the Austro-Hungarian Empire, they were at opposite ends of it. And not only was Marie-Victoire the last of her line to be so intimate with the Rohans, but she kept Antime in the dark about her Stuart ancestry, which in letters to Louis, she referred to as her 'Secret'.

During the First World War, the sixteenth-century palace-fortress of Grzymałów was devastated by the Russians, whose staff occupied it for several months when the front was nearby. Hardly anything survived. Even the roofs had to be replaced. Only the castle's massive walls remained to await postwar restoration. Sychrov did not suffer the same fate, which is why some of Marie-Victoire's letters survived. Rohan descendants probably had no idea who she was, even if they realised her letters were in their archive. And though Marie-Victoire's descendants were well aware of Louis' replies in their secretaire, they wrongly assumed the relatively unknown general to be the internationally famous Cardinal Louis of the scandalous *Affaire du Collier de la Reine*. To add confusion, Marie-Victoire sometimes called Louis her 'father', and herself his 'daughter'. However, these were only affectionate compliments, revealed when she more accurately wrote of him as her 'second father' and 'father of the family'. Presumably echoed in Louis' replies at Grzymałów, her descendants wrongly concluded that Louis must have been Marie-Victoire's father. But no one bothered to check. So there the matter rested, a family secret seldom spoken of even privately, though known to each generation down to the present day ... until the crucial Sychrov letters were discovered in 1999.

Marie-Victoire's return, firstly to Versailles, then to Paris, came shortly after Louis XVIII's restoration in 1814. Three years later came the extraordinary attempt by Westminster to accuse her brother Charles of trying to invade Britain, after which Marie-Victoire wrote another letter to Prince Louis:

> In prolonging the discussion by my disinterest in better serving my brother, I forgot to ask you ... to obtain an audience for me with the British ambassador ... during your absence I could ask him to keep me informed as to where my brother is, and who could better know his residence than Lord Stuart?

Yet again, we meet that man who was one of the very few people in on the secret of Bonnie Prince Charlie's grandchildren, Sir Charles Stuart, British Ambassador in Paris and nephew of Thomas Coutts' daughter Frances, Lady Bute, whom Marie-Victoire's grandmother, Clementina Walkinshaw, had chaperoned for a year before the Revolution.

Her letter continues revealingly, for she tells Louis that her 'health which suffers by all these worries needs a rest. I have neglected the business of my lessons with my English ladies ever since your kind attempts on my behalf.' And that neatly explains the legend in C. L. Berry's biography of Clementina Walkinshaw that one of Charlotte Stuart's daughters became a teacher in Paris. As a child, Marie-Victoire had obviously learnt English from her grandmother, which she would have needed in order to teach her 'English ladies' the French in which all her letters to Louis were written. And that is entirely consistent with her brother Charles' letters at the Bodleian Library, whose English, whilst not perfect, is very good. Yet these lessons cannot have been Marie-Victoire's only source of income if she was able to neglect them. They were probably a distraction and supplement to her joint-guardian's allowance, which would not have gone very far in Paris, particularly as she was living on the fashionable rue de Grenelle just down from Louis' town house at no. 99. And during her first years back in France, her gift of God 'Theodore', namely Antime, was not far away. For Marie-Victoire now wrote to Louis,

> Fearing to be too indiscreet in asking you to help both mother and son, I have already told you of the wish I have of trying to enter my son into one of the Paris colleges, his father having died in the service of the king, he has been educated at the Royal College of Versailles but being unable to go often and stimulate his enthusiasm for his lessons, I am unhappy with him since I myself left Versailles, this Winter I shall only seldom be able to make the journey for reasons of economy, and I shall be very worried about Theodore's progress who will find himself isolated and without any encouragement. I would be very happy, if through your protection, my son could be brought back to Paris, the Minister of the Interior is your neighbour and I doubt not but that he would be happy to acquiesce to your request ... that you might not prior to your departure leave a small portion of

> happiness for this poor widow ... On Thursday I am going to Versailles to see my son ... his health is fine, but it is his learning which is not going well.

No doubt to underline her relationship to the Rohans, though using that name itself might have irritated Louis, Marie-Victoire signed her letter with the single appellation 'Roehenstart' – with neither Christian name nor initial. This was the rebus invented by her parents and often used by both her brother and sister. Yet in the context of Marie-Victoire's letter to Louis it was an artifice. Because she plainly states she was a widow, so by law, her late husband's surname of Nikorowicz was the correct form. She could have used the title 'de Thorigny', granted at baptism by Jules-Hercule, but that didn't allude to her Stuart mother nor emphasise her Rohan affiliation, which she was trying to exploit.

As for Antime's attitude to his education at the Royal College of Versailles[39], it bears more than a passing resemblance to Prince Charles' in Rome three generations earlier. Some genes are obviously more difficult to modify than others. In this same letter, there is also a poignant echo of Marie-Victoire's childhood:

> I am sending you a book which was written in 1785 during the author's trip to Florence ... The letter which you see and which I beg you to read, has often served to keep up my courage during my misfortunes, and I have kept this copy very carefully, and the reading of these great historical memoirs was like a talisman uplifting my soul.

One can easily imagine what the letter she begged Louis to read was about. A little later, she asked him for 'the pleasure of hearing about the princesses whom I have always loved' after he had returned from the exiled Rohans' new home in Austro-Hungarian Bohemia, telling him she has 'prayed for your happy return' after his 'long journeys which always worry me ... I will send someone before eight o'clock to get your news and find out when you might receive me – that is, if you would not prefer to come and visit me.'

During the years 1803-13, Marie-Victoire could not have been in close contact with Louis, but now, in 1820, she is boldly advising him on affairs of the heart, telling him not to have anything to do with a certain lady who, if she 'presents herself to you during your voyage, tell her pitilessly that you want nothing to do with her'. She then goes on to show absolute familiarity with Rohan family matters by intervening with Louis on behalf of 'Pierre Cazeaux, who has lost his place through a great injustice as the guard of the Forest of Saumur', asking that he be reinstated as he is 'worthy of your confidence and has a perfect acquaintance of your properties in the Midi'. The name Cazeaux was doubly interesting. Because 'Henriette de Cazau' (*sic*) was a witness at her sister Charlotte's marriage to de la Morlière in 1804. In another letter, Marie-Victoire asks after several of her Rohan relations: 'I would be very interested to know if the pregnancy of Princess Gasparine is not causing any worry ... Please pass on my respects to the Princess Charles and Princess Berthe. I sincerely hope to hear their health is good and likewise that of the princes.'

The identity complex visible in Marie-Victoire and her siblings' use of various titles and names is also clear from her following comments to Louis: 'I am utterly devoted to the interests of your illustrious house'; but on the other hand: 'If it is necessary then I shall promise never to dishonour the illustrious family from which I come.' The point being, that in the first, she calls the Rohans *his* family, in the second, she calls them *her* family. Who did she feel she was allowed to be: a Rohan, a Stuart, a Roehenstart, or as she signed herself to Louis in 1823, a Rohan Stuart?

Away from the private family circle of her Rohan cousins, Marie-Victoire repeatedly displays her connection with the Paris legal world and the famous Berryer family who knew her and her sister by the titles of the Countess de Thorigny and the Countess de la Morlière. She wrote to Louis: 'Please can you tell me all you can about the success of the case relating to the Duchy of Bouillon,' the papers of which she wanted 'to put under the eyes of my friends so that they might, in case of need, defend your legitimate rights ... Send me prior to your departure the précis of the case and the defence of the judgement. All the material will be read with the greatest interest.' And 'if the Prince Louis does not know anyone from the Paris bar, I would ask a lawyer for a model of the declaration'. Then she 'wishes very much to learn if the case of Liège has been won'[40], and later asks that 'the testimony of Princess Charles (of which I am sending you a word for word copy) will be done as legally as possible'.[41]

One of her most revealing letters to Louis was postmarked 1820:

> I must thank you for your visit ... I completely forgot to tell you something very important ... It will perhaps be given to me to choose a chevalier from amongst the veterans of the Army of de Condé, waiting for the end of five years of the strictest mourning. I shall continue to keep myself far from Society so as to avoid hearing those insults which have been numerous, of being 'stand-offish', '*un Clou de Charette*'. I will never forget this last phrase which was given me by a very kind grand seigneur. I did not see why I should explain my complete indifference to Society by telling him my Secret ... How many volumes are full of the romances of the Stuarts and Rohans? This Breton blood which runs in my veins has not been very comforting. It was necessary, therefore, to take an extreme course so as to moderate one's conduct. And that was in running around the world during the ten years during which I have conserved my liberty. Let others judge if there wasn't more merit in resisting so as to triumph ... There is nothing left, therefore, other than the reasonable choice of becoming united with an old veteran of the Glory.

Marie-Victoire explains here that the 'Secret' of her parentage was the reason for her reclusive life 'far from Society', of being 'stand-offish', which provoked some ill-bred aristocrat into calling her '*un Clou de Charette*' – meaning someone who disdained the nobility, '*La Charette*' being a contemporary expression for the Paris mob during the Revolution. Evident too is her resigned tone, that, at the age of forty-one, she could see nothing more for herself than the companionship of a retired cavalry officer from the Prince de Condé's royalist army, which had fought against Napoleon alongside the Austrians. It must have felt almost a family regiment given that Condé's wife was a Rohan and Cardinal Louis had helped him so much at Ettenheim. But equally clearly, Marie-Victoire would have to wait for the end of her veteran's unusually long period of mourning. So she spent 1821 acting as chaperon to Princess Gasparine de Rohan prior to her marriage to Henry XIX, the reigning Prince of Reuss-Greiz. Marie-Victoire complained to Louis that 'I have used a large amount to settle old debtors' and overspent on 'a marriage trousseau worthy of the august person whom I had the honour of accompanying'.

But when her time with Gasparine ended with the latter's marriage in January 1822, there followed a complete change of plan. Instead of marrying her 'reasonable choice' of Condé's noble French veteran, Marie-Victoire asked Louis to 'honour the promise that you made to come and take tea this evening – I have already invited the respected foreigner ... Please choose between Thursday, Friday and Saturday for giving me the honour of taking tea with the noble and honest Englishman'. This newcomer must have had considerable charm to so successfully eclipse Marie-Victoire's chevalier-in-mourning. Suddenly, her excitement is palpable:

> I know there is no need to stimulate your kindness in doing justice to a poor orphan of the pure blood of the **R**s and the **S**s, but I beg you not to lose courage; ... that would be to give up when everything is going well. Christian charity will maintain your benevolence, at least up until the time of the marriage!! These services are worth more than gold!! ... You were able to see that I had not spoken very frankly of the natural birth. He is as aware of the above as much as we are. He knows perfectly well that the brave Admiral Prince de M. [Armand, Prince de Montbazon] never married the Duchess [of Albany]. I believed it necessary, all the same, to warn Monsieur d'A. that he could perhaps hear repeated in Society the terrible lie that hangs over the head of my respected uncle and guardian, the Prince F. [Ferdinand]. As soon as Monsieur d'A. spoke to me of his hopes for a union I told him about everything quite frankly. He knows that the Prince F., nominated guardian after the death of the Prince de M., only supervised my education and that by having appeared to be interested in me, has fallen victim to this lie ... If it is necessary then I shall promise never to dishonour the illustrious family from which I come. Monsieur d'A. has often said to me that he loves the nobility of our feelings (I am not modest enough not to repeat this compliment!) and that he fully knows I lack certain documents to prove other titles of nobility, but that it is all the same to him, and that I was always in his eyes an **R** and an **S**. Right now I doubly regret that the Princess Charles is not in Paris, who could have told me who has the right and that if I don't have any fortune, at least I possess a spotless reputation. I defy my greatest enemy to say that I have had even a single lover. You will laugh at me for such bourgeois morality, and I believe I can see my friendly and gallant prince smile at my lack of sociability. But for myself I don't regret it, for it has made me worthy of a gentleman who is giving me his name ... In the midst of my antisocial attitude and estrangement from Society I have kept up relations with a few people of note (once or twice a year). For example, I know the person ... to whom you are going on Sunday. If by design or by chance he should speak to you of me, I would invoke your deepest paternal feelings not to deny me.

Though her suitor had evidently heard gossip about Marie-Victoire's birth and parentage, their marriage went ahead. Yet how extraordinarily revealing is her letter. Firstly, it proves she realised the parentage given at her baptism was fiction designed to legitimise her as a Rohan. Because she reveals here that she knew perfectly well that Charlotte Stuart was her mother – which it would have been pretty hard not to – whilst the dutiful Jules-Hercule isn't even considered for paternity. Instead, she tells us that Ferdinand, presumably, had convinced her that Society's gossip was wrong about him being her father and that his elder brother Armand was; which was clever, because Armand had no children and had been conveniently guillotined in 1794, therefore was not around to deny it. In fact, if Armand had actually been her father rather than Ferdinand, then Marie-Victoire and her siblings' conception would have been truly miraculous, because Armand was away at the time, fighting in the American Wars of Independence.[42]

So who was the mysterious Englishman, Monsieur d'A., who had arrived out of nowhere and was so keen to win the hand of a middle-aged widow of natural birth? Before answering that question, it is necessary to remember who Louis de Rohan's grandmother was. She was Princess Louise de La Tour d'Auvergne, the daughter of the Duke de Bouillon, who had married the Duke de Montbazon, Jules-Hercule de Rohan. And it was the same Jules-Hercule who had formally recognised Marie-Victoire at baptism, giving her full rights of inheritance after him. And in inheritance terms, Louise had died first, Jules-Hercule second. Not only that, Marie-Victoire was the granddaughter of Prince Charles Edward Stuart. And his Sobieska mother and Louise's were sisters.

All of this mattered because Louise's nephew was the last Duke de Bouillon who died without heir in 1802. Shortly after the Bourbon restoration in 1814, the rights of succession to the Duchy of Bouillon were awarded to Jules-Hercule's eldest grandson, Charles. However, that decision was fiercely contested by the Bourbons. And not only by them.

It so happened there was a family from the channel island of Jersey called d'Auvergne from which descended two half-brothers. Both joined the Royal Navy. Philip, the elder, became an admiral and Corbet James a captain. They claimed descent from the twelfth century Robert IV, Count of Auvergne, and kinship with the La Tour d'Auvergne Dukes de Bouillon. Louise's brother, the penultimate duke, adopted Admiral Philip in 1786 and in 1791 issued a declaration that he should succeed to the Duchy of Bouillon in the event of his son dying without heir – which is what happened. Infuriated by the French Court's decision to award the duchy to Charles de Rohan, it was Philip d'Auverge, styling himself 'Prince of Bouillon', who so fiercely contested the matter in court. However, the legal costs ruined him and he committed suicide, though not before adopting his younger brother Captain Corbet James as the heir to his title and rights to Bouillon. And it was Corbet James d'Auvergne who was the mysterious Englishman who appeared out of nowhere to outflank the veteran of the Army of Condé with regard to Marie-Victoire's hand in marriage. And that explains another legend in C. L. Berry's biography of Clementina Walkinshaw, that one of Charlotte Stuart's daughters became the Duchess de Bouillon.

It is hard to believe the retired aging bachelor d'Auvergne's sudden romantic interest in Marie-Victoire was not connected with his claim to the Duchy of Bouillon, which had been awarded to her Rohan cousin. But Marie-Victoire passionately believed in her

English naval captain. And where should their marriage take place? Of course, at the Paris residence of the British ambassador, the ubiquitous Sir Charles Stuart, the man who, as we have seen earlier, knew all about Charlotte Stuart's secret children. British consular records give the wedding date as 29 November 1823 and describe Marie-Victoire as 'Dame Victorie Adélaide Roehen Stuart ... widow' and d'Auvergne as a 'bachelor'.

Those consular records reveal more: Marie-Victoire gave her parish as that of St Benoît. But St Benoît had been closed as a church since 1813 and as a parish since 1808. So why did she give St Benoît as her parish? Well, St Benoît's address had been 96, rue St Jacques. And the rue St Jacques was precisely where Ferdinand de Rohan had rented a house from the Abbé de la Villette for Charlotte Stuart, her mother and her three children before the Revolution. In naming St Benoît, Marie-Victoire was absolutely accurately giving the parish church of her childhood home.

Unfortunately, no sooner had Marie-Victoire and her claimant to the Duchy of Bouillon married than problems began. To Louis, she now wrote,

> My good and honest friend, for whom I would like to avoid even the smallest sorrow, had this morning a very unpleasant visit from a creditor set upon tormenting Monsieur d'Auvergne because of his former business people. Since Monsieur d'Auvergne withdrew his proxy they are so enraged that they try to do him all harm possible. You know, my Prince, that to satisfy my heart, and to give proof of the devotion and respect towards the august family which I cherish, that I have always preached peace (before and after my marriage). To be perfectly sure that no court case would be begun I have had nothing to do with business people. I am thus the cause of new sorrows for Monsieur d'Auvergne [who] gave me his word that he arrived here, happy, in good health with four thousand louis d'or in order to await the justice that is owing him!

Time and again, d'Auvergne allowed his wife to act as the interface between his claims and her relations. On his behalf, Marie-Victoire asked Louis to

> prepare a legal declaration which affirms that the Duke de Montbazon acknowledges that he saw in favour of the late Admiral d'Auvergne the sum of 3,000 pounds sterling which was made out to him as a receipt, that this same receipt has been presented to you intact and without any other signature other than that of the Prince de Rohan, that by this reason the recognition of three thousand pounds was perhaps lost. The Admiral, not having passed the succession to anyone else, his sole heir, the Captain d'Auvergne, has a right to be reimbursed which the Duke de Montbazon cannot refuse ... It is said to Monsieur d'Auvergne, 'These are the Princes de Rohan who have the estate of your brother, the Admiral, far from persecuting you, they should agree to your just complaint.'

Marie-Victoire then went on to describe her husband as 'the best of men, and so I feel for him the most sincere affection. I beseech you not to persecute my good and fair benefactor who deserves all the tenderness of his "Victory"'[43] and who 'said that he never knew misfortune (to have debts) other than since he has been involved in a just claim with Prince Louis ... You know how disinterested I am and without ambition. Likewise is Monsieur d'Auvergne. But I cannot resist sorrow when I see my fair friend deceived in all his just hopes'. Shortly after, a new and ominous element began to appear in Marie-Victoire's letters: 'Monsieur d'Auvergne returned yesterday quite ill.'

Louis did not cave in to d'Auvergne's extortion, whilst Marie-Victoire continued naively: 'It is awful that a man of honour is tormented for 200 louis when he possesses more than 2,000 francs in England.' Her tone was becoming caustic:

> Do not fear that I dare to be so indiscreet as to insist on the object of Thursday's request. Your point blank refusal is engraved upon my memory ... The point of this note is to discover if I could on Tuesday morning send for the declaration that you have promised me? I doubt not that your intention is anything other than to entirely conform to the justice due to the admiral.
>
> Victoire d'Auvergne

The letter was postmarked 7 July 1824. Then again that ominous note crept in: 'As Monsieur d'Auvergne is ill it is better not to speak of business in front of him.' And as d'Auvergne's condition deteriorated, so did Marie-Victoire's tone towards Louis soften:

> I was hoping to wish you a happy voyage yesterday, but my duty as an affectionate wife kept me at the side of Monsieur d'Auvergne ... Since your last visit the oppression on the chest of my dear patient became extreme and it is for this reason that the doctor judged that he should be bled ... Please be sure of my desire that all your legal cases turn out in the happiest way for you. I hope with all my heart that all the claims of Monsieur d'Auvergne end amiably with all the parties concerned ... I sincerely wish not to find myself at war with the family that I respect. Monsieur d'Auvergne ... is suffering too much to go out.

Marie-Victoire's second marriage lasted only fourteen months. According to Marshall's *Royal Navy Biography* of 1828, her husband died in Le Havre on 2 February 1825 and was buried in Paris on the 5th of that month as 'Prince Corbet James d'Auvergne, abode Paris, aged 60'. Marie-Victoire's subsequent letters to Louis are on black edged paper:

> It was not a pension of pure favour that was asked for. You know in part how much the venerable friend for whom I mourn had the right to a benefaction from the Bourbons. I admit to you, at the risk of displeasing you, that I believe in your intention of honouring the memory of the English prince who was so unhappy in France.

Apart from the ducal coronet on their seal, this was the only time she openly used the title that her late husband claimed. She signed herself: 'Your very distressed daughter, Victory d'Auvergne'.[44]

Marie-Victoire's two last surviving letters convey her deflation after the stormy emotions raised by the litigious d'Auvergne. Louis' kindness and loyalty to her shines through as she asks him to

> re-read the list of services and to tell me what would be more useful to mention ... It is very tiresome at present to be forced to work on matters of business, but the idea of doing all I can to honour the memory of the best of men excites my courage ... My attachment for you has increased still more in view of the suffering which you have borne with great courage for a year; I confess that it is more than affection I have for you. I feel a sort of veneration for the head of this noble family which so generously gave shelter to our brothers in exile ... I never seemed able to sufficiently show my devotion for my unhappy friend – he used to say that he didn't want to regain his health other than to bring happiness to his 'Victory' ... Forgive me, Prince, I am forgetting myself in speaking of him who merits my regret!

Her tired words recognise d'Auvergne's cynicism – especially that final phrase. She then packed up the apartment in which she had spent her brief second married life and asked Louis for

> permission that the family pictures which were always in the *Gros Caillou* might momentarily be placed in your mansion. I have been told that the new tenants of the apartment I was occupying on the rue de Grenelle cannot keep them as they themselves have a lot of engravings to hang ... Not knowing what apartment I will be occupying when I leave *Tivoli* I would ask you not to refuse my request. There are only two big paintings, the others are busts of an ordinary dimension. The little genre pictures were never taken to the *Gros Caillou*, there are only those of the family ... The bearer of this letter is the daughter of de Carré (an old servant of the Princes de Rohan) ... This is a real service that you do for me in my sad situation; ... you know, my Prince, that I don't have my own place.[45]

The *Gros Caillou* was the area of Paris just south of the Quai d'Orsay where Marie-Victoire lived prior to her marriage to d'Auvergne, after which she lived with him on the rue St Lazare in the district of *Tivoli* just to the north, on the other side of the Seine.

As mentioned above, because Marie-Victoire could reveal the 'Secret' of their birth, her brother Charles tried to hide every trail which might have led to his sister and left orders that all of his documents not already destroyed 'are to be burnt, particularly the sealed parcels marked: "To be burnt at my death"'. But Charles' surviving papers at the Bodleian Library contain several passages which seem innocuous, even meaningless, until put alongside Marie-Victoire's letters to Louis de Rohan, whereupon they betray the close contact over the years which existed between Bonnie Prince Charlie's two surviving grandchildren.

For example, in one of Charles' notes, he jotted down the origins of the d'Auvergne family, mentioning Captain Corbet James' brother, father and uncle by name. On it, Charles wrote a curious comment in Latin: 'The French shouldn't be trusted because they are superficial, deceitful people and immortal God himself considers them impious' – presumably expressing his support for his sister's English husband in the dispute with the French Rohans over the rights to the Duchy of Bouillon. He then added a short history of Tivoli, whence the name of the new and fashionable district in which his sister lived with d'Auvergne, centred on the gardens founded in 1798 between the rue St Lazare and the rue de Clichy. There is also a draft letter to Charles' lawyer after he accused a fraudulent French nobleman of cheating at cards, whom Charles demanded should 'leave Monsieur d'Auvergne alone'. Charles also wrote out the story of the 'Abbé and the Epée', a successful comedy playing in Paris at the time about a beggar boy brought in from the streets of Paris by a good Abbé:

> The child had been ill-treated through some nefarious design ... the youth was the noble heir of a large fortune ... and had been purposefully lost by his interested guardian ... At last ... his uncle, the usurper, was dispossessed and the youth returned to his estates and honours.

The parallels between the beggar boy and Marie-Victoire's son are striking. Both were the same age, both were of noble birth, both were heirs to large fortunes, both were living in Paris. Moreover, the tight purse strings of Marie-Victoire's brother-in-law, John de Nikorowicz, her son's uncle and guardian, were echoed by the beggar boy's uncle and guardian, who tried to keep his estate from him. To cap it all, the beggar boy was called Theodore, Marie-Victoire's pet-name for Antime.

Another glimpse of Marie-Victoire's brother appears in her letter of 1824 asking Louis to provide a reference for someone very close to her: 'In a matter of this type, the testimony of a statesman is indispensible in the eyes of the law. Please reply that you will agree to give your signature ... for a young man who finds himself in the same situation of birth as I do.' The only person known to be both close to her, of natural birth, and in need of testimonies to support claims was her brother Charles.

After d'Auvergne's burial in Paris on 5 February 1825, Marie-Victoire travelled to London, presumably in search of the '2,000 francs in England' which her late husband had claimed to possess there. However, though sole heir under the terms of his will of 8 February 1824, Marie-Victoire inherited less than £100 when probate was granted on 14 May 1825. Her address was registered as 28, Soho Square. Her brother's London home was just around the corner at 63, Frith Street.

With her mercifully brief second marriage over, Marie-Victoire found herself a homeless widow of forty-six without her co-guardian's allowance because her son Antime had just come into his inheritance. Moreover, since 1823, he had been far away from his mother, having become an officer of the Austrian 4th Cuirassiers. Marie-Victoire gave a hint of her plans in one of her final letters to Louis in which she spoke of the Rohans as 'this noble family which so generously gave shelter to our brothers in exile' – namely, the royalists who had fought against Napoleon under Condé alongside the Austrians and remained in that country. Thus Marie-Victoire decided to return to her 'reasonable choice' of the 'chevalier from amongst the veterans of the Army of de Condé' whom she had considered marrying five years earlier and whose 'five years of the strictest mourning' were now over. So she returned to Lwów, the capital of Austro-Hungary's largest province, Galicia, and her son's neighbouring estate of Krzywczyce.

In late 1826, Count Louis Jabłonowski was only just sixteen. Decades later, he wrote his memoirs. In them he recalled his schooldays in Lwów:

> From under the care of three tutors I was released like a bird from the cage and placed in the house of the de Pauws. The lady of the house, a very respectable woman formerly known for her beauty, was from the noble family of de Thorigny, but unsatisfied with this she used to relate that she was the daughter of the famous Cardinal Louis, Prince de Rohan, the unfortunate lover of Marie-Antoinette. Monsieur de Pauw, a decent old soul, having left his home country with the Austrian Army, took part in several campaigns in the hussars, and was administering Krzywczyce, the estate of Antime Nikorowicz, the son of his wife from her first marriage, whilst living in their beautiful town house. They lived pretty splendidly, surrounded by Frenchmen serving in the Army. The commanding officer Fresnel, General Piret, Picard, the Marquis Boquen, the Abbé Parmentier, A. Morris, Charles de Brzezie Lanckoroński, Stadion – the Knight of Malta and General Steininger with his delightful daughter (of sad history) were everyday guests [as well as] Miss Geisruk, daughter of the former Governor.

As usual with such memoirs, the detail is imprecise. Jabłonowski was wrong to assume de Thorigny to be a French noble family, but can be forgiven for not knowing that the records of Marie-Victoire's baptism reveal it to have been given her by Jules-Hercule de Rohan. He also exaggerated in describing Cardinal Louis as Marie-Antoinette's lover and later called him Rohan-Chabot instead of Rohan, a mistake Marie-Victoire would never have made as there was a lot of jealousy between these two separate though inter-married families. Furthermore, Jabłonowski was incorrect to assume Marie-Victoire meant Cardinal Louis if as a sixteen year old he had heard her talking about a 'Prince Louis' as her 'father', not realising this was a metaphor for her 'second father' ... and that she didn't mean the famous cardinal but his great-nephew and namesake, the little-known general. But again, he can be excused, because both Rohans were always referred to as 'Prince Louis'. Also, the name Geisruk is misspelt, the former Governor of Galicia being Count Johann von Gaisruck. Nevertheless, the overall picture Jabłonowski paints is broadly correct and highly illuminating.

The 'beautiful town house' in which Marie-Victoire lived with her third husband may have been the property Antime inherited on Lwów's ulica Ormiańska[46], but was more probably their home on ulica Szeroka[47], later known as Copernicus Street, praised on 23 February 1839 in *Gazeta Lwowska* as one of the city's 'most beautiful houses'.

As for her third husband, Jabłonowski's description precisely fits Marie-Victoire's letter to Louis de Rohan. He was the nobleman, Jean de Pauw, an exiled veteran French royalist cavalry officer whose name appears several times in the records at Vincennes for the counter-revolutionary army, which fought with the Austrians under the Prince de Condé, and whom Marie-Victoire had known intimately in Lwów prior to leaving for Paris after 1814.

So here she is, Bonnie Prince Charlie's middle-aged granddaughter Marie-Victoire with her little court in Lwów, 1,000 miles from the wagging aristocratic tongues of Paris, far from which she told Louis she would 'continue to keep myself', calling this her 'anti-social attitude and estrangement from Society' to which she felt 'complete indifference'. Perhaps here she felt less constrained about the 'Secret' of her parentage, which she and her brother had been sworn to keep as adolescents, which Charles described in 1815 to their mother's old lady-in-waiting as his 'engagement never to break the silence which I have so strictly observed'. And if Marie-Victoire revealed everything in her correspondence with Louis de Rohan, those were private letters to her most trusted cousin, who, in any case, belonged to that tiny group of insiders who knew the truth. But here in Lwów, in her own home, so far from Paris, Jabłonowski's diaries reveal that Marie-Victoire at least allowed herself to mention her Rohan ancestry.

And like in Paris, where the '*Clou de Charette*' shunned the French aristocracy in favour of the milieu of the meritocratic lawyer family of Berryer, so too did that characterise Marie-Victoire's Lwów-based circle whose members did not belong to the Polish aristocracy but to the government and military hierarchy of the Austrian partitioning power. Those mentioned by Jabłonowski include the former French royalist officers, Count Ferdinand Pierre Hennequin de Fresnel et Curel who became an Austrian general in 1817, and Baron Louis Piret de Bihain who became one in 1813. There was also Field Marshal Jean Piccard von Grünthal and General Karl Steininger, whilst the snuff-taking Abbé Parmentier clearly belonged to the more wordly of the priesthood. Another was the Marquis Boquen, whilst the Habsburg Court was represented by Count Charles Lanckoroński, and politics, by the future Governor of Galicia and Minister of the Interior, Count Franz von Stadion as well as the family of the former governor, Count von Gaisruck.

Perhaps it was only a coincidence, but one can't help noticing that, in Paris, the closest lawyer colleagues of the Berryers included the names Piccard, Hennequin, and Bourguignan. The first two were the same names as members of Marie-Victoire's court in Lwów, whilst her brother-in-law Joseph de Nikorowicz – Radziwiłł's Vienna-based adviser – had married the daughter of the French émigré Jean François de Bourguignan, Baron de Baumberg, a professor of law.[48]

Not that Marie-Victoire spent all her time in Lwów. Apart from visits to Vienna, she returned to Paris, where, in the early 1830s, she saw the Berryers, writing to them about 'whist evenings', that 'some of your friends are coming to see me this evening', and 'I was very sorry, Monsieur, to find your visiting card ... I had written two days earlier to one of our friends prior to which we had decided to meet on Wednesday ... to put back this intimate little dinner until Thursday.'

From the same period comes more evidence of Marie-Victoire's contacts with her brother. On 31 December 1833, Charles wrote to his wife Constance in Paris from Castellamare in Sicily that 'Count Alexander Potocki has lost 25,000,000 in landed property'. What possible relevance could this have had? Who on earth was Potocki? And how, in his Sicilian holiday resort, might Charles have heard about a far-off sequestration at the other end of Europe?

At the end of 1833, Potocki's forfeiture was nothing more than local news in the area east of Lwów. It was an act of Russian vengeance for his sons' participation in the 1831 uprising, even though he himself had spent the time living quietly on his estates in East Galicia. Eventually, Potocki managed to reverse the decision, but only after Charles had sent his letter to Constance. The sequestered estate was Satanów, running from that town several kilometres north to Kokoszyńce, along the east bank of the River Zbrucz, which divided Galicia from the Russian-held Polish-Lithuanian provinces on which the uprising had been fought. Facing Satanów on the other side of the river was the castle of Grzymałów, whose estates of Wolica and Kałaharówka were literally a stone's throw across the narrow water dividing them from Potocki's land. Less than three years earlier, on 15 March 1831, the Grzymałów estate had been sold. And who should its new owner be? None other than Marie-Victoire's son Antime, who made its castle his principal residence and the place where Marie-Victoire's letters from Louis de Rohan were kept. Marie-Victoire's brother Charles may have been half a continent away in late December 1833, but for her, the sequestration of Satanów was major local news, and of great interest to her brother, because Potocki's father had been closely associated with the Fergusson-Teppers of their youth, even a partner in their Black Sea Company.

Still more evidence betrays close contact between Marie-Victoire and Charles. On 13 February 1835, Charles received an account from M. S. Bing of Frankfurt for the sale of the 'grand and magnificent palace, number 70 in Vienna'. That building belonged to Count Hubert d'Harnoncourt, whose family had owned it since 1796. He didn't sell no. 70 in 1835, but he did buy no. 71, creating a new palace out of both. The person who in 1835 sold Harnoncourt, the new half of no. 70, was Theresa von Giuliani. And what a familiar background she had ...

In 1736, Francesco Giuliani had been appointed official translator to the Polish embassy in Constantinople and, like the Chevalier de Nikorowicz, provided close diplomatic and trade links between Turkey and Poland. In 1758, the Polish king ennobled Giuliani for these services, and from 1766 to 1770, his son Peter and Nikorowicz's son John were two of the original four pupils at the Royal Oriental School in Constantinople set up by the king to strengthen Poland's diplomacy, crucial to the opening up of the Black Sea Trade. Both Giuliani and Nikorowicz became diplomats there, and the former's brother Henry also studied at the school. Throughout the whole period, the Giulianis corresponded with the Nikorowicz family's key client, Radziwiłł. Put simply, the Giuliani and Nikorowicz families had such close ties that their names even appear together on the same documents. So, whilst it is not clear why Charles received an account for the sale of the Giuliani house in Vienna, it was obviously linked to his sister's Nikorowicz in-laws.[49]

The last link between Marie-Victoire and Charles appears in his letter dated 1 August 1836 sent from Naples to 'Madame Stuart, 4 rue de Harlay, au Marais, Paris'. Charles' obsession with hiding all trace of his sister even applied to his second wife Constance. It therefore must have struck her as strange that he devoted so much space to an apparently irrelevant piece of news from Austria. He began, 'I am sorry to hear the Cholera is raging in Vienna', about which he went on for no less than twelve grief-stricken lines. Abroad again on another solitary peregrination, it probably took a few weeks for the news to reach Charles that, at five o'clock in the morning of 27 April, Marie-Victoire had died at house no. 1132 on Unteren Bräunerstrassen in Vienna – the cause of death, of course, cholera.

Two days later, she was buried in grave no. 55 at the Maria Hietzing Cemetery just outside the Austrian capital. Alongside was grave no. 56, that of Baroness Anne de Bourguignon, who died in 1817, the wife of Radziwiłł's Nikorowicz protégé. Next was no. 57, since 1816, the grave of Anna Leiner von Negelfürst, the mother-in-law of Marie-Victoire's son, Antime. None of them exist any more. They were reused long ago.

Marie-Victoire was not old when she died. Her death certificate from St Michael's Parish in Vienna states simply:

> The high and noble-born Madame Marie de Pauw, née de Thorigny, originating from Tours ... fifty-six years old.

That was exactly the number of years that had passed since 19 June 1779, when the head of the sovereign Princes de Rohan, the dutiful Duke de Montbazon, had brought the infant daughter of his youngest brother Ferdinand and his wife's cousin Charlotte Stuart to the chapel of the Château de Couzières and legitimised her with the title of the Demoiselle de Thorigny. One wonders what the good Jules-Hercule was thinking as he watched the water of baptism trickle from his little niece's innocent brow.

The last of the Duchess of Albany's three 'little flowers' was no more. There was only one member of the next generation, Marie-Victoire's son Antime, whom she used to call Theodore – 'God's gift'.

Antime was five when his father died. His mother was his only family. She not only kept him away from the Rohans but also from the 'Secret' of her parentage, the poisoned chalice of her Stuart ancestry. So Antime never knew he was the unique great-grandchild of Bonnie Prince Charlie. Yet whatever else he may have inherited from that side of the family, his bright-blue eyes certainly came straight from Charlotte Stuart.

Immediately after completing his education at the Royal College in Versailles, Antime became a cavalry officer in the Austrian Army. Now, this might strike one as perfectly normal. In fact, it was very surprising for two reasons. Firstly, whilst his father's Polish family were hereditary chevaliers of the Holy Roman Empire, they had previously been merchant-bankers, diplomats and landowners. They had no military tradition. Secondly, the French-educated Antime didn't join just any regiment, but somehow became an officer of the Austrian 4th Cuirassiers whose commander-in-chief from 1801-35 was the Habsburg Crown Prince and future Emperor Ferdinand I himself. More elite there wasn't.

In her letters to Louis de Rohan, Marie-Victoire describes just how private her life was in the Paris to which she returned after the Bourbon restoration: 'I shall continue to keep myself far from Society', to which her attitude was one of 'complete indifference'. Hardly the words of an aggressive social networker on the hunt for a prestigious career-start for her son. So who found him a position in the future Habsburg emperor's own regiment?

From 1823 to 1828, Antime rose from the rank of cadet to lieutenant and was based at St Georgen near Pressburg[50]. His regimental commander was Colonel Count Carl Clam-Martinitz whose wife was an exceptionally unusual choice for an Austrian aristocrat. In 1821, Karl had married Lady Selina Meade, from an Irish Catholic family, whose ancestor had been James VII & II's attorney general in Ireland. And Selina's brother was Richard, 3rd Earl of Clanwilliam, with whom she had been brought up in Vienna because their mother was Austrian, Countess Karla Thun, and their father had died when both were very young.[51]

Clanwilliam's career started superbly as a member of Lord Castlereagh's suite at the Congress of Vienna in 1814, and soon he became his private secretary. In 1815, Castlereagh went on to negotiate the Treaty of Paris, where for months he lived at the British ambassador's house there. And who might that ambassador have been? Enter once again the now-familiar figure of Sir Charles Stuart, ex-*chargé d'affaires* in Vienna from Selina and her brother's time there, ex-secretary of the British Embassy in St Petersburg from Marie-Victoire's brother's time there, and the British Ambassador in Paris to whom Marie-Victoire's brother appealed for help in 1817, whom Marie-Victoire had asked 'to keep me informed as to where my brother is, and who could know better his place of residence?' Sir Charles' Paris house, which hosted Castlereagh, was also the very place where Marie-Victoire later married her second husband. And, of course, Sir Charles not only knew both Marie-Victoire and her brother, but all about their 'Secret' thanks to the Coutts family of his aunt Frances, Lady Bute. As for Sir Charles and Clanwilliam, their surviving correspondence more than adequately documents their connection[52]. An individualist, romantic, no lover of the Hanoverians, a man famous for knowing everyone and everything, Sir Charles Stuart was the go-between who, in 1823, got Marie-Victoire's son into the Habsburg Crown Prince's elite 4th Cuirassiers commanded by Count Clam-Martinitz, the brother-in-law of Sir Charles' friend Lord Clanwilliam.

Two years later, when Marie-Victoire finally returned to Lwów after 'running around the world' for well over a decade, Sir Charles' influence was also visible in the composition of her little court. Because Count Franz von Stadion was the son of Count Johann von Stadion, Prince von Warthausen, the Austrian foreign minister whom Sir Charles knew well from Vienna, whilst Count Hennequin de Fresnel et Curel was in the 4th Cuirassiers and ranked between Crown Prince Ferdinand and Count Clam-Martinitz.

Antime's military papers state that he was a nobleman with significant private income who had not bought his military title but earned it, that he spoke fluent French, German and Polish, and that he was impulsive as well as brave, honourable, dynamic and good natured. General Roman Wybranowski described him as 'a very kind person, and extremely polite in manner'. Count Jabłonowski added that he was 'the most decent and most noble of men'.

Antime's career came to an end in 1828, when he became engaged to Anna, the daughter of Captain Wenceslas Augustus Leiner von Negelfürst, a retired officer of the Austrian Army descended from a noble family of Baden-Baden. The young couple must have met through the émigré French royalists in Vienna, because Antime's

French aunt[53] and Anna's mother had been buried alongside one another in Vienna over a decade earlier, to be joined in 1836 by Marie-Victoire.

The young couple were married on 19 October 1829 at the parish church of St Paul in Döbling just north of Vienna. At the time, he was twenty-five and a wealthy man as the owner of a mansion in Lwów and the palace, estate and sugar refinery at Krzywczyce. To this was now added Anna's rich dowry, with which Antime bought the Grzymałów estate on 15 March 1831 comprising its sixteenth-century castle, town, extensive arable land, forestry to the south-east, as well as five villages. The castle was a massive, four-bastioned quadrangle built in 1590, situated on a small hill overlooking the River Gniła[54], which formed a lake beneath the escarpment when in flood. Underneath ran subterranean passages, which led to the town from the castle's huge cellars. Such escape routes were more than useful during the seventeenth century, when the castle was besieged by the Cossacks and Turks. Those onslaughts ruined the property, which was then acquired by Field Marshal Adam Sieniawski, the son of Sobieski's field marshal at the Battle of Vienna. By 1731, the castle, town, Greek Catholic Uniate church and Baroque synagogue had all been restored, though the Roman Catholic Church of the Holy Trinity was not finished until 1754. Sieniawski's granddaughter was Princess Elizabeth Lubomirska, reputedly Europe's richest private woman, though, of all her estates, Grzymałów's rich hardwood forests and legendary black earth produced her largest single source of income. The estate also embraced a strange formation of hills known as the *Miodobory* or Honey Woods, which ran in an arc from the north down to Alexander Potocki's Satanów Estate across the River Zbrucz in the south-east. This picturesque name came from the extraordinary quantity of bees which lived there, whose honey was harvested by the local peasants. The area was called 'Swiss Podolia' and was littered with ancient tombs over a thousand years old. The whole area was raised land formed from prehistoric coral reefs which pierced the soil in places, some a hundred feet tall. Its peculiar microclimate produced many rare plants, which nestled among queer rock formations such as the *Okniny* or Little Windows – four small round lakes whose waters were extremely deep and, though bitterly cold in summer, in winter never froze.

Such were the magnificent landscapes of Podolia's high river-cut plateau on which stood the wealthy young Chevalier de Nikorowicz's castle of Grzymałów, whose estate he enlarged by adding the neighbouring properties of Zielona and Pajówka. In the nearby castle of Olesko had been born his warrior-ancestor almost exactly 200 years before, King John III Sobieski. His was the fertile earth of these south-east marchlands, rich with the blood of the soldiers with whom he had beaten back the Turk. And this was the furthest point his descendants would ever live from the rocky shores of Europe's windswept north-west seaboard that once had been the Stuarts' home – a sad path travelled and a long road home, a best-forgotten dream away.

The year 1831 was also the time of the November uprising aimed at restoring Poland's liberty and the cause of Potocki's forfeiture of neighbouring Satanów about which Marie-Victoire's brother wrote to his wife from Sicily. Though fought on the Russian-occupied territory of the old Polish-Lithuanian Commonwealth, nevertheless, Galicia was used as a base, and many idealistic young Poles crossed the border to take up arms and fight. One who rode off to join the uprising was the 'impulsive, brave, honourable and dynamic' ex-officer of Crown Prince Ferdinand's 4th Cuirassiers – a strange echo of Prince Charles, who rode off from Rome at the same age to an earlier Rising, neither more heroic nor more doomed than the other.

Amongst the several political activists whom the Russians had earlier exiled to Voronezh as a preventive measure was the ex-marshal of the Vilnius nobility, Michael Römer. He was the grandson of a Radziwiłł and closely associated with that family. On 1 May 1831, his diary from Voronezh records, 'More Polish officers have arrived here – Apolinary Grabowski, a captain of the 3rd Rifle Brigade, and Nikorowicz, a lieutenant of the cavalry ... Nikorowicz was sick with fever ... They are all going on to Ufa'.

Antime had fought with the Polish 1st Lancers and been taken prisoner. However, as an Austrian citizen with no property in Russia to forfeit, he was already on his way home on 6 January 1832 when, still suffering from a fever which had already lasted seven months, he wrote to Römer, 'We are in Kursk and tomorrow press on further'. Antime told him of the terrible condition of the roads and thanked him for making his imprisonment in Russia one in which he had made so many real friends. Yet, although the uprising was crushed, those who still dreamed of freedom continued to plot, and Antime became president of his district's clandestine association, which held its secret meetings in a back room of Grzymałów's inn.

Just before riding off to fight, Antime had become a father. On 5 November 1830, his first child was born and baptised two days later in Lwów's Armenian Catholic cathedral. The records name the godmother as 'Marie de Pauw' and godfather as 'Captain Jean de Pauw'. Inevitably, the little boy was christened with the name Charles. But Marie-Victoire was the only person there who knew its 'Secret'. Little Charles was soon joined by a sister, Julia Thérèse, born on 21 May 1833, and, six years later, by a brother, Stanislas.

During his children's early years, Antime concentrated on his home and family and, around 1840, converted the austere fortress of Grzymałów into a palace. Retaining the main body of the building with its two rear towers, he added a large, galleried, pedimented portico as well as a Gothic clock-tower containing a spiral staircase. The defensive ramparts were also pulled down, and an 'English' park laid out incorporating the seventeenth-century avenue of massive lime trees planted by the son of Sobieski's old field marshal. To decorate the castle, Antime began to collect works of art, including a fine collection of engravings by Vernet.

Antime not only founded a Greek Catholic church at Krzywczyce but was amongst the first to emancipate his peasants and, by writing numerous articles in the press, was also one of the most vociferous advocates of reform. However, life in the Galician countryside began to be dangerous. In 1846, the Austrian authorities tried to stamp out the nationalistic ambitions of their Polish province by setting the peasantry against the landowners. Given a free hand and open assistance by the Austrian bureaucracy, groups of peasants committed atrocities on hundreds of gentry, irrespective of wealth or any notion of guilt. Antime therefore rented out Grzymałów for nine years and moved with his family to Lwów.

Two years later, the European-wide series of uprisings known as 'the Spring of the Nations' broke out. Again, Antime was amongst the first to join. Again, his hopes were dashed. Though events in Lwów were serious, nevertheless, the minor armed clashes did not flare up into large-scale revolution due to the iron hand of the former Austrian Governor of Galicia, now Minister of the Interior, Count Franz von Stadion, Marie-Victoire's old courtier. It was he who was the probable author of the Austrian-promoted butchery of the Polish landowners, an action which destroyed any hope for unity between the Polish elite and rural population. Stadion also managed to split the political leadership of the revolutionary movement. Patriotic aspirations had crystallised into four main power centres. One was the parallel Polish government called the 'National Council', of which Antime was a member. Another was the Lwów-based chapter of the secret pan-European 'Carbonari' movement with strong links to international Freemasonry. Originating in Italy, its central-European incarnation was dedicated to the overthrow of Austrian rule. Then there were the two military formations: one was the 'National Guard', the other was the 'Academic Legion' comprising a force of 1,200 armed students organised into six companies of 200 men. At the beginning of 1848, they voted on who would be their commanding officer. The man they unanimously elected was the charismatic Chevalier de Nikorowicz. On 23 March 1848, he addressed them with these words:

> Comrades in Arms! You have honoured me with your confidence in choosing me as your commander. I feel it and I am grateful! ... Today all Europe demands the rights that belong to her ... In you rests the hope of our land. Give of yourselves an example to others! And may you convince the whole Nation that you are worthy to carry the arms which the Country has placed in your hands – in the name of Peace, Order and the Safety of the People!
>
> Nikorowicz

The crowd's hurrah which greeted Antime's words calls to mind Glenfinnan, where almost exactly the same number rallied to his great-grandfather, whose ill-fated name was now borne by his eldest son. Of all the Polish military formations active during the Spring of the Nations, General Wybranowski described Antime's as 'the best maintained and organised; ... this formation was kept in perfect military order'. However, towards the end of 1848, Stadion ordered his artillery to bombard Lwów into submission. The Poles had no answer. In Lwów, as elsewhere, Europe's Spring of the Nations proved a premature flowering whose fruits would ripen only later.

That year, Antime's wife died. Three years later, he too was dead. He had gone to the spa at Carlsbad to try and improve his health but died there on 16 February 1852 at the age of forty-seven. In 1870, his daughter, Julia Thérèse, brought his remains back and had them reinterred in Grzymałów's cemetery at the end of the great lime avenue on the high plateau of Sobieski's native Podolia.

After Antime's death, his property was divided. His son Charles received the castle, town and estate of Grzymałów, as well as the palace, estate and sugar refinery at

Krzywczyce. Julia Thérèse inherited that part of Grzymałów called Eleonorówka and Soroka, together with a share of Charles' income. Meanwhile, the youngest, Stanislas, who kept the tradition of uprisings alive by fighting in 1863, received Zielona, Pajówka, Wolica, and Kałaharówka, as well as the mansion in Lwów. Not long after inheriting, Charles swapped Grzymałów for the Rokietnica estate west of Lwów, which belonged to his sister Julia Thérèse's husband, who then bought her younger brother's properties, thus reuniting the whole.

Like his father, Charles also rallied to the Spring of the Nations, though only seventeen, becoming a junior officer in the Polish National Guard. Likewise, he promoted the emancipation of the peasantry. In 1853, he married Aniela, daughter of Baron Joseph Eder, vice-president of the Galician Court of Appeal. But fate gave no quarter to those named Charles.

In 1858, Antime's son quarrelled with a friend. Poland's most famous nineteenth-century horse painter, Julius Kossak was his second when the dispute was settled by way of an 'American Duel'. Two bullets were placed in a bag, one of which was black. When Charles withdrew his hand and opened his palm he saw in it the black bullet. He had one year in which to commit suicide.

Charles settled his affairs and travelled to Versailles. Exactly one year after the duel, he shot himself. Though that was where his grandmother Marie-Victoire first lived when she returned to France and where his father studied at the Royal College, one can only guess why he chose Versailles as the place in which to end his life. He was twenty-eight. Later, an engraved black marble plaque appeared on the wall of the church at Rokietnica. If one moves aside the wooden confessional, its text can still be read:

> To the late Charles Nikorowicz
> who died an unnatural death at Versailles in France on 31 August 1859.
> To the deceased
> from a true friend who as proof of his immortal memory
> has placed this stone here, asking Divine Grace for his soul

No one knows who put it there. No one knows what the argument was about.

Charles' son, named Antime after his grandfather, died in Zakopane in southern Poland in 1908. He was the last of the Chevaliers de Nikorowicz. But through the family's daughters, there were still descendants of Prince Charles Edward Stuart. Yet only one bore her husband a son whose male line survives unbroken to the present day. She was Marie-Victoire's granddaughter Julia Thérèse, who succeeded her brother Charles at the castle of Grzymałów. At the end of the nineteenth century, the distinguished Austro-Hungarian minister and diarist Baron Casimir von Pfaffenhoffen-Chłędowski wrote that she was

> a very attractive girl of Armenian origin, but what was peculiar was that she was an Armenian blonde.

Postscript

When giving talks on the extraordinary yet quintessentially human story of the last of the royal Stuarts and their descendants I am invariably asked two questions: *What happened to the Stuart blood line down to the present day*? and *How did I discover their 'Secret'?* Those questions are connected and best answered in that order.

As related, Bonnie Prince Charlie's granddaughter Marie-Victoire was the only one of Charlotte Stuart's children to have a child, namely her only son, Antime. He had three children, Charles, Julia Thérèse and Stanislas. Of them, Stanislas had a daughter who died childless. So his line ended there. Then there was Charles. He had another childless daughter and one son, Antime jr, who had four daughters. Of them, only two had children, all daughters except for one son who died childless. Those lines therefore moved ever further from the male line of descent from the Stuarts.

Then there was Marie-Victoire's granddaughter, Julia Thérèse (1833-93). It was she and her husband to whom, after her brother Charles, the castle and estate of Grzymałów passed, where Louis de Rohan's letters were kept and which remained her descendants' main home until the Second World War. In 1853, Julia Thérèse married Count Leonard Piniński (1824-86) and their male-line descendants still exist in the person of his great-grandson Count Stanislas Piniński. Theirs is the closest to the male-line descent from the Stuarts. And it is this line that experienced the strange coincidences which led to the discovery of Marie-Victoire's 'Secret'.

Julia Thérèse's husband was not only a talented agro-industrialist, landowner and investor, but also very brave. The son of a father, Count Francis Xavier, who died from wounds received during the Polish uprising of 1831, Piniński joined the National Guard in Lwów during the Spring of the Nations in 1848 as a cavalry officer and, during the Polish uprising of 1863, became the only aristocrat to be charged by the Austrians with sending arms and ammunition to those fighting against Prussian and Russian oppression in the other parts of partitioned Poland. Leonard and Julia Thérèse had four sons, of whom the second, Leon, is important because he was the greatest of all the descendants of Bonnie Prince Charlie.

Count Leon Piniński (1857-1938) was compared by fellow professors to 'the great men of the renaissance ... an astonishingly erudite man of vast humanistic interests'. An internationally recognised professor of Roman Law, he chaired that faculty at Lwów University, becoming its chancellor in 1928. An eminent statesman and brilliant orator, he played a dominant role in the Austrian Parliament, and in 1898, Emperor Franz Joseph made him Viceroy of Galicia. He was also a music and literary critic, composer, art historian, collector, and benefactor. Out of the income from his landed estates, including Grzymałów, he amassed a vast collection of art from the Gothic to contemporary, which he housed in his private museum in Lwów. Having played a key role in the exceptionally important task of persuading the emperor to withdraw the Austrian Army from the Royal Castle of Wawel in Kraków, this supreme monument of Polish culture, which they had been devastating for over a century by using it as a barracks, the Viceroy Piniński published his own restoration project in 1905, announcing that he would donate his main collection to the castle[55]. This he did in 1931, and it remains the most important bequest ever made. To the National Institute in Lwów (the Ossolineum), he donated his library, and to the Polish State Collections of Art in Lwów, he gave his private museum with its remaining 700 paintings and altarpieces as well as antique porcelain, glass, and furniture. A *Doctor Honoris Causa* of three universities, he was the recipient of various awards, an honorary citizen of dozens of towns, and the author of over 140 published works. When the Russians invaded Lwów in 1914, instead of fleeing as others did, he stayed and restarted the educational system, stood at the head of the Red Cross, and did all he could to ease tsarist repression. Short, slender, blonde, with humorous blue eyes, he was remarkably successful with the opposite sex and lived until 1938, when he died peacefully one night in his private museum immediately after playing Beethoven's *Death March* to himself. He married Countess Maria Mniszech but had no children. Instead, he adopted the son of his youngest brother, Alexander Augustus, who died tragically young.

Count Mieczyslas Piniński (1895-1945), nephew, adopted son and heir of the Viceroy Leon, also inherited his father Alexander's fortune. Educated in Vienna at the elite Collegium Kalksburg and the Imperial Cavalry Cadet School, he fought in the Austro-Hungarian cavalry during the First World War, then in the Polish cavalry during the Polish-Soviet War immediately after. Deeply involved in the management and enlargement of his estates in Poland, he nevertheless educated his son in Paris. Hitler's invasion of Poland in 1939 caught him in Lwów, which, days later, was invaded by Nazi Germany's Russian allies. To escape deportation or execution, he was hidden by his Jewish business administrator Simon Kaufman until 1941, when Germany invaded its former Soviet ally. Now Kaufman was in extreme danger. Despite being hidden by Mieczyslas, he and his wife were arrested by the Gestapo in January 1942. However, Mieczyslas had exceptionally high-placed Austrian contacts from his schooldays in Vienna, and the aristocratic Austrian 1st Lancers, including the younger brothers of both the last emperor and prime minister. Somehow, he managed to obtain the Kaufmans' release, even though the Jewish population of Lwów was being sent *en masse* to their death at nearby Bełżec. Even more astonishingly, he managed to get an apparently unique document for them: official written permission signed by the Director of the German Police in occupied Lwów for the Kaufmans to live in his large apartment in the city centre until April that year. Death being the Nazi punishment for Poles even attempting to help Jews, Mieczyslas left for Kraków, where his brother was the commanding officer of the Kraków division of the Polish Resistance[56]. His brother gave him a large amount of diamonds, some to be delivered to members of the Polish Resistance based in Vienna, the rest to be taken with him to his Villa Brunitzki in Abbazia[57]. It was the old premier resort of Austro-Hungary's high society, on the Italian Adriatic, just next to the large port of Fiume[58]. Probably passing them off as members of his family, he took the Kaufmans' two children with him, because Fiume was virtually the only place left in Central Europe from which Jews still had a reasonable chance to escape, and the area was ruled by the relatively benign Italian regime. From late November 1942 until the end of April 1945, with the help of Giovanni Palatucci (murdered at Dachau, honoured at Yad Vashem, known as the 'Schindler of Rijeka'), he ran the Villa Brunitzki as a safe house for couriers from the Polish Resistance on missions to the Vatican, using the diamonds to provide them with money, procure papers or visas, and pay bribes. But General Tito's pro-Soviet Yugoslav communists who seized power at the end of April regarded the Polish Resistance as their enemy. Accusing Mieczyslas of having a radio transmitter and being a 'nobleman', they arrested him and shot him on 9 May, the day after the war ended.

Count Stanislas Piniński (b.1925) was Mieczyslas's only child and the only member of his generation. Told by his father that he didn't 'want him brought up a provincial Polish snob' his cosmopolitan prewar years were nonetheless ones of unquestioned wealth and privilege. Winters were spent skiing in the Haute-Savoie, summers on the Riviera, in Normandy, Brittany, or on the family's Polish estates. His exquisitely dressed father would take him riding in the Bois de Boulogne near their apartment on the rue St Didier in Paris' exclusive 16th *arrondissement*, where he would meet the little Princesses Ysabel and Ariel Faucigny-Lucinge on the avenue Victor Hugo as well as his best friend, Gérard, the son of Count Jean de Boissy d'Anglas, descendant of the famous liberal politician from the Revolution. Educated in Paris at the Ecole Gerson and Lycée Janson de Sailly, his colleagues included Charles and Guy de Rohan-Chabot as well as Olivier and Valéry Giscard d'Estaing, the future President of France. However, the outbreak of the Second World War found him on holiday in southern England with Scottish friends of his father. They, William and Elisabeth Robertson-Butler, had been introduced to one another as visiting scholars in Lwów before the First World War by the Viceroy Piniński, who was so influential there. With the help of these Scots, Stanislas managed to complete his education at Eastbourne College and Radley, though penniless. In fact, they saved his life. Because, after the Fall of France in 1940, the Gestapo came looking for the family at their apartment in Paris. In 1943, Stanislas joined the Polish Air Force as a fighter pilot and did his basic training in Scotland. After the war, a return to Poland was impossible. The country was in the grip of Stalinist terror and the communists had nationalised all the family's property, which, in any case, was in the eastern half of pre-war Poland, which the Soviets had annexed. Worse, his uncle was none other than General Bór-Komorowski, leader of the Warsaw Uprising of 1944 and the Polish Resistance. Freed from Colditz in early

1945 and now in London as commander-in-chief of the Polish Armed Forces, loyal to the government-in-exile and Western Allies, he was sentenced to death *in absentia* by the Soviet communists, and any close relative ran the risk of being used to force the 'accused' back to face execution. Instead, Stanislas went to St Andrews University, where he studied economics and met his future wife, Jean Graham, daughter of James Graham, OBE, and Jessie Cameron Paul.

Now the coincidences began in earnest. Already engaged, Stanislas suddenly discovered that Jean's uncle was none other than the brother-in-law of Elisabeth Robertson-Butler and that her family, the Frasers, were so close to the Grahams that they used to holiday together on the Isle of Arran. It was not the only coincidence. Amongst the names Jean's mother gave her first born was one of which her family had long been proud. That name was Cameron. Because Jean Graham's mother, Jessie Cameron Paul, was the daughter of Jessie Cameron Todd, the daughter of Jessie Cameron of Glenhurich by Loch Shiel[59], the daughter of Margaret Cameron of Goirtean Eorna, the daughter of Mary Cameron, the daughter of Lochiel's brother John Cameron of Fassiefern, who had been imprisoned by the Hanoverians in 1746, 1751 and 1753, who had helped his brothers during the 'Forty-Five, taken part in the Elibank Plot, and whose younger brother Dr Archie had been hung, drawn and quartered at Tyburn without trial in 1753 – the last man to be executed for his part in the 'Forty-Five.

The names of Cameron, Lochiel and Fassiefern had echoed through Jean Graham's childhood. After moving from Glenhurich to Glasgow, her great-uncle's family had named their new home Fassiefern. And throughout Jean's closest family were distributed various objects which had belonged to Colonel John Cameron, Younger of Fassiefern, who was killed leading the 92nd Gordon Highlanders at Quatre Bras on the eve of Waterloo. More than 3,000 highlanders followed his coffin when Colonel John's remains returned to Lochaber, and the epitaph on his tomb at Kilmallie Churchyard by Loch Eil was written by Sir Walter Scott. Those heirlooms included three swords, one of which was a captured French sabre, a powder horn, walnut knife box, and a crystal water glass. There was also the colonel's hide-covered travelling-chest, which stood in Jean's nursery throughout her childhood, as well as a copy of his memoirs with a dedication from his younger brother, Sir Duncan Cameron, Bt, 3rd of Fassiefern. In particular, there was a decanter and four wine goblets said to have been used by Bonnie Prince Charlie when he dined at Fassiefern House on 23 August 1745 whilst the Highland Army picked roses from the bushes in the gardens and pinned them to their bonnets as the campaign badge of the 'Forty-Five, symbolic of the Stuarts' white rose. A century later, two generations of Jean's ancestors lived at Glenhurich House by Loch Shiel, where Lochiel and Fassiefern's first cousin Alexander Cameron of Dungallon had lived. He had been the Standard-Bearer in Prince Charles' army and his sister had married Dr Archie. It was at Glenhurich House that Lochiel, Dr Archie with his pregnant wife, and John Murray of Broughton with his, together with other Jacobite fugitives, hid after the 'Butcher' Cumberland's men had burned Lochiel's Achnacarry to the ground in May 1746.

Over 200 years later, and decades before anyone had the faintest idea about Marie-Victoire's Stuart parentage, it turned out that her descendant Stanislas had married a Scottish girl, who by unbroken female descent was the offspring of those most loyal of Jacobites, the Camerons of Lochiel, without whose 800 clansmen who rallied to the royal standard at Glenfinnan, there would have been no Rising. Six generations separate this closest male-line descendant from his brilliant but flawed ancestor of the 'Forty-Five. And six generations separate his wife from her female-line Camerons of Lochiel. Stanislas and Jean married on 12 May 1951, a union of alarming genetic symmetry. In his 2002 review of *The Stuarts' Last Secret* in *The Spectator*, Hugh Massingberd asked the rhetorical question: 'What better case could be made for the romantic divinity which shapes family history?' – a coincidence born of a chance meeting between two Scottish scholars and a Polish Viceroy in the shadow of King John Sobieski's old mansion in Lwów. Fate quixotic to the end.

That answers the question: *What happened to the Stuart blood line down to the present day?*[60] But what of the second question: *How did I discover their 'Secret'?*

Families can be mighty odd. My mother's is no exception. Any attempt to prise from her or her elder sister information about their Cameron ancestors got nowhere and were re-routed down a *cul-de-sac* of self-deprecating humour, albeit highly entertaining. I gave up trying and, in 1997, reached for a history of Prince Charles Edward Stuart to see what they'd been up to during the 'Forty-Five, a subject I had never taken an interest in before. The reason was that, for years, I had been busy discovering about my father's family, provoked by the fact that I never knew my grandfather, who had been murdered by Tito's communists in 1945, and because my father's past had been a subject hardly ever spoken of due to its painful associations.

By the time I began reading up about the Camerons and Bonnie Prince Charlie, I felt I had pretty much learned all that was worth knowing about my paternal side, something I had to radically rethink when I came across the fact that Charlotte Stuart had given birth to three children by Prince Ferdinand de Rohan. That immediately struck me as an odd coincidence, given that I knew the story in my father's family that Marie-Victoire was the natural daughter of a Prince de Rohan, whose letters to her at Grzymałów were still within living memory.

A couple of years earlier, I had discovered a long-forgotten Piniński Archive in Lwów, the former Polish city near which the Sobieskis had their main estate of Żółkiew, now in the Western Ukraine. That archive is in the W. Stefanyk Library of the Ukrainian Academy of Science, previously the Polish institution known as the Ossolinem, now based in Wrocław. Only recently had it become relatively easily accessible for foreign researchers, and I had obtained from them a large number of photocopies of various family documents. Therefore, no sooner had I come across the eye-catching fact of Charlotte's natural children by the Prince de Rohan, than I was able to go through those photocopies and retrieve Marie-Victoire's Viennese death certificate from 1836. It gave her place of origin as Tours, her status of birth as noble, her year of birth as 1779, and that she was originally called 'de Thorigny'. I saw she had the same Christian name and was the same age as one of Charlotte's daughters.

The plot thickened. Then, having failed to find a noble family called Thorigny which made any sense, I began to wonder, if it wasn't a name, could it be a place?

That took me to a nineteenth-century dictionary of French place names. Sure enough: Thorigny, near Tours, bought in 1757 by Prince Jules-Hercule de Rohan, Duke de Montbazon, sold by him in 1781. So I went to the archives there and to Thorigny itself, where I met the château's present owners who, by chance, had just received an excellently researched history of Thorigny by a local historian, Ludovic Vieira. That led me to Marie-Victoire's 1779 baptismal entry explaining her title as 'the Demoiselle de Thorigny', the 1782 notarial pay-off for 'services rendered' by Marie Grosset, and the highly enlightening memoirs of the great-nephew of the parish priest Abbé Barnabé.

The National Archives in Paris yielded the letters of the 'Countess de Thorigny' and the 'Countess de la Morlière' to the Berryers, thanks to the genius of the now-retired Michel Guillot. But other documents, such as the death certificate of Marie-Victoire's sister and the baptismal certificate of her brother were relatively easy to find in their respective Belgian and Parisian archives. In England, it was the Stuart expert Arthur Addington who tipped me off about the de la Morlière marriage details, of which chapter and verse I received courtesy of that family's relation, Robert Testot-Ferry. Then the ex-Royal College of Heralds' former senior editor of Burke's Peerage, Roger Powell, unearthed all manner of information from the British Consular Records concerning Marie-Victoire's second husband, d'Auvergne. The debtor list is long, and I may have missed some out even in the Acknowledgements in *The Stuarts' Last Secret*, but it would be incomplete without mention of the extraordinary ability of Raymond Poulain of the Friends of the Musée de la Poste in Paris to interpret and decipher postmarks and envelopes, which allowed me to place, date and order Marie-Victoire's letters. There is also the wonderful Maria Muryn from Lwów, a bottomless well of knowledge on the contents of that beautiful city's State Historical Archive, who found me Antime's baptismal entries of 1804 and 1806 and much else besides.

To Professors Bruce Lenman of St Andrews University and Waldemar Łazuga of Poznań University, I am deeply indebted for their advice as well as the foreword and introduction each wrote for *The Stuarts' Last Secret*. Another to whom I owe special gratitude is Professor Edward Corp of the University of Toulouse, whose research into the exiled Stuart courts in France and Italy he has shared with me with unsurpassed generosity. As to the very existence of this book and its predecessor, special thanks must go to Agnieszka Sozańska, not only for her heroic patience and academic discipline during the research work, but for her encouragement that it be committed to paper.

Perhaps one of the happiest episodes occurred thanks to Hana Slavičkova, Helena Śmiškova, and Ondra Śmišek of the Czech State Archives in Děčin. Knowing that the Rohans' old archive from Sychrov was housed there, but that from Warsaw it was one hell of a place to get to, I sent them a letter asking them to check the archive's index for every relevant name I could think of. Their trawl produced a disappointing result – only a few letters between Ferdinand and Louis de Rohan from the years of the

Revolution. I phoned up. Could they possibly send me photocopies? Yes, of course. I waited two months … they didn't arrive. I asked again. Yes, of course. I waited another two months … they didn't arrive. I asked again. Again nothing. Should I make the effort? Was it worth it? Finally, something prompted me to go there and thank God for that. Not only did I meet people as generous and helpful as everywhere else, but when I examined the index of the Rohan Archive, I saw that I had forgotten to include in my list of relevant names one that was absolutely crucial. I forgot, because it wasn't a name, only an alias – Roehenstart – and there it was. But when, as the only person in the modest reading room of the Děčin archive, I received the dusty package of twenty-three letters, I saw that they were not, as I had presumed, unknown letters from Charlotte Stuart's son Charles, but the surviving part of that half of Marie-Victoire's correspondence with Louis de Rohan of which his replies to her had been kept by my father's family at Grzymałów. My thanks therefore to Hana, Helena, Ondra, and whoever else it might have been whose unseen hand ensured I was never sent the thrice-promised photocopies. Or I would never have found the key to the Stuarts' 'Secret'.

The royal House of Stuart seems to have been haunted down the generations by a malevolence of fate, be it the ill-winds that helped William of Orange's invasion, then thwarted Spain and France's attempts at their restoration, or the blighted lives of every one of them and their descendants called Charles or Charlotte.[61] Even the discovery of their 'Secret' is thick with coincidence, such as the wonderfully unreceived photocopies from the Sychrov Archive, the miraculous appearance of Vieira's crucial history of Thorigny, or the extraordinary genetic symmetry of the Stuart-male-line/Cameron-female-line marriage of the family's senior descendant in 1951.

Now take from the shelf, if you will, the 1856 *Militär-schematismus des österreichischen Kaiserthums* and open its musty pages at 419-20.[62] There you will see the proud names of long-dead officers of Austro-Hungary's grandest cavalry regiment, Emperor Franz Joseph's own 1st Cuirassiers. Two will catch your eye: Prince Victor de Rohan (1827-89) and Count Victor Piniński (1830-97). The former was Marie-Victoire's exiled French relation of the Sychrov estate in Austrian Bohemia, the latter was the Polish brother-in-law of her granddaughter Julia Thérèse of the Grzymałów estate in Austrian Galicia. Yet besides them leaps out a seemingly impossible third person, a man called … Charles Edward Stuart of Albany. Who on earth was he?

This book's foreword recounts the story of the English naval officer, Thomas Allen, whose sons John and Charles were the 'demonstrably false' Sobieski-Stuarts who claimed to be grandsons of Bonnie Prince Charlie, the younger being the father of Marie of the oft-repeated but much confused legend of the Château de Beaumanoir. But he also had one son, whom he christened Charles Edward Stuart of Albany.[63]

Of all the multiplicity of careers that son could have chosen, of all the various regiments, in all the different armies, of all the countries and empires of Europe, the mad hand of chance chose to place him at exactly the same time and place alongside the two Victors – a *bona fide* Prince de Rohan and Count Piniński, both genuinely related to the last Stuarts and their descendants – a juxtaposition of grotesque proportions.[64]

However, history's mischief was not done yet. Because, on 16 May 1874, this spurious Charles Edward Stuart of Albany married Lady Alice Hay. And her grandfather just happened to be ... King William IV, the Hanoverian usurper! Whoops ...

Nothing but coincidence – a last laugh echoing down the silent corridors of Europe's once-gilded past.

Addendum

A document discovered on going to print may shed light on Marie-Victoire's 1820 letter to Louis de Rohan (p. 149), containing the enigmatic phrase after the word, triumph: 'I saw no other course other than being done with this disaster at precisely the point when I could no longer fear anything from the perfidious and seductive child. This grey hair which will soon cover my brow will show contempt for love, were I to be so mad as to be attracted by it'. Read in context, her passionate blood had proved hard to control, forced her 'extreme' decision to leave Lwów, so as to 'moderate' her 'conduct'. Obviously something very serious had happened there before 1814. So, in 1820, she resigned herself to becoming 'united' to the veteran of de Condé's army, royalist officer, Jean de Pauw. A clue is in a Warsaw archive (AGAD, Ks. Metryk. Rz. Kat. Archidiecezji Lwowskiej, A-74595, 63) where a baptism in Lwów is recorded for Zenon de Pauw, born 27.7.1813 as the son of Jean de Pauw. Because Marie-Victoire appears as the mother. But was she? (a) Only the Nikorowicz family took part, the godfather was John, and the priest was Mark, Marie-Victoire's brothers-in-law. (b) But Mark was an Armenian Catholic priest. Why would he baptize the Roman Catholic baby of Roman Catholic parents in a Roman Catholic church? (c) Marie-Victoire's Paris letters prove Antime was there too. She writes of no other son, of being a widow, and of ten years of liberty in 1820 (Antime's father died in 1810). (d) In 1826 Jabłonowski lived with Marie-Victoire, knew her family well, but only mentions Antime. (e) Sir Charles Stuart arranged for Antime to join the elite 4th Cuirassiers of Crown Prince Ferdinand. Zenon was but the employee of Antime's daughter at Grzymałów, as manager of the steam mill. (f) Zenon lived, died and was buried at Grzymałów, but did not live with the family. (g) Two children of Grzymałów's last owner (Countess Julia Pinińska , 1885-1975) are still alive. Their mother passed on every detail of family history. She remembered Zenon at Grzymałów, but as de Pauw's son, not Marie-Victoire's. Had he been her grandmother's uncle, she would known about it. If Zenon was de Pauw's illegitimate son, Marie-Victoire might well have wanted to help her friend by standing in as mother. In 1824 she asked Louis de Rohan to help 'a young man who finds himself in the same situation of birth as I do'. But her in-laws had no interest in de Pauw. Or was Zenon Marie-Victoire's illegitimate son? Then they would oblige. She was their sister-in-law, of passionate 'Breton' blood, who could only 'moderate her conduct' by the 'extreme course' of leaving Lwów, to be 'done with this disaster', to 'no longer fear anything from the perfidious and seductive child'. Jabłonowski described de Pauw as 'a decent old soul', fond enough of Marie-Victoire to suggest 'becoming united' in 1820. Had she become pregnant in 1813? Might he have stood in as father, perhaps even married and divorced her for the purpose? Whatever the truth, the above illuminates Marie-Victoire's emotional personality and reasons for leaving Lwów.

Notes

1. Since James VI & I inherited the throne of England and Ireland nearly a century earlier, the Stuart kings had done all they could to promote unity by calling themselves Kings of Great Britain. This appellation was why they considered themselves James I, James II and James III – not of England, but of Great Britain, and therefore not because they didn't care about their ancient throne of Scotland.
2. The Stuarts' religious toleration remained a hallmark of their future exiled courts, even in Rome, where, though Catholics themselves, they always provided for the religious needs of their Protestant adherents and visitors from Britain.
3. E. Corp, *A Court in Exile, The Stuarts in France, 1689-1718* (Cambridge University Press), pp. 314-15. Professor Edward Corp is the leading authority on the Stuart courts in exile.
4. Today, Šiauliai in Lithuania.
5. Then called Ohlau, located near Breslau, today called Wrocław and the largest city in the south-west of Poland.
6. The Act of Settlement of 1701 and the Bill of Rights created a situation, prior to the Act of Union of 1707, in which the English parliament, without consulting Scotland, decided that the Crowns of England, Ireland and Scotland would not pass according to the established tradition of England and law of Scotland, namely from James VII & II to James VIII & III, but that the succession would be reversed back through James VII & II, Charles II and Charles I to James VI & I, then down through his daughter Elizabeth to her German daughter Sophia, Countess Palatine von Simmern, then to Sophia's non-English-speaking son, Georg von Brunswick-Lüneburg, Elector of Hanover, even though over fifty people were closer to the throne than he was. It was also determined that, in future, only members of the Church of England could inherit the throne of Scotland. England's behaviour was widely perceived as arrogant and the principal cause of the 1715 Jacobite Rising, which was mainly motivated by a desire for Scotland to withdraw from the Union.
7. There has been much confusion concerning this palace. Prior to the Stuarts' tenure, the Palazzo del Re (the King's Palace) had been called the Palazzo Muti, as it belonged to the Marchese Muti. However, adjacent to it, but standing on the west side of the Piazza Pilotta, is another Palazzo Muti, which belonged to a cousin, also with the title of the Marchese Muti, but which retained its name after 1719. In the 2002 edition of the present work, the front elevation of the latter Palazzo Muti is illustrated, with the side of the Palazzo del Re visible at the end of the street on the right-hand side, which was where the *facciata* of 1747 was created to celebrate Prince Henry Stuart's appointment as cardinal, because that was the part of the Palazzo del Re in which his apartment was located. The Palazzo del Re passed to the Marchese Sacchetti during Prince Charles Edward's tenure and then to the Casali family, which is why, after Charles' death in 1788, it became known as the Palazzo Casali. To confuse matters further, in their famous views of Rome from the mid-eighteenth century, both Giovanni Battista Piranesi and Giuseppe Vasi deliberately called the Palazzo del Re by its old name of the Palazzo Muti so as not to compromise British grand tourists who bought

the print when they returned home from Rome to Hanoverian Britain. And most who went to Rome usually visited the Stuart Court, not just out of sympathy or curiosity, but because it acted as a form of embassy with regard to Roman Catholic Europe, as there were no diplomatic relations between the Vatican and Britain due to the fact that the Pope did not recognise the House of Hanover's right to the throne.

8. The son and heir of King James VIII & III's illegitimate half-brother, the marshal of France and 1st Duke of Berwick and Liria.
9. Balhaldy's real name was MacGregor, but his surname had been outlawed.
10. There is a painting in the Scottish National Portrait Gallery of Charles dressed in his suit of Highland clothes, wearing a blue bonnet and white cockade, painted by the Scottish artist William Mosman in 1740 after Jean-Etienne Liotard's pastel portrait of 1737. A marginally later oil-on-canvas version by Liotard is in the same gallery. The book of dances was almost certainly *A Collection of Country Dances written for the use of his Grace the Duke of Perth*, by David Young, 1734/7, from *The Drummond Castle Manuscript* in the possession of the Earl of Ancaster at Drummond Castle. A facsimile is in the Special Collections section of Glasgow University Library, and the title page is illustrated in an article by Douglas Smith published in *The Fifteen: The Journal of the Northumbrian Jacobite Society*, November 2007, no. 8.
11. Which in English means 'Charles' Year'. Phonetically *Thearlaich* is very close to Charlie, whence the popular appellation of Bonnie Prince Charlie.
12. The Lake of the Caves.
13. Bergues, near Dunkirk.
14. Aachen.
15. Charles was called *le Prince Edouard* by the French, whilst the 'whore' was Louis' mistress, Madame de Pompadour.
16. This scene has been invariably, but wrongly, described as occurring in Florence in 1784 or Rome in 1786. The above information is taken from Corri's autobiography, which forms the preface to his *The Singer's Preceptor* (London, 1810). Corri (1746-1825) was a pupil of Nicola Porpora, under whom he studied in Naples, after whose death he lived in Rome. Corri moved to Edinburgh in 1781 and London in 1790, where, interestingly, the composer's publishing house used the Prince of Wales' feathers as its trade mark. He became one of Britain's most influential teachers of singing.
17. Carolus Rex 1777.
18. King I cannot be, nor condescend to be a duke, Rohan am I.
19. The Rohans' exotic title of Duke de Rohan-Rohan was acquired to outdo the Chabot family, who, now calling themselves Rohan-Chabot, had inherited the title of Duke de Rohan through the daughter of Duke Henri de Rohan. This, however, didn't prevent strategic inbreeding, and through his mother, Ferdinand de Rohan's great-great-grandparents were the couple in question, Henri Chabot and Princess Marguerite, Duchess de Rohan in her own right.
20. Today, the *Mairie*.
21. Louis XVI's foreign minister.
22. The privilege of princesses and duchesses of the blood royal to remain seated in the presence of the queen.
23. In English, his name was William Ross (1762-90). The grandson of a poet, John McKay, he worked as a parish schoolmaster until his death at the age of twenty-eight. Written upon hearing the news of Prince Charles' death, the above two of the fourteen verses and chorus were translated in 1932 by John Lorne Campbell.
24. It pleases to cherish hope; it does not please to always cherish it in vain.
25. Hope though infinite I will always pursue.
26. He was also the son of Charlotte's stepmother's sister, Princess Caroline zu Stolberg-Gedern.
27. Henry had been appointed Bishop of Frascati in 1761, and the Villa Muti there was his favourite country residence.

28. In various surviving documents, she is described as Marie or Victoire or their equivalents in English, Polish or German, though Victoire was her everyday name. For the purpose of this book, the author has chosen to use the name Marie-Victoire.
29. There is no indication from the baptismal entry whether this *ex aqua* baptism took place at the surgeon's house, elsewhere, or at the parish church; however, it can be safely assumed that it was not the latter.
30. After whose daughter Marie-Victoire was apparently given her third name of Adélaïde, as mentioned earlier.
31. The title used by Clementina.
32. Douglas being one of Charles' main aliases.
33. 'His Royal Highness' refers to Henry. This and other letters were sent to Louis' brother, Prince Victor de Rohan, and mainly concerned Henry and the Rohans' attempt to reclaim the estate of Oława in Silesia, which had belonged to the Sobieskis but had been confiscated by the invading Prussians. Neither family ever succeeded.
34. Long Street.
35. A chevalier or ritter was the equivalent of baronet.
36. From 1766-70, Nikorowicz's son John was one of the first four students at the Polish Oriental School in Constantinople founded by King Stanislas Augustus to train Polish diplomats in the Turkish language so they could be significantly more effective. Such a diplomat-linguist was known as a *dragoman*.
37. See note 42.
38. The cardinal being, of course, Henry Stuart.
39. Today, the Lycée Hoche.
40. The case of Liège was a counter-claim to the long-contested rights of succession to the Duchy of Bouillon, described below. This counter-claim was lodged in 1817 by the heirs of the siblings of the 5th Duke de Bouillon, whereas the Rohans were the heirs of the siblings of the 6th Duke.
41. 'As legally as possible' obviously means 'in the most correct legal form'.
42. She correctly calls Armand 'the Prince de Montbazon' – Jules-Hercule being the Duke de Montbazon. Because this was the title used by the second oldest of the four Rohan brothers, Louis and Ferdinand being the youngest. Like Marie-Victoire, her brother Charles must also have been told that Armand was his real father, and that Ferdinand was only his 'guardian' who 'supervised his education'. Indeed, Ferdinand's letters of the 1790s to his brother, Cardinal Louis, reveal that he was very interested in the education of a young boy, though naturally no name is given. Thus, in his letters from Munich dated 1800, it was almost certainly Ferdinand whom Charles was addressing as his '*Tendre Papa*', a metaphor natural in the context, elsewhere describing him as his 'uncle and protector', though this could possibly refer to Louis at Ettenheim. And if Charles believed his real father to have been Armand, it fully justifies his 1813 attempt to save something from the Rohan estate on St Domingo, because it was Armand who originally bought it. It also explains his 1811 letter in which he states he has no father, even though Ferdinand was still alive at the time.
43. D'Auvergne's name for Marie-Victoire.
44. The reference to the Bourbons refers to Admiral Philip d'Auvergne's help to the French royalist underground movement on Jersey during the French Revolution, as well as to the Count d'Artois who had a base there from 1792; see D. Hamilton-Williams, *The Fall of Napoleon: The Final Betrayal* (1994).
45. Those 'busts of an ordinary size' would have included the pastel portrait of Marie-Victoire illustrated in this book.
46. Armenian Street.
47. Broad Street, today called Copernicus Street. The city centre house was mentioned in the press because the De Pauws' heirs had just sold it.
48. P.-N. Berryer, *Souvenirs de Berryer*, vol. I (Paris, 1839), pp. 301, 308, 323, 325, 327, 363; P.-N. Berryer, *la Vie au Barreau* (Paris, 1910), pp. 146, 165.

49. J. Reychman, *Życie Polskie w Stambule w XVIII w.* (Warsaw, 1956), pp. 74-81.
50. Today, Svätý Jur near Bratislava in Slovakia.
51. Selina and Richard's sister, Lady Caroline Meade married another great Austro-Hungarian noble, Count Pal Széchenyi, who became one of the emperor's chamberlains.
52. See, for example, the National Library of Scotland, MSS 6203-16.
53. Baroness Anne de Bourguignan, the wife of Joseph de Nikorowicz, as described above.
54. Rotten Water.
55. Piniński's close friend, Count Charles Lanckoroński, was likewise instrumental in persuading the Emperor, and today, his Italian Renaissance paintings also adorn the Royal Castle. The present custodian, Anna Petrus, ranks them as the most important gift ever made, apart from the Piniński collection of over 350 works of art. Although the negotiations concerning the Royal Castle were led by Piniński, another to play a crucial role in recovering the Wawel was Count Stanislas Badeni, Marshal or Speaker of the Galician Parliament when the Emperor finally agreed in 1899. See www.lwow.com.pl/petrus.html
56. The Armia Krajowa or Home Army, Europe's biggest and best organised.
57. Today, Opatija in Croatia on the Istrian Peninsula.
58. Today, Rijeka in Croatia.
59. Three of whose four grandparents were Camerons, and whose father's ancestor fought at Culloden.
60. Stanislas and Jean are the parents of the present author, whose only son, Alexander Leon, descends through his maternal grandfather, Count Jan Badeni, from Catherine Sobieska, King John III's sister, who married Prince Michael Radziwiłł – which is why, in the eighteenth century, the Radziwiłłs were the Stuarts' closest Polish cousins.
61. For details, see the postscript to *The Stuarts' Last Secret*.
62. Less traditionally minded readers wishing to save themselves a lot of trouble may prefer to do a Google book search instead: http://books.google.pl/books?id=3fnY5RbGtaoC&pg=PA420&dq=victor+pininsky
63. 1824-82.
64. This son of the younger Sobieski-Stuart charlatan cannot be held responsible for the fact that his father christened him with a false name, and in later life, he reverted to his family's real surname of Allen.

Suggested Further Reading

Bogdanowicz, M. Rosco-, *Wspomnienia* (Kraków, 1958).

Chłędowski, K., *Pamiętniki* (Kraków, 1951).

Jabłonowski, L., *Pamiętniki* (Kraków, 1962).

Balleine, G. R., *The Tragedy of Philippe d'Auvergne: Vice Admiral in the Royal Navy and Last Duke of Bouillon* (Chichester, 1975).

Beauclerk-Dewar, P. & Powell, R., *Right Royal Bastards: The Fruits of Passion* (Buckingham, 2006).

Berry, C. L., *The Young Pretender's Mistress* (Edinburgh, 1977).

Bongie, L. L., *The Love of a Prince: Bonnie Prince Charlie in France* (Vancouver, 1986).

Corp, E., *The King over the Water* (Edinburgh, 2001).

Corp, E., *A Court in Exile: The Stuarts in France, 1689-1718* (Cambridge, 2004).

Corp, E., *The Jacobites at Urbino: An Exiled Court in Transition* (Basingstoke, 2009).

Duffy, C., *The '45* (London, 2003).

Franklin, R., *Lord Stuart de Rothesay* (Worcestershire, 1993).

Gibson, J. S., *Lochiel of the '45* (Edinburgh, 1994).

Haynin, E. de, *Louis de Rohan: le Cardinal 'Collier'* (Paris, 1997).

Lenman, B., *The Jacobite Risings in Britain 1689-1746* (London, 1980).

Martin, G., *Histoire et Généalogie de la Maison de Rohan* (Lyon, 1998).

McLynn, F., *The Jacobites* (London, 1985).

McLynn, F., *Bonnie Prince Charlie* (London, 2003).

Perrault, G., *Le Secret du Roi: la Passion Polonaise* (Paris, 1992).

Pininski, P., *The Stuarts' Last Secret: The Missing Heirs of Bonnie Prince Charlie* (East Linton, 2002).

Pininski, P., 'The Stuarts' Last Secret: The Children of Charlotte, Duchess of Albany', in E. Corp (ed.) *The Stuart Court in Rome* (Aldershot, 2003).

Pininski, P., 'The Royal Stuart Bloodline after Bonnie Prince Charlie', *The Stewarts*, Vol. 22, No. 2 (Edinburgh, 2005).

Pininski, P., 'Charles Stuart, Lord Stuart de Rothesay (1779-1845): Ambassador Extraordinary', *The Stewarts*, Vol. 22, No. 3 (Edinburgh, 2006).

Pininski, P., 'Royal Stuarts in the Heart of Europe: The Polish Connection', *The Stewarts*, Vol. 22, No. 4 (Edinburgh, 2007).

Pininski, P., 'Rohan – Stuart: Breton Nobles – Princes Baroque', *The Stewarts*, Vol. 23 No. 1 (Edinburgh, 2008).

Pininski, P., 'The Last Stuarts: More Secrets', *The Stewarts*, Vol. 23, No. 2 (Edinburgh, 2009).

Pittock, M., *The Myth of the Jacobite Clans* (Edinburgh, 2009).

Prebble, J., *Culloden* (London, 1961).

Reychman, J., *Życie Polskie w Stambule w XVIII wieku* (Warsaw, 1959).

Sage, H., *Une République de Trois Mois: le Prince de Rohan-Guéméné* (Verviers, 1909).

Schuchard, M. K., 'The Young Pretender and Jacobite Freemasonry: New Light from Sweden on his role as "Hidden Grand Master"' (revised), in *The Consortium on Revolutionary Europe, 1750-1850* (Florida State University, 1994).

Sherburn, G., *Roehenstart: a Late Stuart Pretender* (Edinburgh & London, 1960).
Skeet, F. J. A., *HRH Charlotte Stuart, Duchess of Albany* (London, 1932).
Speck, W., *The Butcher* (Oxford, 1981).
Stopka, K., *Ormianie w Polsce Dawnej i Dzisiejszej* (Kraków, 2000).
Taylor, H., *Prince Charlie's Daughter* (London, 1950).

List of Illustrations

1. King James VIII & III (1688-1766), Prince Charles Edward's father. This portrait hung in his wife's bedroom in the Palazzo del Re in Rome, the original of which was painted by Martin van Meytens in 1725 to celebrate the birth of Prince Henry. The original is lost but this 1730 copy by the Stuarts' court painter Antonio David is the only known version by that artist, who also painted the 1729 portraits of Charles and Henry at the Scottish National Portrait Gallery. (Property of the Piniński Foundation, Warsaw)
2. Queen Clementina (1702-35), née Princess Sobieska, granddaughter of King John III of Poland, and Prince Charles Edward's mother. This painting hung in her husband's bedroom at the Palazzo del Re and is a pendant by Antonio David to the portrait of James. They were the couple's favourite portraits and they ordered a number of copies in 1727-28 from the English artist E. Gill but resigned from the commission because they were unhappy with the quality. (Property of the Piniński Foundation, Warsaw)
3. Prince Charles Edward Stuart (1720-1788), miniature by Jean Daniel Kamm (1748), after the lost original by Louis Tocqué completed in January 1748 and then given by the prince to the first great love of his life, his maternal first cousin, Princess Louise de Rohan, Duchess de Montbazon. (With thanks to John Nicholls, MBE, Chairman of The Fifteen – The Northumbrian Jacobite Society)
4. Charlotte Stuart, Duchess of Albany (1753-89), by Hugh Douglas Hamilton, the daughter and heiress of Prince Charles by Clementina Walkinshaw. Legitimised by her father and granted the rank of Royal Highness with the right of succession, she was recognised by the Pope, the King and Parliament of France, as well as the Grand Duke of Tuscany, but survived Prince Charles by only a year, dying from cancer of the liver just weeks after the outbreak of the French Revolution. (With thanks to the Scottish National Portrait Gallery)
5. Prince Henry Stuart (1725-1807) by Maurice Quentin de La Tour. Until 2009, this portrait was believed to be of Prince Charles Edward. It was started in January 1746 and finished in February 1747, before Henry's appointment as Cardinal in June 1747. It was commissioned whilst Henry was in Paris during the winter of 1745/46, when he believed he would soon be sailing with the French fleet to join his victorious brother in Britain prior to a glorious Stuart restoration. (With thanks to the Scottish National Portrait Gallery)
6. Marie-Victoire, the Demoiselle de Thorigny (1779-1836), the daughter of Charlotte Stuart and Ferdinand de Rohan. Legitimised at baptism by her uncle, Jules-Hercule, Duke de Moutbazon and head of the sovereign Princes de Rohan, she alone kept the bloodline going. This portrait of *c.* 1800 shows her just prior to her marriage to Paul Anthony, Chevalier de Nikorowicz, the rich, discreet merchant banker to the Stuarts' closest Polish cousins, the Princes Radziwiłł, from which family Prince Charles suggested finding a bride for his younger brother Henry in November 1746. (Property of the Piniński Foundation, Warsaw)
7. General Prince Louis de Rohan (1768-1836), painted in 1830 by Alexis Valbrun. Louis was the grandson of Prince Jules-Hercule, Duke de Montbazon and Marie-Victoire's long-standing confidant. Of their intimate Parisian correspondence from 1815/16 to 1825 some twenty-three of her letters survive in the Rohan archive from their estate of Sychrov in the Czech Republic. Of the many links between Marie-Victoire's cousin, Prince Louis, and Sir Charles Stuart (ill. 9), who helped her brother in 1817 and son in 1822, the most intimate was via the vastly rich, very beautiful but extraordinarily eccentric Wilhelmina de Biron, Princess of Courland, Duchess de Sagan, who was Louis' ex-wife and Sir Charles' ex-lover. (With thanks to the Státni Zámek Sychrov, the Czech Republic)

8. Bonnie Prince Charlie's unique great-grandchild, Marie-Victoire's son, Antime, Chevalier de Nikorowicz (1804-52), painted *c.* 1823 when he became an officer of the elite 4th Cuirassiers of the Habsburg Crown Prince Ferdinand, arranged in 1822 by the British Ambassador in Paris, Sir Charles Stuart. Because his mother never told him her 'Secret', Antime's was the first generation not to know that Marie-Victoire was the heir of the last Stuarts. (Property of author's family in Kraków)
9. Sir Charles Stuart (1779-1845), Lord Stuart de Rothesay, painted in 1830 by Sir George Hayter. Seen wearing the robes of his 1828 peerage and the chain of a Knight Grand Cross of the Bath, he was British Ambassador to France from 1815-24 and 1828-30. In Paris, he not only knew Marie-Victoire and her brother, but also their 'Secret' thanks to the Coutts family of his aunt Frances, Lady Bute, who had been chaperoned for a year in Paris by Clementina Walkinshaw. It was Sir Charles who found a position for Antime in the Habsburg Crown Prince's 4th Cuirassiers through his friend, Lord Clanwilliam, whose brother-in-law, Count Karl Clam-Martinitz, commanded the regiment. (With thanks to the UK Government Art Collection)
10. Antime, Chevalier de Nikorowicz, *c.* 1828, painted by Leopold Fertbauer, shortly after he left the Crown Prince's 4th Cuirassiers and prior to his marriage in 1829. Antime fought in the Polish Rising of 1831 and, during the Spring of the Nations in 1848, was unanimously elected commanding officer of the 1,200-strong Academic Legion. (Property of the author's family in Poznań)
11. Antime's eldest son, *c.* 1836, who was given the ill-fated Stuart name of Charles, never before used in his father's family. He joined the Spring of the Nations in 1848 but, ten years later, lost an 'American duel', whereby he had to commit suicide, which he did on 31 August 1859 in Versailles. (Property of the author's family in Warsaw)
12. Antime's daughter, Julia Thérèse, Countess Pinińska (1833-93). Of the family's daughters, she was the only one who bore her husband a male heir, whose line survives unbroken to the present day. She also succeeded her brother Charles as the heiress of Grzymałów Castle, which remained her descendants main home until 1939. (With thanks to Maria Księżopolska, née Pinińska, Connecticut)
13. King John III Sobieski (1629-96), Prince Charles Edward Stuart's great-grandfather, engraved in 1684, the year after his magnificent victory at Vienna over a Turkish army of almost 100,000, described by Lord d'Abernon as one of the eighteen battles that changed the course of world history. A brilliant warrior and passionate lover, his letters to his French wife are one of the great works of the Baroque. (Property of the Piniński Foundation, Warsaw)
14. Prince Charles Edward Stuart (1720-88), by Giles Hussey *c.* 1735, who became known as Bonnie Prince Charlie because his Christian name in Gaelic was *Thearlaich*, similar in pronunciation to Charlie. (With thanks to D. S. Lavender Ltd, Conduit Street, London)
15. A plan of Edinburgh published in the 1745 edition of *The Gentleman's Magazine and Historical Chronicle*. (Property of the Piniński Foundation, Warsaw)
16. A plan of the Battle of Prestonpans, or Gladsmuir as it was originally known, fought on 21 September 1745, published shortly after in *The Gentleman's Magazine and Historical Chronicle*. A Jacobite officer, Lieutenant Anderson, was a local farmer's son who told Lord George Murray of a secret path through some marshland, enabling the Highland Army to start their move at 4 a.m. and launch a surprise attack at 6 a.m., which secured victory within minutes, inflicting heavy losses on the Hanoverians. Prince Charles Edward personally insisted on the best possible treatment being given to his enemy's wounded and prisoners. (Property of the Piniński Foundation, Warsaw)
17. A map of Culloden or Drummossie Moor from the 1871 edition of *The Memoirs of the Chevalier de Johnstone*, showing the coastline and woods to the left (north), with the steep-sloped River Nairn and high moorland beyond to the right (south). It is clear from this how limited was the choice of battlefield given Prince Charles Edward's conviction that the Jacobite Army's provisions at Inverness had to be protected at all costs. Lord George Murray argued against giving battle, and for dispersal and a guerrilla campaign. But Sir John O'Sullivan saw the weakness of this and pointed out that the Highlands were at the end of a long, hard winter and so food was very scarce, the area left in their control was relatively small, and that half the

army was non-Highland in origin. Lord George then argued for positioning the army on the higher ground and slopes of the River Nairn; however, this contained the fatal flaw of leaving the road to Inverness wide open. (Property of the Piniński Foundation, Warsaw)

18. The Order of the Battle of Culloden, as illustrated in the 1871 edition of *The Memoirs of the Chevalier de Johnstone.* Apart from the various regiments, it also shows the gun placements. The Hanoverians stood to the east, with their backs to Nairn and the icy-cold wind and sleet, whilst the Jacobites were to the west with Inverness behind them. (Property of the Piniński Foundation, Warsaw)
19. An article in *The Gentleman's Magazine and Historical Chronicle* from late April 1746 announcing the outcome of the Battle of Culloden. (Property of the Piniński Foundation, Warsaw)
20. The *de jure* King Charles III in 1776 in Florence, an engraving after the original portrait by Ozias Humphrey, RA. One traveller wrote of him, 'When a young man he must have been esteemed handsome... he is by no means thin, has a noble person and a graceful manner ... on the whole he has a melancholy, mortified appearance'. (Property of the Piniński Foundation, Warsaw)
21. Clementina Walkinshaw (1720-1802), Prince Charles' third love after his cousins Princess Louise de Rohan and Princess Marie-Anne de Talmont. She was from a loyal Jacobite family and the mother of his daughter and heiress, Charlotte Stuart, Duchess of Albany. She was also the great niece of 'Bobbing John', 6th Earl of Mar (Duke of Mar in the Jacobite Peerage), who by his ineptitude snatched defeat from the jaws of victory during the 1715 Rising. (With thanks to the Derby Museum and Art Gallery)
22. Prince Jules-Hercule de Rohan, Duke de Montbazon (1726-88), the 'dutiful' head of the Rohans, whose family solidarity was legendary. This 1780 likeness is the only image known and shows him as he was when he baptised his niece, Marie-Victoire. (With thanks to Prince Raoul de Rohan, Devon)
23. The 1779 baptismal entry for Marie-Victoire (1779-1836), Charlotte Stuart's daughter by Ferdinand de Rohan. From the Parish of Veigné near Tours, it is signed by Prince Jules-Hercule de Rohan, Duke de Montbazon, who legitimised her and granted her the title of the Demoiselle de Thorigny. (With thanks to the Archives Départementales d'Indre-et-Loire, Chambray-les-Tours)
24. The Château de Couzières in the Parish of Veigné in whose chapel Marie-Victoire was baptised. Her title of the Demoiselle de Thorigny came from the neighbouring château which, like Couzières, was a fief of the Rohans' Duchy of Montbazon. (Property of the Piniński Foundation, Warsaw)
25. Prince Ferdinand de Rohan (1738-1813), Archbishop of Cambrai and Count of the Napoleonic Empire, the brother-in-law of the Stuart Princes' first cousin Princess Louise de La Tour d'Auvergne whose husband was Prince Jules-Hercule de Rohan, Duke de Montbazon, Henry Stuart's ADC in 1745. (With thanks to Josselin de Rohan-Chabot, Duke de Rohan, the Château de Josselin, Brittany)
26. Part of a letter from Prince Ferdinand de Rohan to his brother, Cardinal Louis, dated 17 April 1795. Sent from Venice to Ettenheim, Ferdinand describes the help that Thomas Coutts the banker is providing. (With thanks to the Státni Oblastní Archiv Litoměřice at Děčin in the Czech Republic)
27. Cardinal Louis de Rohan (1734-1803), Prince Ferdinand's elder brother and the hero of the scandalous *Affaire du Collier de la Reine*. After the French Revolution erupted, Louis, who was Prince-Bishop of Strasbourg, retreated to the safety of Ettenheim in the eastern part of his principality, where he helped his relation, the Bourbon Prince de Condé, form a counter-revolutionary army and where he looked after Charlotte Stuart's children. (Property of the Piniński Foundation, Warsaw)
28. The death certificate of Charlotte Maximilienne, daughter of Charlotte Stuart and Ferdinand de Rohan, who lost her baby and died in childbirth after her first pregnancy at Huy near Liège in 1806. (With thanks to the Archives de l'Etat at Huy, Belgium)
29. The 1744 letter of Gregory, Chevalier de Nikorowicz (1713-89), to King Augustus III of Poland, in which he refers to his patronage by the Stuarts' closest Polish cousins, the Princes Radziwiłł, and requests diplomatic protection and tax exemptions for his trade and espionage mission to the Court of Persia at Esfahan. (With thanks to the National Library in Warsaw)

30. The Palace of Sychrov, north of Prague. Purchased in 1820, it was the Rohan family's main home until 1945. After their escape from the French Revolution, the Rohans never returned permanently to France, and it was here at Sychrov that Marie-Victoire's letters to Prince Louis de Rohan were kept. (With thanks to the Státni Zámek Sychrov, the Czech Republic)
31. An envelope written in 1824 by Marie-Victoire and addressed to Prince Louis at his mansion on the rue de Grenelle. (With thanks to the Státni Oblastní Archiv Litoměřice at Děčin in the Czech Republic)
32. The back of an envelope sent by Marie-Victoire to Prince Louis on which she calls herself 'Rohan Stuard d'Overgne'. In French and Italian, the letter 'd' is phonetically the same as 't' and Stuart is often spelt this way. For example, the old Bologna guide of *c.* 1793 describes Charlotte Stuart as 'Carlotta Stuardo' and the marble slab from her grave was spelt 'Stuarda'. Likewise, 'd'Overgne' is also phonetic, the correct spelling of her second husband's name being 'd'Auvergne'. (With thanks to the Státni Oblastní Archiv Litoměřice at Děčin in the Czech Republic)
33. One of Marie-Victoire's letters to Prince Louis, in which she refers to her son's education at Versailles. Though she describes herself as a widow and a mother, she uses the alias 'Roehenstart', a rebus of Rohan and Stuart, as a sort of maiden name. Her brother Charles and sister Charlotte also used the name at times. (With thanks to the Státni Oblastní Archiv Litoměřice at Děčin in the Czech Republic)
34. One of Marie-Victoire's letters to Prince Louis, in which she refers to her 'Secret', to the 'romances of the Stuarts and Rohans' and to her 'Breton blood'. Both the Stuarts and the Rohans descended from ancient Celtic families of Brittany. The Stuarts' protoplast was Flaald, eleventh-century hereditary High Steward of Dol, whereas the Rohans' ancestor was Guethenoc, Viscount de Chateautro en Porhoët, who built the massive fortress of Josselin in 1008. (With thanks to the Státni Oblastní Archiv Litoměřice at Děčin in the Czech Republic)
35. One of Marie-Victoire's letters to Prince Louis in which she refers to herself as an 'orphan of the pure blood of the Rs and Ss' and writes of her 'natural birth'. (With thanks to the Státni Oblastní Archiv Litoměřice at Děčin in the Czech Republic)
36. The second page of the previous letter in which Marie-Victoire admits her mother 'the Duchess' was 'never married', and appeals to Prince Louis to help reassure her future second husband d'Auvergne with regard to any gossip 'he could perhaps hear repeated in Society'. (With thanks to the Státni Oblastní Archiv Litoměřice at Děčin in the Czech Republic)
37. The 1804 '*ex aqua*' baptismal entry for Marie-Victoire's son by Paul Anthony, Chevalier de Nikorowicz, in the records of the Armenian Catholic cathedral of Lwów. Born prematurely, he was not expected to survive, was immediately anointed with the water of baptism, and temporarily given the name of the saint's day upon which he was born. That name was 'Zenon' from Zenodoros, meaning 'Gift of Zeus'. Careful of her Catholicism and 'bourgeois morality', Marie-Victoire preferred the Christian equivalent, 'Theodoros', meaning 'gift of God', which is why 'Theodore' became her pet-name for her son. (With thanks to the Central State Historical Archive of the Ukraine in Lwów)
38. The 1806 record of the '*in baptismo et in confirmatione*' formal christening ceremony at the Armenian Catholic cathedral of Lwów. By this time, Marie-Victoire's son had become healthy. His temporary name of Zenon was now replaced by Antime and Mark and his godparents were appointed. As Marie-Victoire's only child, he was the unique great-grandchild of Prince Charles Edward Stuart. (With thanks to the Central State Historical Archive of the Ukraine in Lwów)
39. The Castle of Grzymałów, *c.* 1900. Some 80 miles east of Lwów, the estate was bought in 1831 by Antime de Nikorowicz, and it was here that Prince Louis de Rohan's replies to Marie-Victoire were kept until the First World War, when the Russian Staff occupied the castle in 1914 and devastated its interiors. (Property of the Piniński Foundation, Warsaw)
40. One of the drawing rooms at Grzymałów Castle, *c.* 1900. The family's oldest documents were kept in a secretaire here, some of them dating back to the fourteenth century. Amongst them were the letters of Prince Louis de Rohan to Marie-Victoire, which were the key to unlocking the Stuarts' Last Secret. (Property of the Piniński Foundation, Warsaw)
41. Genealogical table.

Index